D1094414

BURT FRANKLIN: RESEARCH & SOURCE WORKS SERIES 283

Essays in History, Economics & Social Science 39

SPECULATIVE NOTES

AND

NOTES ON SPECULATION.

SPECULATIVE NOTES

AND

NOTES ON SPECULATION,

IDEAL AND REAL.

BY D. MORIER EVANS,

BURT FRANKLIN
NEW YORK

BURT FRANKLIN, Publisher
235 East 44th St., New York 10017
Originally Published: 1864
Reprinted: 1968
Printed in the U.S.A.

Library of Congress Catalog Card Number: 68-58216
Burt Franklin Research & Source Works Series 283
Essays in History, Economics, & Social Science 39

TO

JAMES JOHNSTONE, ESQ.,

AS AN OLD FRIEND AND AN AGREEABLE COMPANION,

𝔗𝔥𝔢𝔰𝔢 𝔓𝔞𝔤𝔢𝔰 𝔞𝔯𝔢 𝔍𝔫𝔰𝔠𝔯𝔦𝔟𝔢𝔡,

WITH

EVERY FEELING OF RESPECT AND ESTEEM,

BY THE AUTHOR.

CONTENTS.

TO THE PUBLIC.

———◆———

A few of these papers have, during the last twelve months, appeared in the "London Review," the "Bankers' Magazine," and other publications; the great majority, and the longest of the series, are now presented for the first time.

London, March, 1864.

SPECULATIVE NOTES.

I.

IT is a beautiful afternoon in March, crisp, clear weather, and the sun in shining throws his bright rays over the façade of the Royal Exchange, the frontage of the Bank, and the surrounding buildings. The reflection is caught by the upper stories of the Globe Insurance Office, in the heavily glazed windows of which floods of light dance. The busy throng is streaming past the Mansion House—the great, stern Hall of Justice—up the Poultry and Cheapside, either westward or in other directions.

The whirlpool of traffic centred near this spot is, as usual, exhausting itself through the assistance of all classes of vehicles, from the neatly-appointed brougham taking up some City magnate, to the fully-freighted omnibus which, laden inside and out, rolls ponderously along, or the adventurous hansom which, driven at furious speed, threads the intricacies of the maze with apparently hazardous, but almost recognized certainty of success.

I am making my diurnal jog-trot round, and am the personal witness of this scene; for know, courteous reader, the nature of my avocation is so singular that it rarely or ever commences before other people have concluded their day's work; and though it is unnecessary further to illustrate this peculiarity, it will serve to explain what may appear exceptional in itself, if it were not cursorily alluded to.

On this special occasion, unfortunately, I am later than usual—the banks and other great public establishments have closed, and I am looking in every nook and cranny for a belated individual, who, either through accident or design, remains beyond the hour when it is reasonably supposed the tide of business has ebbed out for the day.

My simple object is information—information, however, that can be obtained only in particular channels, and from practical sources; and which, though eagerly sought and relished by the public, is scarcely sufficiently valued, considering the labour its collection entails. For years it has been my practice, and still is, if in any doubt of gaining what I am seeking, to rush to the great thoroughfare by the Mansion House to watch the current of human life—seething and battling as it does with every difficulty to make its way onwards—as in its midst I can generally discern some one or other who will gratify my curiosity by giving the desired intelligence.

On this —— March, 1860, I am in a peculiar dilemma. I have missed everybody, even my last resource—the burly bank porter—who, as far as his limited knowledge extends, will answer my most pertinent inquiries with grave solemnity, if they do not impinge upon the secrets of the much-revered parlour, the dreaded inroad upon the privileges of the charter, or a rumoured late interview between the Governor and the Chancellor of the

Exchequer. I am, therefore, compelled to adopt my final ruse for keeping pace with the course of events, and letting nothing escape me.

Like the detectives—some of whom actually cross my path, and in turn for a moment eye me suspiciously, though the majority know my form and features well—I am on the spot scanning particular styles and particular gaits, with reserved objects little dreamt of by the manner in which I carry out these my peculiar land-line surveys. For some time I wait patiently, but apparently without prospect of success, and the only reward for my perseverance is the kindly recognition from the insides of cabs, or the outsides of other conveyances, of friends who are in too desperate a hurry to fly the living maëlstrom to attend to me or my wants, though sore many may imagine my distress to be.

At length I fancy I descry a style and appearance about which there can be scarcely any mistake, and which, if they shall represent in real reality the personage supposed, will relieve me from much of my difficulty, and at least satisfy my anxiety on points of importance, of little or no weight to him, but of vast interest to his willing recipient.

I am right in my conjecture, it is one of my very best friends, one who can afford me the special knowledge I wish to secure, and who I feel will not hesitate or be stinting in his supply, if there be any to give. He approaches; his bearing is slightly imposing, being above the middle height, and exhibiting some regard to a substantial style of dress: he comes up, pressing through the crowd, who seem disposed to give him 'vantage ground. He is well enveloped in his fashionable brown coat; he walks jauntily, but not with a supercilious or ostentatious air, and as our eyes meet he vigorously rubs his delicate, pulpy, well-formed hands.

"Ah! Ah!" he says, with a smile, and his bright eyes twinkle; "this is glorious weather—they have been doing something over the way, to-day—taking it in by sackfuls—money I should think will be cheap after this."

"Have they?" I respond. "You are just the person I was in quest of. Detained late westward, I have not long reached the City. What has been doing?"

The speaker's playful allusion to the "doing of something over the way" is in relation to enormous bullion operations at the Bank, whither large sums have been sent during the day. The sequence of his volunteered information is, that fine weather, with good bullion arrivals, will produce a favourable effect upon the money market.

I inquire the nature and extent of the transactions at the Bank. I am replied to in the same jocose vein, but find myself furnished with precise information. What the course and transactions at the Stock Exchange? No absence of intelligence of the principal movements and fluctuations, given in the same off-hand style, tinged with a spice of irony upon men and things in general. Has there been any fact of importance in the open money market—such as joint-stock bank stringency, or probability of increased abundance? He is not at a loss upon any of these questions; he answers glibly, but unerringly; and, finally, parting to catch his omnibus, asks with mock solemnity, if I can tell him the last price of Chinese Turnpike Bonds, since he purposes shortly making a considerable investment.

My end is accomplished, and he is soon lost in the human maëlstrom; but I have followed as long as vision enabled me his retreating figure. I am satisfied at having so amply gratified my thirst for knowledge of the day's proceedings, yet, at the same time, I cannot help reflecting that in following my cherished pursuit I make huge sacrifices that no emolument can ever repay.

How, on my way to my office, to shape and put into proper guise my required store of well-collected facts, the thought haunts me of his comfortable, easy, and steadily-attained position. How rebellious my heart rises, which at other periods is tractable and thankful, imagining the surfeit of pleasure he must enjoy in hastening home to spend his evenings with his wife—perhaps his little ones. And here am I working night after night into the silent hours for at most a precarious existence if head or hand should fail.

I, who at all times and in all seasons relish a sparkling or facetious colloquy, feel a peculiar description of *melancholia* follow this interview and conversation; but after chewing the cud of sober thought, I surmount my short but sharp hypochondriacal attack, and putting my back to my evening's labour, manfully go at it, and struggle through.

A month subsequently, I am in the City rather earlier. I make my accustomed calls, and among other places at the joint-stock banks. An unparalleled fraud has been discovered—a fraud that appeared likely, when its magnitude transpired, to shake confidence to its centre; and when I inquire the perpetrator, I am told it is William George Pullinger—the individual who but a few weeks previously, inspired in my breast those transient feelings of envy, which certainly for the moment disturbed me more than I ever remember to have been before by any analogous circumstances.

The event, and its antecedent incidents, teach me a very useful lesson. There is no desire on my part to exchange places with the jocose conversationalist who, with such a weight of penal responsibility upon his shoulders, could maintain so bold a front and display such bland, facile manners; and seldom since have I exhibited a disposition to shift the yoke, which my friends and neighbours assure me, I am destined for some time to bear.

II.

THE manners and customs of the English in banking and discounting, as in everything else, are liable to change. The proof of this, if it were required, is to be found in the experience of the last ten years, and it is daily becoming more than ever apparent. The growth of the joint-stock principle, at first tardy and slow, has at length so rapidly expanded that it appears difficult in the slightest degree to arrest its progress. If the celebrated Abraham New-land, in his straight-cut brocaded coat, as he is repre-sented in his portrait in the lobby of the Bank parlour, or the crusty but honest, straightforward old Fuller—he who reproved one of his best customers on the point of ex-travagance for ordering a second pint of beer—could rise from their graves and witness the wonderful and almost magical alterations in the system of business, they would pray like Count de Lorge, when relieved from the Bas-tile, to be carried back to their imprisonment, believing that the system could not last, and that the world was coming to an end.

It requires no great stretch of imagination to lead us back to Lombard Street, or other precincts of the general banking community, to trace the difference in the style and manners of transacting the financial engagements of the day—for even, as Mr. Ruskin would say, the very stones themselves speak and tell of the decided and important change that has come over the monetary world in this respect. Those who are old enough to remember the dull dark route of Princes Street, with the one or two private banks carrying out their operations in that locality, with low ceilings, brass-railed counters, and clerks dressed in sober black, with the inseparable white neckerchief, must marvel much at the difference now presented, when contemplating the huge fabrics raised on the same spot by the London Joint-Stock Bank and the Union Bank of London, filled with the busy bustling body of clerks comprising the respective staffs of those establishments.

The London and Westminster Bank, with its modest portals in Lothbury, which seemed the entrance to a moderately well-to-do mercantile firm, has swelled its proportions into such a conspicuous building that it now stands face to face on approximate terms of equality with its neighbour and old opponent, the Bank of England, and showing, if not in masonry and solid granite, commensurate dimensions with that ancient establishment, at least a more satisfactory feature in the one essential thing to the maintenance of prosperity,—viz., a better dividend. The London and County Bank, following the example set by its more wealthy and important compeers, has not been slow to imitate the movements of its predecessors; and if an increased business is to be acquired by handsomely-fitted, convenient, and commodious premises, assuredly the new range of buildings in Lombard Street will, with the existing satisfactory management, achieve that end.

The attention that of late years has been bestowed in rendering banking premises more useful and ornamental, is a subject of congratulation; and when piles arise like those of the Oriental Bank, they remind one greatly of fabled Eastern magnificence, blended with every comfort that may be considered desirable for the *employé*. Perhaps for their position and situation, the City Bank and the Bank of London present less attractions than others in this particular; but they have at the same time been more recently developed, and when the next cycle of improvement in architectural adornment shall arrive, no doubt they will be found expanding in similar proportion to the rest. *Ex necessitate* they will be compelled to do this with the view, not only of affording augmented facilities to their customers, but of keeping pace in the great race of banking competition.

Even the poor little London and Middlesex Bank*— scarcely the violet of our banking *bouquet*, seeing that it emanated from the hydra-headed Unity Company, which in turn has, figuratively speaking, eaten up its directors, shareholders, and, at last, its original projector and first manager—has endeavoured to struggle into a position, and with circumscribed, but well-arranged offices, offers an attraction of mahogany, glass, and fretwork probably greater than it can provide in the shape of extended credit and capital. To finish up this catalogue *raisonnée*, it is necessary, of course, to include the three largest amongst the most recent additions to our banking organizations, the Metropolitan and Provincial, the Alliance London and Liverpool, and the Imperial Bank of London. The directors in these instances very prudently have not rushed into excessive outlay—perhaps those associated with the Imperial have been the least discreet, but that has occurred through old connection with the Commercial —and they will do well to bide their time before they rear

* While these pages are passing through the press, the Bank is declared to be " in course of liquidation."

up palatial institutions and expend an undue portion of
their limited capital in Portland stone, iron-palisading,
and highly-burnished door-panels. Their time will come
in due season, if they shall be successful, to emulate the
extensions and embellishments of their prosperous neighbours, and till then we would venture to whisper, " Be
watchful, cautious, and content."

But while these changes and modifications have been
pursued vigorously and almost unceasingly by the joint-
stock banks, have the private banks taken any measures
to increase their conveniences and to make any architectural
display ? They have certainly, and in a very fair ratio,
attempted to make themselves seen and appreciated.

Acquiescing, at length, in the dictum that the age of
appearances demanded that improvement should be made,
and that it was necessary to move, if only partially, with
the current, Jones, Loyd, and Co. ; Smith, Payne, and
Smiths ; Glyn, Halifax, and Co. ; Roberts, Lubbock, and
Co. ; Drewett, Fowler, and Dimsdale ; Stone, Martin,
and Co. ; and several others, have from time to time
rebuilt, enlarged, beautified, and in other ways given a
better tone and aspect to their establishments ; and these
alterations have naturally been accompanied by attention
to ventilation, greater space, and more accommodation,
both for customers and clerks.

Barclay, Bevan, and Tritton, with the Quakerly element
of a dislike to change, have at last succumbed to fashion,
and they announce, first, the absorption into their bank
of the old firm of Spooner, Attwood, and Co.; and secondly,
the immediate reconstruction and rehabilitation of their
premises. The mystical influence of progress has therefore been at work even among the patrons of the broad-
brim, brown cloth, and small continuations. This, at

least, says much for the steady course of the movement, and the persistent force of its career.

Perhaps the sole remaining old-fashioned house, in every degree, is that of Messrs. Currie and Co., of Cornhill. It is nevertheless strong and solid in its antiquated notions, and if it is not prepared at once to go with the stream, it may be fairly calculated that in a few years it will have to do so. There is, however, occasionally a charm in entering into one of these quiet and unobtrusive establishments after having previously encountered the great rush and noise of business in other of the more prominent banks; and the contrast, it must be admitted, is singularly striking.

With the additions and improvements by the private banks necessary to keep headway owing to the rapid growth of the joint-stock principle, the discount establishments have been gradually conforming to the order of the day, and may be said to have made no inconsiderable advance. The old but convenient offices of Messrs. Overend, Gurney, and Co., when Mr. Samuel Gurney was the presiding genius, assisted by his active and vigilant junior, Mr. D. Barclay Chapman, were, before the death of that revered philanthropist, too circumscribed for their pursuits; and he, recognizing the necessity for change, entered into the spirit of the movement, made the requisite purchases, and the improvements in the house "at the corner," as the establishment is familiarly designated, were without delay accomplished.

The firms of Messrs. Higgs and Gandle, and Messrs. Colls, Thompson, and Harris, had they lived, would have been compelled to adopt the same course, but they were worked out before the new era commenced, and are now only names numbered with the past. Messrs. Alexander

and Co., it might have been expected would have made
extensive modifications in their premises, but they seem
to have been satisfied with slight amplification and rearrangement. Still they are conveniently situated, and
allow the transaction of business with all the ease and
necessary facility.

The great mistake of the National Discount Company,
when they entered on their career, was alleged to be the
rushing into "bricks and mortar," which originated in
the circumstance of the purchase of premises in Cornhill,
and the erection of that massive and costly edifice at the
top of Birchin Lane. If this investment interfered, in
the earlier stages of their business, with their development, there has since been less reason to regret it, the
directors having, after all, turned it to good account,
through advantageous sub-letting and the enhanced value
of the site.

The London Discount Company, during the brief
period of its existence, was content to occupy offices of
adequate but not immoderate dimensions, and when it
wound up they were not found to be a clog upon the
realization of the assets. The Joint-Stock Discount
Company have commenced with very fair prospects of
success, in premises suited to their wants and requirements; and if the same caution guides them in their
future arrangements, no complaint will be preferred against
them for having launched into an extravagant expenditure
in building or external decoration.

All these changes, all these modifications, are, however, typical of one thing, which is, perhaps, the greatest
misfortune of the age—a love of show, that may lead eventually to excessive expenditure, and sometimes to embarrassment. Instances have been seen of the great mistakes

which frequently arise from this state of affairs, in the tendency to encourage a desire for outlay, which is permeating every rank and condition of life. Bank partners, bank managers, and the principal officials of these establishments, possess the means, either through property, stipend, or allowance, of supporting the character and profession which the taste of the hour inculcates; but it is not setting a healthy example to clerks, subordinates, or the rising generation, to make a display, which is more properly that allied with the spendthrift, than with the cautious, plodding, accumulating banker.

Exceptions there are to the present rule, but we fear they will prove rare indeed, in which this show of gaud and glitter is carefully avoided, with the view of building up solid strength and prosperity in preference to achieving ephemeral popularity; and they merit this passing allusion to illustrate the fact, that although the multitude represent the great worshippers of folly and extravagance, the world has not absolutely run stark staring mad.

Incomes may be spent of £5,000, £10,000, or £15,000 a year, but this kind of outlay, though it may sustain carriage, horses, liveried servants, and marine residences, would be more appropriately devoted to increasing the amount of Consols, Bank, or India Stock, and Exchequer bills, for the support of credit and fair fame in the days of adversity. Bank and other managers may drive their broughams, and give the most splendid entertainments, probably with the object of securing business and increasing their connections; but these practices may have their risk and disadvantage, since they please more the personal vanity and taste of the individuals themselves, than they add to the well-being or prosperity of their respective institutions.

III.

A GOOD dinner is a thing always to be enjoyed; not, how-ever, alone, for that would simply be gluttony personified, but in the society of a few choice spirits whose friendship and conversation will assist the process of digestion, and give real zest to the festival, even if it be of the plainest kind. Gastronomy most people hold to be an art which should be highly revered—some few, perhaps, for its satisfying powers, but the great majority for the tone it imparts to the social circle, and its genial influence upon those who can properly appreciate the honoured customs of our country.

The set dinner party is all very well in its way, lead-ing to fresh acquaintances and the exchange of mutual courtesies; ordinary dining is what must be done, and, as a requirement of nature, should be attended to, without too great a trespass upon time or upon pocket; but the dinner *impromptu*, the unexpected invitation, the uncer-tainty of knowing whether you will be able through pressure of engagements to get there or not, is the dinner to work the brain, send the fancies reeling, and rub off the rust from the human cob-webbed machinery acquired by overtaxed exertions.

Such an invitation I received some months ago, and as it was merely proffered from a shake-hand acquaint-ance, very doubtful was I at first whether I ought in

justice to myself or my daily routine of labour to accede
to the proposal, but although it was made at 1 o'clock
p.m., and we were to dine at 5, at the West-end (with
strict injunctions not to dress), the favour of my company
was asked in so frank and straightforward a manner that
I could not find heart to refuse. Intuitively I almost felt
that I should be at home, and one of the guests, who had
accepted in an equally unceremonious manner the offer,
being a friend, I broke through my general rule of refusing, and at the hour named reached the appointed place,
where the reception was of the most hearty character
imaginable.

What if our company on the present auspicious occasion be limited and select? What if it include only
three of mature years and two comparative juveniles?
Shall it be less instructive or entertaining than if it comprised a numerous and mixed assemblage, every one imbued with his or her own importance, and impressed with
the notion that what he or she uttered was the best thing
said this season, believing, complacently enough, that
everybody else was nobody!

We can dismiss the juniors, for they have been eminently gratified with the prandial exhibition, if faith is to
be placed in the frequent ejaculations of " capital !" and
" excellent !" as the turtle has been duly qualified with
the ever-present punch à la Romaine, and the successive
relays of fish, flesh, and game have gradually disappeared;
and, allowing them to finish a hurried dessert, they may
take their departure for the small house in the Haymarket,
to criticise my Lord Dundreary, and see " if he is a fellah"
they can understand.

We of the heavy, austere school, though permitting the
pleasures of the play to despoil us of part of our company,

are not readily disposed to abandon the table and the creature comforts of life, to sacrifice the remainder of the evening, when probably the special three congregated together may not, at least for years, if ever, meet again. Brought by an extraordinary accident into each other's society, this *impromptu* dinner has so far gone off amazingly well : not the slightest jar—everything running on smoothly as a river, the greatest and uttermost regret being that this uncommonly comfortable alliance had not, under similar circumstances, been effected before.

One, a *millionaire* in figures, but extremely careful, can enter into the *minutiæ* of operations of a most extensive character. If more accurately described, and in language better understood, he would at once be recognized as a power in Lombard Street, whose friendship the wealthy and affluent are glad to seek, though it may not always serve them in their direst need.

The other, hale, bluff and exuberant—exuberant even in distress, and whom no adversity, stinging as it may be, can turn from the hopeful aspiration of surmounting all difficulties, when from their accumulative force they are apparently insurmountable.

Myself, verging towards the age when the joyfulness of youth has mellowed down into that happy quietude betraying a consciousness of having done my best to serve the public, the great arbiter of opinion, and those with whom I am associated, finishes the photographic group which it is desirable to put forward to lead to the little *scena* about to be detailed.

It does not matter much, but the central figure of the sketch has, to use the phraseology of the day, more than once made a sensation in financial circles. The truth need not be concealed—it is a patent fact ; and being an individual of sanguine temperament, he never hesitates to avow it. Not that he has gone on the principle of two bankruptcies and a fire, making a man's fortune; quite the contrary. Every time he has failed, it has been a thoroughly legitimate smash, leaving him denuded of the last vestige of his property. Yet, optimist as he is, he still lives for the bright side of the picture. This he, if consulted on the portraiture, would admit is not an overdrawn account, particularly when compared with many others he could at a short notice exhibit.

We have got well into the dessert; we have passed compliments on our retiring friends; the wax candles are lighted, and claret is being freely passed. Waiters move noiselessly about, the heavy damask curtains, with their bullion fringe, are drawn, and the fire burning up brightly gives an air of coziness to the antique, but well arranged apartment, and sends a good glow through you. It may be the wine, it may be the conversation, or it may be a happy combination of both; but certain it is that the time passes rapidly, and no one would imagine, that either of the three, had any responsibilities which could interfere with this pleasant, but short-lived career.

We are men of money, and without investigating what our immediate resources are, our thoughts naturally turn towards rates of discount, the state of money—that inscrutable mystery—the action of the foreign exchanges, and last, not least, the supply of gold from those wonderful localities, Australia and California.

Soon threadbare are worn the arguments of the bullionists, and the inconvertibles; each one has a theory of his own to frame a panacea for all existing evils; but while these respective views are enforced with vigour, and combated with courtesy, currency controversy, in the accepted sense of the term, is avoided, much to the comfort of all.

But in the midst of the debate there creeps out the word " speculation ;" and, as if by magic, the whole conversation at once takes another direction. Either by personal experience, family relationship, or through other sources, each one has something to say of the dreadful effects and consequences, of this paralyzing influence whenever it is in full sway.

Our friend the *millionaire* in figures, with his placid face, and smoothly trimmed hair and beard, remembers the great quicksilver and cochineal speculations, which swallowed hundreds of thousands of pounds, and beggared hosts of families. The lotteries of Cornhill he speaks of with great facility ; the days of Bish, Luck, Hazard, and the general multitude of ticket-sellers, being quite green in his memory. He mentions the prizes that men and women secured on their sixteenths ; of the rage for particular numbers, and of the crowded thoroughfares at the time of the drawings, to ascertain the declaration of the fortunate figures. The demoralization created by the railway mania, he thinks was nothing compared to the mischief produced by the lotteries, the propensity to gambling being spread by them through all circles, whilst the beneficial results to the public were *nil*, contrasted with the advantages conferred by the iron-way system.

I, myself, throw in a few observations respecting the railway mania, and the great monarch of the period—the mighty Hudson. I sketch off the rough, burly appearance of that potentate, the date of his decadence, and allude to his subsequent dethronement, and departure from the country. This brings me to the Australian and Californian speculations of 1851-2, when companies with small capitals, and £1 shares, were the great *furore*—when two or three descriptions went to enormous premiums, but never, with a single exception, realized anything for the fortunate shareholders, save the handsomely-tinted scrip issued by the directors, and the elaborately-prepared prospectuses, with the careful assays of the gold-bearing quartz, acquired by the usual chemical tests.

It was indeed, I remark, a fever-heat of excitement when, on the authority of one of the first brokers of the day, I was informed that steady-going bankers, church pluralists, and others of the wisest in the land, were exchanging Consols to purchase Aguafria gold-mining shares, Australian freehold, the British and Colonial, and Golden Mountain of Mariposa shares. These " golden dreams," became "waking realities " in less than twelve months ; the majority of the companies—and their name was legion—were speedily extinguished ; a few dragged on a hopeless existence, but only to remind those, who had not forgotten the voice of the charmer at the great meeting at the London Tavern, informing them, that California and Australia, merely required British capital, and British energy, to develope their resources, though not precisely in the fashion he indicated.

But even when the panic came—for panic it was in one sense of the word, though not in another—the shares sinking gradually to a low point, there were then a few inconsiderate, and foolish people, who trusted to rescuing a prize, here and there, out of this vast lottery of blanks. I related how on one account day, as I was passing to get the prices of various securities, I met an acquaintance, a jobber, who, pushing across 'Change, displayed a bundle of scrip in his hand. It was a parchment issue, respectably printed, with several recognizable signatures at foot—everything, as bankers and brokers say, in order.

"Here," said he, "we have come to a pretty state of things at last—London and California gold-crushers going at anything—a nominal price to close a deceased account. I must clear them out, for the parties are determined to have no such securities among their investments. You see, I do not give them a good character to take you in ; but really, fifty won't hurt you at 1s. per share. Recollect, fifty at 1s. per share, one pound paid—you may either obtain a winding-up 2s. 6d., the full value at a distant date, or perhaps untold riches."

"Nonsense !" I rejoined ; "you know that I am no speculator, and have little faith in any of these sorts of operations."

"Ah, but," said he, "this is no ordinary speculation ; it is a great risk—a dead loss, perhaps, of £2 10s. But, on the other hand, it may turn up trumps. Recollect Australian Agricultural shares at £24 and no buyers, and subsequently at £266 ! You have heard that deposits of those shares for bad debts, made the owners' fortunes."

What force of logic could stand against this ? I knew the facts he was reciting were true. Within my own knowledge had come a great deal of the special movement, which in a few months, had so metamorphosed the character of that particular property that, though I fain would have avoided the tempter, still the risk was so small, that I almost involuntarily said yes ; having been bitten, as it were, with a notion that they might some day or other, realize a value, better than their then nominal quotation.

The jobber was a man of discernment ; he saw my hesitation, and bantering me more fiercely than ever, offered to give me credit for the amount, if I could not immediately hand over the cash.

Here was great leverage; my pride was now attacked, as well as my pocket. I fumbled among my papers; the necessary sum was forthcoming, and without asking any contract to seal the bargain, took my scrip, and hurried away.

"That was a speculation, indeed," chimed in our friend, the close-bearded *milliomaire* in figures : "the worst of speculations—a risk apparently without the slightest chance of success ; the deep burial of money under prospects, the most discouraging."

"But let us hear the result," said the hale, burly, trading optimist. "I am not so sure, but we shall find our mistake in that respect. In my early experience I have found the grain of mustard seed, in the shape of capital, productive of the most important consequences."

"Admitted," said the *millionaire*, "but not when thrown into a hazardous mining adventure."

"Stop, friends," I cried ; "you both are right, and both are wrong. In my case, the speculation has turned out a bad one ; for the scrip of the London and Californian Gold Crushing Company—Californian Crushers, as they are called in the market—still remains at the bottom of my security box, as inanimate and unproductive, as any stock can be, and to the extent of that £2 10s. I have despoiled myself and my family, of what we might have otherwise enjoyed. But what a fortunate thing it would be, if all the other operators in that great period of fraud and peculation, could place their losses or outlay, at that *minimum* amount. Many boxes, I fancy, could be found at bankers, and in brokers' counting-houses, which contain shares and scrip of the issues of those days, repre-

senting more than £1,000,000, if cleared out at their
original, or cost valuation. *Millionaire* must not, however, be so hard on my poor speculation; for the grain of
mustard seed in the shape of capital, has in many instances,
been highly productive; *videlicet,* the first price for outlay
in the Devon Great Consols, and also in that of the Burra-
Burra Mining Company."

"Replenish your glasses," said Optimist, whose face
is now beaming with kindly feeling, and whose eyes
glisten, as he intimates that he will give us an anecdote of
his own, in connection with a speculation, in which he has
been engaged, and, mark you, this time with profit.

"Nothing," he adds, as he smacks his lips and takes
wine, "is like claret for keeping the nerves cool, and the
head clear, when absorbed in heavy operations.

"You shall hear my story of a small speculation,
which will perhaps afford its lesson in its way—though I
often shudder at the misery, and anxiety, I passed through,
before my object was attained. It was a speculation—a
real speculation in every sense of the word, but it was my
first, and I trust it will be my last appearance, upon the
London Stock Exchange."

He lights a cigar, rolls the end carefully, and proceeds :—

"You must know friends, that it was in one of my
periods of financial depression—and they have not been
unfrequent—I was at home, moodily looking over that
crowded sheet, called the railway share list, when my eyes
lighted upon the Lombardo-Venetian Stock. Though
absorbed in other business, gigantic transactions in iron,
coal, and minerals, I had watched the course of events
during the Italian war with very great interest, and I felt
sure the time was approaching, when it would suit the

policy of Napoleon to bring it to a close. From the strain on my mind of other engagements, I fancied a little change would prove beneficial, and I meditated a trip to the metropolis, and at the same time a venture in Lombardo-Venetian shares. It was fresh in my remembrance that when they came out, they were well spoken of, that they rapidly went to a premium, and were one of the prime favourites of the day. My cogitations in the railway were solely on this subject. Had I as a military man been planning a campaign, my mind could not have been more completely centred in the one idea. Lombardo-Venetian shares had been up to four premium; they were now thoroughly prostrate, and at a discount, every day being quoted at a further fall."

"Yes," said I, "every day's intelligence brought in floods of sellers, the Paris, as well as the English houses, operating largely."

"Well, I felt perfectly satisfied that the war could not last for ever—the early engagements had been won, but still there were those, who considered that the struggle would be long and obstinate; nevertheless, that did not deter' me from following out my inclination. When I reached town all my available cash was £1000. I went to a London banker, and consulted him, upon what I termed, my investment. He shook his head doubtfully; he was not favourable at such a moment, to placing money in such a security, but if I thought of doing it he could introduce me to a broker, who would transact any *bonâ fide* business I might require. Clever bank manager—link the first: I sought the broker—link the second: here was I on the high road to gambling, and my hobby riding with all the easy grace of a lady's park hack. The broker was a first-class man, enormous connections, clients little lower than Bank and India directors, huge offices, clerks rather fussy and uncivil. My introduction is sufficient; he listens to my views, pauses at my san-guine estimate of Italian politics—but he executes the order, and off slides my last £1000 ready cash into Lom-bardo-Venetian shares. The contract is made out, the commission paid, and I return to my hotel, and still cogi-tate on these shares. I have a friend in the country who has plenty of cash, and the thought strikes me, that if I can borrow £2000 of him, it will increase my interest in this great line, and *when* the rise comes—as I feel sure it must—I can pay him with £5 per cent. in-terest."

" Well," said close-bearded *Millionaire*, " that is rather sanguine reasoning, *a fortiori*, of that event having taken place."

" Then," continued Optimist, " I can see you are no speculator—perhaps operator, is the better word to use, or you would not have made that remark. When you operate or speculate, you look straight ahead, avoiding all doubts and contingencies, and only see success. Well, I believed I only saw success. I write to my friend; it is a day or two before I receive the answer; but meanwhile Lombardo-Venetian shares are, to quote the daily oracle, ' steady, with a tendency to advance.' This is comforting, though no substantial change has taken place. The success of the Piedmontese and French troops is more encouraging, yet, nevertheless, the Austrians exhibit no want of energy. My friend sends me in due course the £2000, and though in a degree, still ignorant of the actual manner in which I intend to employ his advance, he enjoins caution in my use of it, knowing how unfortunate I have been before in a variety of transactions."

" Humph," surlily growls *Millionaire,* " determined to be ruined."

" Again I go to the same broker," rejoins Optimist in apparent glee, "who readily enough transacts my business; but, having other views on investments, he thinks I am placing too large an amount of capital in one undertaking (to use his own phrase, 'too many eggs in one basket'). He does not know my real object or intentions. The account day arrives. My shares are delivered to me, and I go to another banker with whom I have relations, and deposit them with a promissory note for another loan. Deep as I am in Lombardo-Venetian, I am not sufficiently deep, for I make another heavy purchase, greatly to the astonishment of the steady-going broker, who deals principally with Bank and India directors. All this time I have merely been stemming the tide against sales; but the market, fortunately for me, keeps steady. The rise that I am looking for, however, has yet to come, and I return to my home in the country to wait for it."

" Not a promising state of things," I remark.

" No," says Optimist; " but I had fixed my mind upon the result, and believed I could wait patiently. But how changed in the next few days was the aspect of the market! The news from Italy was discouraging; prices' fell, and with them the quotation of Lombardo-Venetians. Not such a fall, however, as would make the heart quake, but just that turn to indicate an approaching reaction. My spirits drooped. I was out of sorts. I hardly mixed with my family, and for a night or two I could get no rest. My wife, dear darling ! who has shared a good deal of misery with me, soon divined the cause. She was sure there was something on my mind. It was no use struggling against the fact, so, from first to last,

I made a clean breast of it. From a cousin on her side
I had borrowed the £2000, and if it were lost, and particularly in share operations, it would break the family
connection. Each morning's post brought the London
share list, and there was always a rush by myself and my
son to look at the prices. Back another quarter per cent.,
and the market showing great heaviness. Oh! fool that
I was ever to enter into this speculation. Surely you
have gone through enough pain in other difficulties, I
used to say, arguing with myself, to have avoided increasing it by such a venture as this. Could you not have employed your money better, in your own legitimate channels,
and perhaps with fairer prospects? What will the world
say if, after all your experience, you are once more ruined,
and that by a few thousand Lombardo-Venetian shares?
All this time the market was in a very unsatisfactory state;
the reaction which had set in was gradual, and it required
but another half per cent. fall, to place me in that position
from which there could scarcely have been a recovery.
The anxiety I experienced threatened to terminate in
madness. My brain seemed on fire, and the weight of
suspense was most overwhelmingly oppressive."

"It was a great mercy," says *Millionaire*, "you were
not thrown on a bed of sickness."

"At length," continued Optimist, "a pause ensued in
the movement of quotations; a slight rally followed,
which subsequently resulted in a rise of a quarter, to a
half, per cent. The intelligence then came of the battle of
Solferino, and at once greater activity was apparent; the
list of prices now daily presented improvement. How
jubilant immediately became my spirits! Of course I was
right; my speculation was sound, and had been most
soundly conceived. Another half per cent. rise, and I

should secure a moderate profit; if further good news came, what was there to prevent me clearing £3000 to £4000? What a pity I had not sought other means of obtaining advances; for the greater the holding, the greater would have been my returns. This was the reverse of the gloomy forebodings of the previous fortnight, and I now pretty clearly saw my way out of the wood. My wife was elated, my son was elated—we were in fact all elated together. In the midst of our rejoicing arrived the telegram, with the intelligence of the armistice, and treaty of Villafranca; this, when it was confirmed, as you know, terminated the war, the first sensible effect of which, was exhibited by the increase in value of Lombardo-Venetians, my favourite securities. I honestly confess I did not wait for the full improvement, but realized, and not only secured my original investment, but repaid the £2000 borrowed, and discharged the loan, leaving myself a clear gain of upwards of £2700. But fortunate as was the result, the torture I passed through, the harrowing influence exercised upon my home, when the great secret was revealed, and the enormous risk involved, determined me, if I could possibly restrain myself, to avoid ever again entering the arena of the Stock Exchange. Since then, I have lost nearly £3000 in a contested election, and several other large sums in mercantile adventures, but never have I known the exhaustion, produced by the alternation from apprehension to joy, and the intermediate stages of languor, which I experienced during the comparatively short interval, absorbed in the conception, and completion, of those very doubtful share operations."

Millionaire confesses with a sardonic grimace, partially occasioned by the smoke of a very fine flavoured old Cabana, first penetrating his nostrils, and then getting into his eyes, that the result might have been considerably worse, for those very transactions might have brought Optimist to bankruptcy,—whereat the latter shudders, having already passed through the process; and I add that I only hope the experiment once tried, will never be repeated, for usually if such engagements are successful, they are either followed till a fortune is assured, or, on the other hand, ruin entailed.

Watches are at this point consulted; the hour is found to be growing late, and the company, after once more pledging each other, agree to separate, none the worse for this review of some extraordinary operations.

IV.

IT is quite certain, looking at the events now passing
around, that we are going through a transition stage, in
the banking progress of this country. Every day fur-
nishes evidence of the fact, and so strongly is this becoming
apparent, that the sooner the public prepare to recognize
the change, the better will it be for all interested. The
struggle, as in the case of the common road carriage
against canals and railways, has been proceeding for some
few years, but it has now arrived at a point, when it is
self-evident, that a crisis has been attained, and that,
whether "for good or for evil," the Joint-Stock Bank
will supersede the Private Banking system.

The Duke of Bridgewater, Mr. Felton, and other great
celebrities connected with the development of the arterial
canals, scarcely supposed that, in the course of less than half
a century, their most cherished notions of the facilities
afforded by their watery routes, would be for the most part
superseded, by the extraordinary speed of the locomotive
on the iron road. George Stephenson had not then
emerged from the coal-mines to give practical effect to his
inventive genius; and his son Robert, was only a boy taking
his first lessons in engineering, from the rough examples
afforded by his father.

In the course of thirty years, however, the principal

districts of the north experienced an enormous alteration, and the carriage by the common road having disappeared through the competition of canal conveyance, the latter, in its turn, sensibly suffered as soon as railways became popular, and the success of goods traffic was established. Even at the advanced period of our own day, we have seen the last vestiges of the old road and canal business drop, as it were piecemeal, into the possession of the rulers of our railway system—first the great Pickford, and secondly the universal Chaplin and Horne, having, in one shape or the other, completely absorbed it.

Paterson, when he organized his plan of the Bank of England, old Jemmy Wood of Gloucester, when he sold grocery on one side of his counter, and changed bank notes on the other, and Mr. James William Gilbart, when he was guiding the London and Westminster Bank in its important battle against the Directors of the Bank of England, respecting the acceptance of bills, never imagined for a moment, that the banking system would have so steadily but surely expanded, or that the principles which have regulated business at these various epochs, would have so gradually but radically altered.

Paterson was considered a dreamy enthusiast, but he established the great basis of our London banking operations. Jemmy Wood was the perfect type of the original country banker, springing from the trading masses and taking his position among his fellow-men. Gilbart must be acknowledged, with the aid of his directors, and the establishment with which he was associated, to have given great impetus and vitality, to the Joint-Stock principle as developed in the metropolis, and reflected in the provinces. But they have passed with their generation ; matters have essentially varied in the banking world, and now we have

come to a period when it is inevitable that the system of
Private firms, will have to make way for its more powerful antagonists, the Joint-Stock Banks, conducted both on
limited, and unlimited liability.

The private banks have at particular junctures experienced reverses of magnitude, and in times of panic have
failed, causing misery and privation to depositors and
note-holders.   They, then however, scarcely entailed
such frightful damage, as was created by the suspension
of Joint-Stock Banks; and those who are old enough to
remember the crash following the stoppage of the Northern
and Central Bank, and the Imperial Bank of Manchester,
will admit that the suffering occasioned by those disasters
was of the most distressing character.   To bring the facts
down to a more recent date; the loss and misery occasioned
by the break-up of the Western Bank of Scotland, the
Northumberland and Durham, and one or two other
banks, at the time of the crisis of 1857, were enormous,
exhibiting the effects of bad management, and of placing
too great confidence in individual officers.

Whilst this condition of affairs has existed in exceptional instances, the Joint-Stock principle has nevertheless been making important progress, and the elements
of its success are much superior to those furnished by the
Private system.   And this can be very shortly illustrated.
The private bankers, as a class, have struggled manfully
and vigorously against the tide of competition which has
set in so strongly against them, and though they have
every now and then been able to place barriers temporarily in the way of their antagonists, they have never
been able permanently to impede their operations.   The
exclusion of the Joint-Stock Banks from the privileges of
" the clearing" was, for a short time, the stronghold of

the Private bankers, and like other ancient fortifications was considered impregnable.

Direct assault was at first tried by the Joint-Stock Banks, but it did not avail; the Committee were immovable, and refused to listen to any terms. A guerilla mode of warfare was then adopted, and when sudden pressure upon tills, for note and cheque exchanges, was found inconvenient, then at last the Private Banks gave way, and the Joint-Stock Banks vented loud pæans of triumph. Thus was the important difficulty surmounted, and the Joint-Stock Banks were furnished with the facilities which were alone required, for the ultimate enormous expansion of their transactions.

To obtain the privilege of " the clearing" was a matter of life and death to the earlier banks, but when they had " fought the fight" and gained admission, their successors, as a recognized rule, were allowed to enter after an acknowledged probationary term.

It was said when the important firm of Messrs. Strahan and Paul failed, that the Private Banking interest had received " a heavy blow and great discouragement." The same cry was raised in relation to the Joint-Stock Banks, when the Royal British Bank closed its doors, and several of the directors fled to avoid the consequences of their conduct. These two startling catastrophes occurred so near each other, that the iniquity exposed in the one had hardly faded from the public mind, before it was revived by the fearful irregularities exhibited in the examination of the other.

But yet there was an important dissimilarity in these events. The Royal British Bank failed simply through mismanagement. Had the board of directors been true to themselves and their trust, pursuing a straightforward course, their business, which was sound, would have increased, and they would now have had the control of a good and healthy concern. It was not so in the case of Messrs. Strahan and Paul. There the business was drooping through the surrounding competition of the West-end branches of the Joint-Stock Banks. Sir John Dean Paul ventured largely " into the philanthropic and director line," with an eye to connection, but without important results. The bank was not doing well, and therefore Sir John and his partners entered into speculations. These did not succeed; and to make up the deficiencies, appropriations were made of customers' securities, which eventually produced bankruptcy and disgrace.

The enormous difference between the Joint-Stock and the Private Banking systems is not to be found in the ordinary way of transacting business, or the readiness with which accommodation is afforded. It exists essentially in the security presented in the aggregate by the Joint-Stock system, and by the allowance of interest on deposits and current accounts. The amounts that accrue in individual cases may, either from deposits or balances, be small, but being, like the sands of Pactolus, golden, they recommend themselves greatly to the attention of every one in these days of thrift and perseverance.

Through the steady accumulation of custom attendant on this system, the Joint-Stock Banks, both in London and the provinces, have achieved a position which is not likely to be assailed by any innovations the Private Banks may attempt. Some hustling and jostling will be sure to ensue between the unlimited and the limited liability banks, because they are now engaged in a great competition; but beyond this their position cannot in the least be interfered with.

The Private bankers, on the other hand, must, in course of years, decay. Not that there is a probability of any serious failures or disasters : they will quietly liquidate under favourable circumstances, or transfer or amalgamate their businesses with existing powerful Joint-Stock institutions, as was the case in Messrs. Dixon and Sons' amalgamation with the Union Bank of London, and more recently by Messrs. Heywood, Kennard, and Co., and Messrs. Hankey and Co., joining with the Bank of Manchester, Limited, under the title of the Consolidated Bank ; and Messrs. Loyd, Entwistle, and Co., of Manchester, being swallowed up by the Manchester and Liverpool District Bank.

Honourable exceptions there will, no doubt, be, in which several of the private bankers, principally West-end and Lombard-street establishments, will maintain their *prestige* from acknowledged wealth and resources ; but the days of Private Banks, as a system, are numbered. They cannot now rush into the breach, and endeavour, at all hazards, to wrest business from the Joint-Stock Banks by allowing interest on deposit and balances : they have overlooked or refused to recognize that element too long.

If it has become a fashion to run after Joint-Stock Banks, and encourage the growth of the principle, it has taken such deep root that it threatens within the next twenty years to encircle the whole banking interest. The Private Banks now seldom, not at least in the ratio they did, secure new accounts. The widely-spread connection of the Joint-Stock Banks, either through directors, shareholders, or managers, so completely monopolizes this branch, that the Private Banks never possess a chance—the " touting," to use a vulgar but expressive

term, being so universal.   Where, then, is their resource ?

Extensive mutations will, in the natural order of
things, take place; old firms will die out; the majority
of successors will pass their accounts and their business
to Joint-Stock Banks; and the few who will remain
through ties of affection and old acquaintance will not be
worth keeping, and must be ultimately relinquished. The
alterations that will take place in the metropolis will
occur immediately after, if they do not at the same time,
in the provinces; and we are now on the eve of events
of this character, which will prove more important as
every year revolves.

V.

GAUNT panic, with uncertain gait and distorted visage, stalks hurriedly through the land. Like the leper of old, downcast in mien and paralyzed in limb, his presence is the signal for immediate apprehension, lest his contagious touch should strike with disease sound constitutions, and bleach white the bones of living men. The slightest blast from his lividly scorching breath remorselessly crumples up credit, and destroys, as by the fell wand of the necromancer, the good fame and fortune acquired by long years of toil and steady accumulation.

Gaunt panic, appear when he may—and the vaticinators say that his appearance is decennial—seldom or never passes through the land without functionally disturbing the great centres of finance and commerce, and impressing, in his route among his victims, some whose resources, however enormous, are thrown out of reckoning, or direct reach, by the vicissitudes that invariably accompany his career.

Gaunt panic has held unsteady sway at antecedent epochs, which would seem to mark his coming much in the order that chronological historians aver ; and if those years of 1836-37, pregnant with American distress, shadowed forth the influences of his unwelcome visit, equally disastrous were the signs presented when, in 1847-48, he again entered the palace of the millionaire and the hovel of the peasant,—the memorials of that period exhibiting the most startling losses.

It needs little effort of memory to recall most fearful visions of the dark days of 1857-58; of the convulsion that then rooted up credit and caused the collapse of firms, the strength and enduring powers of which it was supposed were proof against the assaults of this terrific and insatiate monster. Is there to be a repetition of this great sorrow for financial or speculative sins committed since that date? Is this Cimmerian gloom once more to throw its death-like shadows across the commercial horizon, and bring disasters, and its train of discouraging consequences, in the course of the next five years?

Some economic writers have sounded the passing bell, or, perhaps, to speak more appropriately, the warning-note, desiring the public to prepare for that crisis which it is presumed will come according to the natural cycle of events as illustrated by seeming precedents. With the future I will not attempt to deal; any immediate prognostication in relation to that is, to my mind, somewhat premature; but of the past I may freely speak, and, in the character and under the guise of a vision, tell of what I then heard and saw.

It is the year 1857 : the month is dull dreary November, and the panic is raging with most ungovernable fury. Houses have failed by the score ; the Bank directors have run up the rate of discount, not without reason, to 8 per cent.; it is on the eve of touching 9, and no relief in view. "Things in general," to use commercial phraseology, "are bad indeed." The private bankers stand aghast through the great lapse in confidence ; the joint-stock banks, consolidated as their resources are, exhibit the uneasiness inseparably allied with this continuous scene of disorder ; and the important problem for solution is, who may be considered safe and who not ?

Bank managers, careworn and restless, remain to the last minute that intelligence of credit is available ; bank directors, those on the *rota*, and those who, if they desired, could leave, keep watch with managers, eagerly investigating the various reports brought in from time to time, and haunt the several parlours of these establishments, in the presence of the gloom and gaslight, like weird spirits of the night.

Rumour, with her thousand tongues, is now employed as well as she can be. She has already toyed with the position and stability of more than two sound banking establishments ; she has wrecked Liverpool and Manchester firms by dozens, and Glasgow, shaky enough without, is, if you give credence to her stories, thoroughly undone. Happily, the majority of these statements turn out to be untrue ; the mind is relieved, but still the prospective apprehension increases.

In the midst of this perilous turmoil comes a report, shadowy at first, but subsequently in a measure confirmed, that a particular important leviathan house is in straits; not exactly through want of property, for that it possesses to repletion, but owing to the difficulty experienced in realizing it ; and the tale goes, that unless the Bank or the other great financial corporations interfere, the crash will be dreadful. This comes upon me with more amazement than anything else I have heard during this portentous crisis ; but unsubstantial as the rumour is, knowing the pressure existing everywhere, I fear it may be true.

Worn with several days' exertion and anxiety—for it would be difficult to explain or render intelligible to others, save those who have personally gone through a panic, what the sensations are as the various phases succeed each other—I return home, restless and uncomfortable; first, through the night influence of an implacable November fog—secondly, in consequence of the weight of the responsibility of my position. I endeavour to sleep, but all my efforts are unavailing, and in a feverish dose my mind wanders, and combining the progress of events with a little fanciful illusion, presents a sketch not far removed from stern reality.

Through the dark portals of the Bank comes, emerging into the broad thoroughfare, the form of a stalwart gentleman, a little too burly, though tall, for grace in figure, but still erect, walking easily, in a manner which to a casual observer would indicate a person of position and means. He is well, but not extravagantly attired; a long blue frock coat, with velvet collar, black vest and black trousers being the style of his scrupulously neat and unexceptional apparel. There is not the slightest display in the shape of jewellery; no exhibition of chains or rings; everything is nicely ordered and well arranged.

In my vision, I think he appears thoughtful, that he scarcely walks with his accustomed dignity, and that his cheek blanches as he communes with himself upon the importance of the mission on which he is engaged. That mission is one, so it seems according to the instincts of my perception, fraught with the most momentous consequences, not to him alone, but to others financially connected with his foreign relations, and whose future is, as it were, so completely identified with his own. Steadily he leaves the Bank, pressing towards other large monied institutions where conferences are requisite to elucidate and explain certain apparent difficulties raised by those who appear dissatisfied with his supposed resources.

And now, in my vision, it seems to me that his cheek blanches whiter than ever, as an inner thought becomes self-revealed, and the cherished hope of a life may, if his present end is not attained, be irretrievably destroyed. The annihilation of that one resolve, the darling project of his mature years, will be to him in its poignant influence more than a death mercantile, or final disruption of credit.

It is sufficient that the one bright, burning thought has become so self-revealed—for its nobleness of purpose has reinvigorated his being—and in my vision, I think I see him smile benignly, and with upraised eyes pursue his course with restored complacency and increased strength.

My vision gradually extends. I watch him into neighbouring banks; he is there received with marked attention; his views are canvassed, and, entitled as they are to weight, formally discussed. Assistance and co-operation it is admitted will be required. These are not denied; but it is essential that the Bank of England shall countenance the proceeding, and then all will be as it should be. This is the important mission in which the great financier is engaged—engaged, not to extricate himself solely from temporary difficulties, but to save and relieve others who would be most extensively compromised by his collapse.

In my vision, I follow him home to his quiet apartments in a fashionable neighbourhood; but here again there is no display, comfort, not luxury, being his prevailing taste. He is intensely disturbed. His mind, though vigorous, and his health good, he cannot altogether repel the shock occasioned by the inroad of the gaunt monster panic; and, burying himself deeply in his correspondence and his securities, he passes despondingly through the night. One hope there is, and that one hope is a load-star in the midst of his heavy affliction.

It seems to me in my vision, which at particular points occasionally becomes confused, that I compress into it the events of two or three days. Evidence there is certain that I accompanied the same figure into the Bank to consult with the court upon what was to be done under the peculiar circumstances, but a little respite was considered necessary to ascertain in what shape they would be able to furnish the required support. Pending this short delay the most serious apprehensions are aroused, and the remembrance of my vision is, that many houses, if not banks themselves, would have disastrously suffered if this leviathan capitalist had not received a little indulgence.

My vision is not protracted, though meanwhile the commercial atmosphere is fully charged with the hot breath of scandal; other capitalists of high position and wealth are said to be conniving at difficulties placed in the way of an arrangement, because rumour, quite as busily employed as ever, affirms that these great houses would be perfectly willing to see the sacrifice of a competitor accomplished, to increase their own connections, and obtain a portion of the *flotsam* and *jetsam* usually secured on the break-up of a large establishment.

Fortunately, if rumour has in the least indicated the truth, these individuals are doomed to disappointment, for after a very short delay I see my friend emerge once more from the Bank portals, accompanied by those whose presence prove to me that the desired assistance has been afforded, placing his affairs beyond the reach of further prejudicial molestation, whatever may be the current of events, or the process of exhaustion produced by the progress of panic. My vision is brought to an end as I see him return to his home in the Albany, with thankful heart and inclined head, reiterating once more the expectation of yet perfecting the dearest object of his long-toiling and self-abnegating career.

To put at rest idle reports and to counteract those which may have already gone abroad, it is publicly announced that the Bank of England and some of the joint-stock banks have agreed to assist the principals of a large American firm, who have deposited securities far in excess of the aid required, until they shall have ascertained the course of their engagements on this and the other side of the Atlantic.

Four or five years have elapsed; they have passed away with the most unparalleled speed; this great American house has reared its head again, its engagements of the panic period of 1857 have been in due course and without the slightest impediment honourably liquidated, leaving the chief partner with a most princely fortune, and the affairs of the firm progressing more prosperously than ever. The transactions of other competing houses have diminished, whilst those of the revived establishment have increased.

With the rebound in values succeeding the crisis, the investments held in partial suspense have advanced to a point not before touched. Everything in the neighbourhood of Old Broad Street is more encouraging than ever. The one thought, the day and night dream of that great capitalist's existence, is steadily assuming form and substance, and an auspicious occasion is alone wanted to make the event known throughout Europe, and thence throughout the world.

The time arrives: it is made under solemn trust and in a manner the least ostentatious. Simply a correspondence between himself and those eminent persons selected to carry out his wishes, intimate that George Peabody has made an appropriation of £150,000 from his colossal fortune immediately available for the benefit of the London poor. Thus the one cherished hope of his life is realized—he has achieved the summit of his ambition; and now for years of peace and retirement, not altogether from business activity, but that ease and leisure which his *status* and resources will permit.

Once again I see him as he returns from Guildhall, after receiving the thanks of the City of London, and the honoured gift of citizenship for the fund created, and I mark the same benign countenance, the same conscious dignity of worth; but the hair is a little more silvered, and the step less firm than prior to his day of financial trial. That dark, sombre morning has at length been followed by bright, glowing eventide.

VI.

It is impossible to overrate the advantages, social and financial, which have accrued from the gold discoveries in California and Australia. Although America first derived importance from the acquisition of an extensive auriferous territory, and was immediately placed on a footing of equality in this respect with Russia, it was not long before England secured similar auxiliary power from the active exploration of her own colonial dependencies. If California may be considered to have relieved the United States of a portion of her surplus population, and at the same time have afforded them scope for the exercise of their enterprising and acquisitive talent, so has Australia also proved a safety-valve to Great Britain in furnishing homes and resources to hundreds of thousands who would, under other circumstances, have remained in poverty and wretchedness.

France has not yet been sufficiently fortunate to increase her trade or relations by the discovery of gold in her own locality, or that of her southern or western possessions; but it is still probable that the period is not far distant when she will stand in a position equally favourable, and furnish her proportion to the general supply of the total of the precious metals produced and distributed throughout the civilized world.

The history of California dates back only a few years. Its purchase from Mexico, and the doubtful nature of the bargain, were the first distinguishing events in its chronology. Then came the reports of secret riches, fabulous in their nature and extent ; then their development on a progressive scale, and at last confirmation by veritable monthly exports to the mother country. The rush of emigration that ensued, the rapid expansion of business, and the subsequent growth of cities and towns, from the plateau site of San Francisco to the less populous districts in the mountain ranges, fill up the outline of this rapid sketch. From 1848 to 1850, or in a space of about two years the settlement had been formed, its trade opened, and its gold production raised from £11,700 to £5,000,000 ; the latter having since increased to £11,000,000 per annum. Wonderful as these results appear, they are no less extraordinary in the case of Australia. Colonized as the localities were long before it was even premised they contained the boundless wealth they have since realized, they had themselves been found to be valuable adjuncts to the commerce of the United Kingdom ; and the exports of wool and hides, and eventually tallow, gave them an importance which was readily recognized by all interested in their progress.

It remained, however, for the perseverance of a Hargreaves to demonstrate in a practical manner the existence of that which the researches of philosophers had indicated as probable. Murchison, Clarke, and other geologists had for several years intimated—the second with more precision than others (possibly from the advantage of local residence)—a conviction that the stratification of the Australian Cordillera was favourable to the existence of gold ; but with the exception of the case of Macdonald, a shepherd, who occasionally on his return to Sydney from the interior exhibited small specimens, no actual results were obtained.

In 1851, three years after the discovery of the auriferous resources of California, New South Wales was pronounced, on the authority of the government, to be rich in alluvial and quartz deposits, and active exertions were immediately made to test their capabilities. The inhabitants of Port Philip, who had then recently obtained a separate government, jealous of their reputation, commenced extensive explorations, which were rewarded by the development of Ballarat, Bendigo, and Mount Alexander. The total value of gold exported from Victoria and New South Wales in the first year did not exceed £1,000,000, each contributing nearly half, but New South Wales the larger proportion. The aggregate lately has greatly increased, Victoria producing nearly the entire sum—the shipped amount for 1861 being about £9,000,000, while New South Wales contributed only a few hundred thousands.

It may, from these figures, be estimated that the production of Australia and California is nearly equal, if the former does not in reality exceed the latter, owing to the amount retained in trade and colonial circulation, more particularly since the establishment of a mint. Taking the aggregate exports to be at this present time £21,000,000 per annum, the influence that such an addition to the precious metals has exercised upon the markets of the world, remote or otherwise, must have been enormous. The expansion of business, the opening of new channels for enterprise, and the consequences which attend these sudden mutations, have not been unaccompanied by disaster.

Increased trading, legitimate in the first instance, has led to speculation; speculation carried beyond due bounds has led to loss; and fortunate have been those whose earlier profits have either covered or diminished their later sacrifices. But admitting that partial mischief has ensued from the rush of adventure in connection with Australian and Californian trading, the result has not been without benefit. Few of the firms which failed, seeing the improvident nature of their consignments, could have hoped to escape the effects of a general collapse, when it was apparent that the supplies forwarded were wholly disproportioned to the requirements of either community.

From the severity of commercial panic and financial embarrassment California has suffered in a greater degree than Australia; and although the "go-a-head" principle of our trans-Atlantic neighbours has assisted them in recovering their *status,* the pecuniary losses experienced during the banking crash in San Francisco were extremely heavy. In this state of affairs the stability of our banking system has presented merits of no ordinary description; and notwithstanding, as experience has painfully demonstrated, that joint-stock undertakings can be brought to a stand when all sound principles are discarded, the protection they afford depositors, under the most discouraging circumstances, is better than that attained through any other medium.

The inefficiency of the American principle, except in so far as concerned the bankers themselves, was strikingly illustrated when the San Francisco suspensions occurred. The diggers, who had placed their hoards in the custody of these establishments, commenced a run, and they were paid as long as the coin and notes in the tills lasted; but

immediately the houses closed there was nothing further
to be realized—the balance-sheets exhibited by the respective parties showing that the whole property was sunk
either in inconvertible securities represented by land, state
debts, or, to use a Wall-Street technicality, " other in-
tangible nonentities." A list of shareholders, weak
though it might appear, would be far preferable to the
doubtful alternative thus presented.

But one phase of speculation, which at the time
attracted general attention from the avidity with which
the public engaged in it, has apparently wholly subsided,
and will in all probability never revive. Allusion is made
to the companies organized with the view of more rapidly
testing the resources of these new El Doradoes. Who
does not remember the scores of undertakings brought
forward for obtaining leases of land, both in California
and Australia, and despatching staffs with the requisite
machinery for carrying out mining according to the most
improved theories ? The Fremont grants and the Segen-
hoe estates were marketable at a price, although in the
first case there was no legal transfer, and in the second
the land was not auriferous or the prospects encouraging.
One pound shares were freely manufactured, and as the
scrip sold, and directors entailed little responsibility
further than signing their names and squandering the
subscriptions, the operation was continued till unpleasant
revelations caused a general explosion. It is curious
enough that France was the spot whence these bubbles
sprang. Shortly after the confirmation of the Californian
discoveries there were a host of small undertakings matured under the titles of " The Miner," " Associated
Company of Explorers," " The Company of Pioneers,"
and other distinctive appellations; but they were never

successful, and the shares had only a limited circulation. These projects, however, when fostered by English capital, and patronized by English directors, created a temporary mania, it being difficult during the height of the short fever to procure any of them under a premium.

The rage for speculating in them is, of course, not to be compared to the career of gambling which inaugurated the extension of the railway system ; but for the period it lasted there was great activity in all descriptions, and the transactions interfered with business in other and more permanent securities. And where are they now— even the best of them—the Agua Fria, the Nouveau Monde, the Colonial Gold, or the Port Philip,* with the multitude of others which it is scarcely necessary to mention ? All, or nearly all, have gone through the process of liquidation, but not before the whole of the capital has been expended, and further liabilities have, in some cases, been incurred. The directors and proprietors have found to their sorrow that neither in Australia nor in California can labour be so conducted as to produce through the management of a Company a profit proportional to the outlay.

In instances where the most studied economy has been enforced, the results have been highly satisfactory ; but in many cases, instead of the projectors and superintendents endeavouring to advance the interests of the shareholders, they have only sought to promote their own personal objects, and fritter away the funds entrusted to their care. Several of the undertakings were, without doubt, made the medium through which designing men fleeced the public of considerable sums, circumstances which subsequently transpired showing in the clearest

* This Company, under a reformed mode of working, pays a dividend to its proprietors, and now promises to be developed.

possible manner that they never contemplated quartz crushing, assaying, or any of the other operations connected with the legitimate working of the enterprise. Their sole object was "share rigging," and general plunder in the strictest sense of the term; many of the companies never having to this day afforded the least explanation of the disposition of the funds provided by the proprietors, or returned a farthing of the deposits.

Of the whole list of forty or fifty associations—the shares of every one of which were negotiated at quotations averaging from 50 to 200 per cent. premium—but one can be said to have been successful. It was remarked at the period, that "the one pound share gold-mining mania might be regarded as a lottery of the most doubtful character," and so it has turned out, there having not been a single prize to compensate for the abundance of blanks.

From £4,000,000 to £5,000,000 of capital has been sunk in these worthless undertakings, and the shareholders have the melancholy satisfaction of knowing that their money has been irretrievably lost, although the details of expenditure will never be forthcoming. As a lesson of experience to small speculators, the recollection of this epoch should prove useful; but the sacrifice large as it may have been considered in some quarters, will constitute a very small debit in the general account of the profit and loss between England and Australia, and America and California.

VII.

SPECULATION now-a-days is not what it was some eighteen or twenty years ago. True it is that great advances have been made in all descriptions of scientific and other improvements, and the association of capital with labour has produced results astounding even those who inaugurated the movement. From these, and other sources, have sprung adventures of a multifarious character, all of which have led to attempts at money-making, more or less successful, according to the various epochs at which they have been introduced. From the date of the South Sea bubble to that of the final dissolution of the Royal British Bank—which, as a remarkable coincidence, terminated its career in the very quadrangle of the old South Sea House—schemers have been found ready to take advantage of periods favourable to the floating of any nondescript project, the creation of a fertile brain or unscrupulous conscience. The rotatory motion of Dame Fortune's wheel, accelerated by the propensity to acquire wealth by a royal road, or a more circuitous route if necessary, has, however, not always achieved the desired object; and many there are who can bear painful testimony to the disastrous consequences of having been associated with Stock Exchange operations.

It has been said that "money and morals" are not always closely identified, and the lust for obtaining riches will very often interfere with the rigid exercise of honest and upright principle. If recent experience may be accepted as a criterion of the truth of the observation, the frauds perpetrated upon the public go far to establish the soundness of the axiom. It is impossible to glance back at the history of the last ten or fifteen years without being struck with the rapid increase of crime, produced by adventurous speculation, and supported at all risks when loss or discomfiture is at hand.

What can be more appalling than the revelations of the Sadleir forgeries, the Crystal Palace delinquencies, or the disastrous career of Redpath, Pullinger, and other notorious culprits. Saddening as these are, they appear to be of one and the same class, all pourtraying unhealthy eagerness to obtain wealth at whatever cost or sacrifice. The Exchequer Bill frauds, which in their day produced a profound sensation, originated in a temporary expedient to supply the funds requisite to liquidate the losses incurred through transactions in various kinds of securities, and which then were the popular medium for business.

But if isolated cases exist in which such discoveries were made, they were far from being of the startling or frequent occurrence as those which have recently attracted attention; and it is evident that the tone of financial morality has experienced considerable deterioration since the ever-memorable railway mania of 1845. Indeed, it is a common subject of remark among parties who have watched the career of events, that the gambling encouraged through the fictitious value which shares attained has done much to aggravate the existing evil—the looseness of principle and the sacrifice of probity to secure the golden prize, having been only too freely 'sanctioned in circles where a higher sense of moral rectitude should have prevailed.

Speculation, as formerly conducted, was very different to what it now is. Between the two systems there scarcely seems any affinity. At the period alluded to, the days of the Spanish, Portuguese, and South American loans—not so far back as the time when the several contracts were concluded, but later, rather about the date of the entire conversions—or confiscations, as some have not inaptly termed the process of reduction and curtailment carried out—there was a serious amount of fluctuation in prices, and the rage for dealings of this description was much more prominent than even at this juncture. Although Consols and other English securities were negotiated to a great extent, the foreign market was the scene of the principal operations, and the herds of petty jobbers who infested the neighbourhood of Capel Court gave vitality to business, and increased, if possible, the extraordinary animation usually witnessed in that locality. The Hebrews, as a nation, have always constituted a considerable majority of the operators, but in addition, numerous aliens and others, who in periods of political disturbances left the place of their birth and made England a refuge, became connected with the Stock Exchange, and for want of better means of employment, or probably a readier way of obtaining a precarious livelihood, followed the course of prices, and were speculators for the "rise" or the "fall" as the inclinations, and an appreciation of the daily intelligence received, induced them to act.

At that time, being placed in a peculiar situation—in fact, in a degree associated with one of the old contracting firms—I was brought in contact with many of these outsiders, and had opportunities rarely enjoyed, of watching the ravages of the cankerworm that has eaten to the core of many an honest heart, and blighted the most brilliant prospects of many a happy family. Old and young, rich and poor, have I seen drawn into this inextricable vortex, each struggling with his own particular views to attain the one grand object, but never in reality gaining it; and when disappointed and heart-broken, sinking into decrepitude, and at last the grave. No long list of railway shares, guaranteed or un-guaranteed, existed then; no miscellaneous companies or joint-stock bank securities, unlimited or limited; these were little known or understood. For speculation—for making a fortune, or more likely, losing one—the Penin-sular or Transatlantic bonds exhibited attractions of the most remarkable character, and in these the great bargains were effected.

But transactions of this character, desperate though they were, and involving as they almost invariably did enormous losses, were managed with more scrupulous re-gard to honour than in the present day. Men, it is not to be denied, overspeculated and failed, and in some instances fraud and chicane were established; but in the aggregate the failures never exhibited, as they do now, an almost disregard of moral responsibility, and those principles supposed to cement that confidence which is the basis of society.

One remarkable instance I may mention, of the dread infatuation attending a speculative career, which came under my own notice; the individual in question being related to the most noble Spanish families. He was a fine young fellow, who having received all the accomplish-ments that careful culture and a first-class education can bestow, left Madrid for this metropolis, to enter into a mercantile life. With the best introductions, and capital to boot, he soon gained admission into the highest City circles, and here his first fatal step was made. He happened to be thrown amongst those intimately mixed up with the extensive business of the Mendizabals, and other similar firms, whose entire concerns were one vast game of speculation—London being the centre, and Paris the next great mart of their transactions.

Although repeatedly warned of the influence of a "first bargain," especially if it show a profit, he listened to the voice of temptation, and was speedily trepanned. His own sources of information were good, and had faith been preserved by the governments of Spain and Portugal, he would have realized an enormous fortune ; but their conduct, disgraceful as it was at that period with respect to their foreign credit, soon produced one of those marvellous convulsions which brought ruin and despair to parties not prepared to believe in their irregular proceedings.

My poor friend Perez Y—— suffered with others, and after passing through the ordeal of inability to pay his "differences," again entered the arena with ardour to retrieve his position, but with very meagre success. Occasionally there was a bright hope, a notion that the fickle goddess would favour him ; yet the glorious opportunity never arrived, and he was shortly reduced to comparative beggary, with little or no prospect of relief.

A long friendship, however, had been maintained between us, and despite his confirmed monomania for speculation, I felt I could not wholly discard one who was in all other respects a most amiable and pleasant companion. Eventually he left the country, and my sphere of occupation having changed, Perez Y——, and the Spanish, Portuguese, and other foreign securities dealt in, were temporarily forgotten.

Whenever I visited the City, I nevertheless made inquiries of some of our old acquaintances, who could only give me partial intelligence respecting my missing friend, and that was not of the most satisfactory character. I nevertheless gleaned that he had visited Paris, Frankfort, and Amsterdam, following his infatuated vocation, and losing caste in most places through the unfortunate results of his operations.

One evening, when I had just finished my last slip— part of the shreds and patches that give consistency to the general contents of a daily broad-sheet—I was startled from a momentary reverie by a sonorous knock at the door of my chambers.

Before I had time to collect myself and intimate that the party might enter, a little girl, meanly attired, thrust a note towards my table, and without the least further inquiry, disappeared. I instinctively seized the missive, and recognized the handwriting: it ran as follows :—

> " ——— Buildings, ——— Street,
> " Stepney Green.
>
> "Mui Amigo M——, I have managed to reach England again, and have lived in seclusion here some weeks, broken up by disease and want. Few are now left me of my old acquaintances. Have you the inclination or time to pay me a visit? *Donde estan tus flores brillante juventud!*
>
> " Weeping yours,
> " P. Y."

I confess I was singularly affected by this epistle; it touched an old chord, and I at once resolved to seek his abode. From the address, I could tell he had taken up his quarters near a spot where he had previously been compelled to sojourn through a pressure of circumstances. Gathering together my papers, I hurriedly arranged them, and was speedily in the broad glare of the public thoroughfares. Fleet Street was soon passed; Cheapside in succession, and then the Bank.

Impelled by curiosity, instead of continuing a direct route, I turned aside, and threading the narrow passages at the end of Bartholomew Lane, wandered in several places where in earlier days Perez and I had frequently been together. Little alteration had occurred in their appearance. The same dull heavy air seemed to pervade the neighbourhood, and although improvements had made progress, their irregularity indicated no settled order or system.

It was rather advanced in the evening, but the lights and sounds proceeding from many of the local refectories plainly indicated that although the business of the day had passed, many of their frequenters remained. A thought suddenly struck me as I approached one from which my poor friend had on several occasions addressed me letters. Entering, I explained my object, viz., to ascertain if any of his old acquaintances still resorted there, and was fortunate enough to discover two who remembered him well, and who were thoroughly acquainted with the whole of his antecedents. The elder gentleman also was not entirely unknown to myself, and volunteering to accompany me, we made our way thence through Bishopsgate, across Spitalfields, down Whitechapel, on to Mile End, and reached in less than an hour the place designated in the note left at my chambers.

"Ah!" remarked my companion, looking at the row of small tenements towards which we were directing our steps, "this is what a great number of them come to. It is a desperate game; but some fare even worse, distressing as the case may be—suicide, expatriation—all the fearful consequences of this kind of life!"

This was delivered in the style of an apostrophe, for he well knew that I was acquainted with many similar instances, from which the most fearful results had accrued to individuals thus compromised.

Having arrived at our destination, my knock at the door was soon answered. I inquired whether Mr. Perez Y—— was residing there.

"Oh! you mean the gentleman that's ill," said the girl attending the inquiry, and whom I recognized as the bearer of my summons.

"I mean a foreign gentleman—a Spaniard," was my response.

"Yes; the poor gentleman that's ill, you mean," repeated the girl. "You're the friend then," continued she, "that he has been expecting all the evening; he'll be glad you've come."

Motioning us to follow, we ascended a narrow staircase; the dilapidated state of the house and its confined position betokening the poverty of its inhabitants. Our progress was, however, arrested by a peremptory hush, and the appearance of the doctor afforded the opportunity for ascertaining the state of the health of his patient. He gave an unfavourable account of the ravages of the disease—consumption in its worst form—and said it was, in his opinion, a question of only a few days. As the poor fellow was partially delirious, he advised caution in the proposed interview.

The dim light from the piece of candle that guided our footsteps cast a heavy shadow on the wall as we passed onwards, and prepared us in a measure for the spectacle we were about to witness.

There, on a low trestle bed, was stretched the care-worn invalid. His naturally well-formed frame had been so completely invaded by disease, that he was merely the shadow of his former self. Sallow in complexion when in health, the contrast was now indeed striking. The lines of his features were sharp and distinct, and his high pale brow was well developed beneath his crisp, curly black hair. It was true he was "wandering," as the nurse said, when she applied a saturated handkerchief to his mouth to relieve his thirst, for he knew no one. I endeavoured to obtain a recognition, but in vain. He rolled in his bed, not as if in agony, but as though he were enjoying himself in society.

Talking in his native tongue, the motion of his hands and his significant gesticulations seemed to indicate that he was impressing advice upon an imaginary acquaintance. I could distinguish at intervals something of what he said, but from my imperfect knowledge of Spanish, I was unable to catch everything. The strongly and oft-repeated exclamation, as he raised his head, of " *Si, senor, vende tu camisa y comprate los vales* " ("Yes; sell your shirt, and buy the bonds "), was sufficient to inform me that he supposed he was in his accustomed haunts, sur-rounded by the associates of former periods. It was remarkable that at that very time a sensible rise had taken place in Portuguese, one of his favourite securities; and the people of the house mentioned his partiality for reading the foreign news, and his constant inquiries respecting the price of stock.

Thus we found poor Perez previously to his death, and thus we left him. Still the same strain during the brief interval that preceded the termination of his earthly career. His wants were quickly provided for, and helping hands were ready to be extended from several quarters, but their assistance was never needed. With "the ruling passion strong in death" he passed away, and furnished another example of the mysterious influences which control and regulate our different destinies.

VIII.

IT is not denied by the most ardent friends of the Bank Charter Act that there are peculiarities in its operation which require amendment. They would be most willing to facilitate the requisite changes without making concessions to popular clamour, or to the advocates of inconvertibility. The experience of two serious panics since the Act came into force has been obtained, and shown how incapable it is of carrying out in their full integrity the principles which were so strongly asserted to be the basis of the new law. But while it is allowed that the Act has not worked as well as it should, it has still not altogether failed in its attempt to regulate the machinery of the currency.

The great misfortune seems to be that in maintaining the privileges of the Corporation and of the proprietors —a point invariably looked to in any negotiations between the State and the Governor and Company of the Bank of England—conflicting interests must arise ; and it can hardly be otherwise with the present constitution of the latter. The Bank is divided into two departments—one the banking and the other the issue— and they can never work quite satisfactorily together. However conscientiously the directors may desire to conduct the business of their great establishment, there must always be the two objects in view : first, as is supposed,

to regulate the currency; and next, to look after profits
and to earn an average amount of dividend. In these
days of competition, when most of the great metropolitan
joint-stock banks can distribute to their proprietors profits
equal to 20 and 22 per cent., the return of 8, 9, or even
10 per cent. to bank stock proprietors seems insignificant.

It must be allowed, of course, that there is some dis-
tinction between the body corporate of Threadneedle
Street, and the London and Westminster, and the London
joint-stock banks, as regards the class of transactions
into which they enter; but the position of the former,
with the large facilities it possesses, ought to ensure it a
greater proportion of profit. It is true there is much
dignity about the Bank of England; the office of Director
is a post of high honour, and the supreme seats of Governor and Deputy-Governor place their happy occupants at
the highest elevation of financial rank. It is, unfortunately, owing to this very dignity, refusing to stoop down
from its lofty eminence, that the Bank is prevented from
securing a much larger share of business than it has
hitherto enjoyed. In the competition which is now taking
place between the joint-stock banks, limited and unlimited, and the private banking interest, the Bank of
England may be compelled to move on, but this movement
will, it is feared, require more ability than at present
pervades the councils of the Court. If there be any
real genius among the six and twenty high-class
names constituting the direction, it is probable that the
routine of the establishment prevents its development.
Unless some vigorous attempt be made to enforce attention to the question, it cannot be hoped that any immediate success will ensue. The Court has the privilege of

exercising its own free will, without control; and it is hard to surmount any objections raised by the Governor and his deputy on the other side of the purple cloth, at the meetings in the Bank parlour. These meetings, indeed, have become quite farcical, important as their deliberations ought to be. At these half-yearly Courts, instead of merely announcing the dividend, and receiving a few stated compliments and adulations from self-complacent proprietors, the great financial questions of the day should be discussed, and information elicited of the progress and movements of banking in general.

What the East India Court meetings formerly were, the Bank of England meetings should be at present; but its debates have gradually dwindled to such a degree that now, if the proceedings occupy more than a quarter of an hour, the proprietors are surprised. In days gone by Mr. Parry de Winton, the ever-present Mr. J. H. Clark, Mr. Weedon, and Mr. Fielder, would attack the Court, but never on great points. Where now is Mr. Thompson, with his one stereotyped question, "Do the branch banks continue a source of profit?" All these gentlemen appear to have retired, and left the arena to be filled by Mr. Alderman Salomons, Mr. Matthew Clark, and one or two others, who are quite satisfied to obtain an assurance that everything is progressing well; and who, in return, pass cut and dried votes of thanks, uttering a few platitudes to embellish the mock formality. This will not much longer be tolerated. The endeavour of one almost unknown proprietor, recently, to break down the barrier of official dignity between the proprietors and the Court, should be resolutely followed up by some of the most influential on the list.

It will be difficult at first to enlist parties ; but only let one or two Court meetings take place at which there is a disposition exhibited to probe the topics of the day, and the information demanded must then come out, and the Court and the public will thereby be enlightened. If this be not done, the somnolence and apathy of the body of Bank stock proprietors will not escape the notice of experimenting financial authorities, and the Court and their privileges will be speedily interfered with. The Court may be in some measure to blame for not taking the initiative in reformation, and making the most complete use of the facilities they enjoy ; but, at the same time, the proprietors should remember that they have a duty to perform, and if they believe the Court require prompting, it is their province to take united action to accomplish that end. This proneness to allow the Governor and Deputy-Governor to have too much their own way has always been the anomalous feature in the history of the corporation ; more especially, however, in the last five or six years ; the great struggle with the discount brokers, and the earlier publication of the *Gazette* returns, not having provoked the discussion those matters deserved. This may eventually prove the rock on which the establishment will split ; for if, in common parlance, the proprietors do not look after their own affairs, other persons will not do so for them.

It has always seemed to be understood that Mr. Gladstone has entertained the notion that a State Bank should be organized, not alone for the convenience of the Treasury, but also for the benefit of the public exchequer. Those who profess to be acquainted with the idiosyncracies of his subtle, symmetrical, financial mind, have every now and then given inklings that at a future day, if he remain much longer in power, some demonstration will be made which will be the precursor of an important change. He, it is positively asserted, sees the impracticable points of the Bank Charter Act, and his microscopic vision will ere long penetrate the details. In what manner his views may shape themselves no one would attempt distinctly to prophecy, but his predilections would, there is little doubt, lead him to increase the power of Government over the establishment, even should he not interfere with the privileges of the Corporation at the end of the term for which they have been granted.

The Charter runs for some period yet; meanwhile various mutations may occur, but it is not impossible that Mr. Gladstone's impressions on the subject have been shared by others, and that when the proper season arrives, it will be much more completely ventilated. The banking and financial community are undergoing quite a *bouleverse-ment*—for the better or worse, a date within the next decade will decide. It will consequently be necessary for all who have monetary relations of importance, to watch their growth, augmentation, and maturity, with a vigilance that was never thought of in the past; and if we should at any moment approximate to the formation of a State Bank, the groundwork of such relations would be of a most delicate and complex character. A State Bank might or might not be advantageous to the country; its arrangement would require to be most strictly checked and guarded against official peculation and jobbery; and while there are many who altogether disapprove of creating such an institution, a great number of thoughtful and recognized economists would, on the other hand, give to the project their support.

IX.

SHADOWS OF THE PAST.—A WALK ROUND 'CHANGE.

I AM, I believe, a thoroughly confirmed monomaniac. Perhaps this arises from what may not improperly be called my surroundings. From whatever cause it proceeds, there is no denying the fact that I have become so completely identified with the City, in the general, if not abstract sense of the term, that I fancy I am somehow or other welded into a portion of that great heaving mass of machinery, which throbs, and vibrates in its daily action through sources innumerable, influencing the banking and financial transactions of the entire world.

This spice of egotism—for that, I have no doubt, the assertion will be dubbed by even my best friends—must not be ascribed to any vanity, but, on the contrary, principally to a destiny which seems to have exercised full sway over my short but eventful life, and that in close connection with the use and the abuse of money, and its multiplied relations as represented on 'Change.

I was born within a stone's throw of the great national establishment, as the Bank is sometimes called, and nurtured in one of those very large red brick mansions which were formerly to be so frequently met with in and about the Mansion House. The antiquity of my home was evidenced in its huge, cavernous cellars, its long, massive staircases, its balustrades of heavily-fashioned

mahogany, its wide hall—almost sufficient to turn a
coach-and-four in—and its long iron link extinguishers,
which hung gloomily pendant from either side the door-
way. The sombreness of the house affected me almost
from infancy, my mind was fashioned for sober thought,
and parental guidance confirmed my staidness by directing my attention in affairs mundane to that important
centre of operations embraced within a circuit of Threadneedle Street, Lombard Street, Cornhill, and Lothbury.
My proclivities for making acquaintance with these sorts
of things were thus developed at an early date, and
have since gradually progressed, through study and observation; but, happily, I have been able to repress the
evil genius Avarice, though I have not been so fortunate
as to avoid incurring the calumny of being thought rich,
when I know full well I am comparatively poor; a fact
that will hereafter be discovered, to the intense satisfaction of my numerous enemies.

Assuming that my thoughts were directed in my infan-
tine days, not to the acquisition of, but to a general knowledge concerning the circulating medium, it is sagely
related of me, that when I was ill and blind, through a
most severe attack of measles, I resolutely refused to take
my medicine, until the doctor administered consolation in
the shape of a penny, which immediately opened a way
for the passage of the draught, and put me on favourable
terms with him for the future !

" Good Doctor Headington," as he was familiarly
styled, was a type of the school of the last generation ; the
fine old gentleman in the neatly crimped frill shirt, knee
breeches, and black silk stockings with buckled shoes.
He soon became a fast friend of mine, having predicted
clever things of me, because he believed there was

"something in the boy." Our acquaintance ripened and grew into a firm friendship, which was only severed when *pallida mors* loosened the silken cords that bound us together.

Shades of the past, ye come looming up in all your greatness; wave not at present your sable plumes to remind me of what I am and what I shall be, but bear awhile and suffer me feebly to trace a few scattered memorials of names and things that hold sweet, though in many cases painful remembrance among the living! Stand back! compress your fretting feathery heads, room ye shall have, and plenty, to put in form your darkening presence when the grand master Time shall call all home!

It is not surprising that with my education, commenced in that old gaunt house, one of the residences of the merchant princes of the Steelyard days, I had, before I was fit for migration to a country school, explored the most remote corners of the metropolis, but particularly those brought within the sphere of immediate notice. What portion of the Royal Exchange was I unacquainted with?—where was the nook or corner in 'Change Alley that I had failed to investigate, not for archæological researches, but for mythical lost bank-notes, lottery bills, and cherry-stones?—who more frequently than myself traversed Sweeting's Rents to look at the picture establishments which exhibited the chief caricatures of the day, before the celebrated H. B. lived, or poor Seymour had passed away?—or who, when in funds, better enjoyed his glass of gingerade from Colsey's cool fountains, than the sketcher of this sketch?

And all this, to say nothing of the chevying under the piazzas of the Exchange, the drumming on the settles, to arouse the vengeance of the gilt cocked hats and the

silver-mounted staves of office, regularly encased in their
snug watch-boxes at each end of the building.

Who more punctual in his attendance than myself on
the 1st of May, when from the old Post-Office, the mail
coaches, and mail carts, started in gay procession for
their journey, with the horses richly decked in ribbons
and flowers, and the mail coachman and guards—a time-
honoured race—dressed in their gorgeous liveries of scarlet
and gold? Does not my mind wander back to those friends
in the Dead Letter Office, who were always promising to
procure me—but never did—a treat in the shape of a ride
with their relative, the puissant guard of the York mail,
so that I might have the satisfaction of seeing how he
arranged the bankers' and money parcels, and fixed his
pistols, and short blunderbuss, previously to starting in his
curiously-contrived seat at the rear of that vehicle?

Does not the acuteness of that disappointment, which
for years I was unable to surmount, especially when I heard
the sharp twang of the long mail horn—and which was
not removed till I had the satisfaction of being sent to a
boarding-school on the Great North Road, when, on one
occasion, on my return for the holidays, having missed
the ordinary coach, my friends, to my delight, made
terms with this very tall bewhiskered gentleman to drop
me at my destination,—shadow forth something of being
intended by nature to be thrown into the midst of the
great vortex of financial life?

Was I not interested to find I had not mistaken my
companion?—was he not marvellous in his stories, during
that ten or twelve miles' ride, of highwaymen, mail rob-
bers and wayfaring tramps?—did he not make my blood
leap in my veins when he described, midst clumps of
trees, and in sheltered ravines, the possible places from

which an attack on the mail might be attempted ?—were there not special points he showed me at which the notorious Turpin and his associates, had made their haltings, when escaping the vigilance of the authorities ?

All this told with the shadows of trees in a clear autumnal evening throwing their arms in lank and fantastical array across the road, impressed itself upon me with a peculiar charm ; but the time was, alas ! too short for its continuance. A smart whirl of the coachman's whip, a cheery Oh ! Oh ! to the horses, a hurried good-bye from a small upturned face to another looking down with kindly sympathy, and my greatly coveted ride was at an end.

How is it that in that school, whence has emanated talent to grace the best of the professions, my mercantile and financial capacity is speedily discovered ? Is it because I am a City-bred boy—a true son of Cockaigne, born within the sound of Bow bells, and having some slight knowledge of things east of St. Paul's ? Is it because I know the purlieus of the Mansion House, speak with confidence of Rothschild's counting-house in New Court, and unravel the mysteries of the pulling down of Old London Bridge, showing with pride my small minature Bible made from the foundation stone ?—or, further, is it because, naturally of a prudent and careful turn, I husband my weekly allowance, and am enabled to make advances, at the current rate of interest, to the more spendthrift class, who will revel in the luxuries of French rolls, raspberry tarts, and candied horehound ?

The latter position, I have often thought, made me a little looked up to, not because I was usurious, since there was an absence of anything approaching that in my financial arrangements, but from the simple fact, that if a fellow was in a mess, either in arrears for rabbits' food, or in debt to James the gardener, for plants and seeds, an application to the " copper merchant " would set them free, and end in a saturnalia round the old walnut tree, which would have thrilled with delight the heart of a Faun.

Did this foreshadow in the slightest degree my future connection with the money market, or those haunts sacred to the high name of £ *s. d.*? Could the fact of my having started on a sheet of foolscap, with a good goose quill, raised weekly by eleemosynary aid, the journal called the *Academic Chronicle*, typify in the least a relation at some distant day with the press literature of England? Yet so it was, and so it is ; and the world goes moving round.

Shades of the past, ye are pressing on with solemn grandeur ! Those large funeral urns speak of great names, and symbolize in eloquent, but silent force, the strong grief felt for worth departed. *Sic transit !*

I have left the chrysalis state. I have been working, and have worked upwards. I have worked into the heart's core of the City of London. Steadiness in conduct, and punctuality in the performance of my engagements, has thrown me into strange channels. If not a Whittington at the very outset, I have not forgotten his story, problematical though it is in some of the details, and, following his example, have made available for beneficial purposes my leisure hours.

By strange, but fortunate coincidence, I am brought in contact with the principal monied powers of the period —the great Nathan Meyer Rothschild, the Barings, the Goldsmids, the Cohens, the Carbonnells, the Mendizabals, and others of that class, who lived to secure enormous wealth, before the new principle of the Credit Mobilier, or, as it is styled in some quarters, confederated capital, was called into existence, to compete with the operations of their successors.

What if my introduction to the important representative of the Rothschild family, is in the character of a flying Mercury, with the intelligence of the West India Relief Loan having passed the House of Commons. Is it not of vital interest to him to know the fact, though it is at an advanced hour in the evening, seeing that in the course of a few days, he will probably be called upon to contract, what is afterwards known as the "Black" Loan. He evidently considers it so, or he would not on a foreign post night admit me on passing a simple name into his presence, and receive from my own lips, the message I am desired to convey. There, at the old establishment in New Court, I am face to face with the greatest millionaire in Europe; he, with his heavily hanging, but smiling countenance, questioning me, after he has satisfied himself of the correctness of my intelligence, on small points of every-day news. How snugly he sits ensconced in his easy chair—with a sofa at hand for a lounge after the fatigues of business—his broad table before him smothered with correspondence. How sagacious he looks from beneath his full eyebrows, as he plays with his loosely-adjusted white neckerchief, and then pulls together the ample folds of his dark coat. The result of that interview I can never forget.

Subsequently, although but a growing youth, I meet him frequently on 'Change, at the pillar where he accustomed himself to stand, surrounded by his friends, on Tuesdays and Fridays. Among them are Thomas Massa Alsager, then styled the Mirror of the Times, and the

good old soul Daniel Hardcastle. If he desire to speak,
or communicate with me, I boldly go into the group
of Exchange brokers, and receive my information; if
not, I pass before him; his quick eye detects me:
there is nothing to say, and I move away. If I visit
New Court before he returns, I am sure to encounter
a bevy of poor Hebrew suppliants for alms, who besiege
him going and returning, clustering round him as if they
were his closest kith and kin.

Who is here entering 'Change from the southern
entrance, and walking steadily, not as in subsequent
years, bowed nearly to the ground with age and in-
firmity? It is plain Isaac Lyon Goldsmid, afterwards
Sir Isaac Lyon Goldsmid, who in his later years, receives
considerate attention at the hands of royalty, and is
possessed of property second only to a Rothschild. He,
with his venerable appearance has come to meet that fine,
tall, gentlemanly man attired in black, who, with imposing aspect, is in the midst of a host of Spaniards, and
Portuguese, debating dry topics of finance. That individual is the celebrated M. Mendizabal, the future
Chancellor of the Exchequer of Spain, whose eventual
career did not escape condemnation when his policy
became developed. Mr. Isaac Lyon Goldsmid has
objects in view—so has M. Mendizabal; they know each
other, and their sapient glances prepare either not to be
taken by surprise. They have both probably huge operations on foot in the Peninsular securities—perhaps in
the contrary direction; and if one elicits much intelligence from the other, fortunate will be the gainer.

I lose them as the attendance on 'Change increases,
and the general hum of voices, first droning, then
becoming more powerful, rises at length, into ineffective

competition, with the noise from the warning bell. There
are others I see mingling in the crowd, old Thomas Ward,
and Joseph Somes, the leviathan shipowners ; they are in
the heyday of their prosperity ; their argosies of wealth
are upon all seas ; their vessels stand registered for every
land. They meet their friends in their respective walks,
and are recognized with much deference.

Shades of the past, I again invoke your aid ! Let
your cypress tresses fall lightly about your brows, and
cloud not too heavily our present dreamland ! The silver
arrow has sped, the column is broken, but the great day
will adjust all !

Pluto and the furies, have designed a huge conspiracy.
They have attempted to drive Plutus and his worshippers,
from their acknowledged throne. A great conflagration
has taken place—such a one has not been known for a
quarter of a century. The lurid skies spread the information far and wide, and all attempts to arrest the
mischief are unavailing. The old steeple of Bow is
lighted up, till the dragon becomes in the pale grey light
indeed a dragon of fire, and the dome of St. Paul's, with
its dark rotundity, rises up in full dimensions, leaving
the small turret at the summit, and the gold cross,
thoroughly illumined by the sapphire hues which shimmer
through the sky. It is an intensely cold night, and an
intensely cold morning ; but all the appliances of skill
cannot stay the destruction that is going forward. The
Royal Exchange is evidently doomed, and with it the surrounding piles of buildings. The grasshopper for a while
maintains his supremacy, but only in a blackened and
charred position, and he, like other elevated celebrities,
finally staggers and falls.

Lloyds, the old-established shipping institution, the

contiguous offices, the premises in Sweeting's Rents, are more or less injured, if not permanently rendered useless, and the scene is one of universal destruction. The crowds, numbering hundreds of thousands, closely impact round the Mansion House, Cheapside, Old Princes Street, Moorgate Street, Threadneedle Street, Bishopsgate, Leadenhall Street and Cornhill, are surging to and fro, battling for precedence to get near the spot, and witness the endeavours of the fire brigade to check the fury of the maddened elements.

The roads and passages near the spot, are sheets of ice—the frost, which has not exhibited the remotest sign of giving, having acquired greater strength from the general outflowing of water. The branches from the engines, as they are directed with precision against the burning building, shoot forth their hissing streams, which are lapped up by the many-tongued flames emerging from the windows, or drape the frames and the surmounting *chevaux de frise,* with fringes of icicles of the most massive description.

I am here again, active in the body of the masses in front of the Exchange, probably more by accident, than design. Many I recognize, drawn hither by the unpleasant knowledge that their offices are uninsured and that their losses, however soon the fire may be got under, must be considerable. Following this catastrophe the confusion for days, weeks, and months, is extremely great. 'Change removes to the quadrangle of the South Sea House, and there is not sufficient accommodation. Lloyd's business is carried on in the upper apartments of that old-fashioned building, and committees are formed to superintend arrangements, and devise regulations, to obviate, if they can, immediate inconvenience. Moving in one shape or other, I become concerned in the practical evolvement of the plans devised, and thus am established once more on the ground identified with my old pursuits. *Tempora mutantur!*

The new Royal Exchange is designed; fierce competition rages, and the best architectural proposal unfortunately is shelved. The structure in its fresh form progresses, and in the course of a few years is completed, but scarcely to the satisfaction of any save the Gresham committee. Meanwhile numbers of the visitors of the old institution are called away; others depart through broken fortune; a few ascend to high estate and diplomatic appointments, leaving the writer still to commune with the shadows of the past, in his every-day walk round 'Change.

X.

THE days of premium-hunting have not passed. It was supposed, till within the last few months, that the rage for share subscription would never again assume a magnitude, likely to be dangerous to the general community. That supposition we must now admit to have been fallacious, unless we perversely shut our eyes to what is hourly passing before them. How long the present fever-heat of speculation will be maintained it is impossible to predict, but from what has recently occurred, it is to be expected that it will shortly decline. The public must be prepared for reaction, and when the reaction comes, fortunate will be the loanholder and the shareholder, if he escape without being plunged into that vortex of ruin and loss, associated with Stock Exchange panics. It must be evident, looking at the rate at which speculation has progressed since the commencement of last year, that we have incurred an enormous amount of liability in the shape of foreign loans, and the various enterprises, submitted for support.

Money, to the extent of many millions, has been subscribed to assist the necessities of Turkey, or to develope the resources of Egypt, and Morocco; and, whilst Portugal has not failed to come again into the market as a borrower, Peru has been allowed to consolidate her debt, though on a doubtful footing; Venezuela bringing up the rear, with two new financial arrangements. Russia and

Italy have likewise sought supplies, but they have not been altogether successful. It is illustrative of the rampant eagerness which has existed for the adoption of new foreign securities, that facilities for obtaining aid, have been so readily afforded to one or two of the states named in this list, particularly after the experience gained through former forced conversions, and the wholesale sacrifice of arrears of interest, when it has been found necessary to seek indulgence on the plea of inability to maintain intact original engagements.

Foreign loans, however, so long as dividends are paid and sinking funds are kept in work, may not prove the worst of investments, though they very frequently produce pressure when they too rapidly accumulate, and the instalments have not been spread over a sufficient period to make their payments fall with a due regard to the prospects of the future. But whilst we have been spreading our gold broadcast in distant countries, and sending the proceeds of these transactions away, we have not been neglecting enterprise at home. Numerous banks have been formed; hotel companies without number have been started; and there seems no character of adventure, to which limited liability, will not in the course of a short time, have been applied.

It would be, perhaps, impossible for a speculative epoch to pass over, without being fraught with considerable mischief. The old story of money and morals not closely consorting together, has been too frequently realized to doubt the truth of the adage; but it must be allowed that recently, the amount of transparent jobbery almost recognized in the light of day, has exceeded that known to have existed in the great bubble period of 1824-25, or the later railway mania of 1845-46.

In the Spanish-American loan days, when Peruvian was sold by auction from the benches of the old Royal Exchange, and when the value of the shares of the mining companies then issued, reached almost fabulous premiums, the operators and jobbers—and they were jobbers in every sense of the term—made fortunes few knew how, though every one sought to inquire. But it was a long time before irregular dealings were discovered, and not till the loan had become nearly valueless, and the companies had gone through such serious vicissitudes as to bring them to the verge of bankruptcy, that persons, who shall be nameless, were found to have committed great wrongs, not only against the public at large, but also against their own particular friends.

The knavery of the railway mania took even a stronger hue and colour; but bad as it was it scarcely approaches, in open trickery, and lucre-hunting, the promotion system, and share rigging of the present day. The Railway King, as poor Hudson was then called, and some of his associates, were roughly handled for their questionable proceedings; but if the history of the present speculation shall ever be faithfully written, succeeding generations will be inclined to draw a comparison, and to regard their conduct with much more leniency than we have been hitherto accustomed to accord it.

If in the days of the railway speculation, engineers, lawyers, and contractors, were supposed to have secured the greatest share of profit, the promoters, lawyers, and directors have on the present occasion, not neglected the opportunity of taking care of themselves. Most unblushing have been the appropriations made for services in the establishment of banks, and most unscrupulous the conduct of the worthies in seeking to get the best of each other in their temporary arrangements, for dividing the spoil when it has come within their grasp. The majority of the promoters have emerged from a school that was little likely to elevate their original education, or inculcate principles of strict honour in the management of the affairs they might happen to undertake.

Many of them have comprised discarded actuaries and secretaries of defunct life and fire offices, which, shooting up like mushrooms on an autumn morning, collapsed as soon as a breath of adversity assailed them; and they have made a good market of their ingenuity and talent. By nature men of reckless character, they have not hesitated to enter into engagements which prudent individuals would have avoided. By dint of impudence they have gone for high prizes, and in several instances have secured them. Supported by one or two sharp-practising professionals, whom it has of course been necessary to pay well for their assistance, the game has been bagged, in the ratio of £6,000 to £10,000 for a bank, £3,000 to £5,000 for a first-class hotel, and £1,000 to £3,000 for a mining or manufacturing adventure! A regular tariff has consequently been established upon which these company-mongers have constantly traded, and traded so successfully, that several are reputed to have become small millionaires, who can command their £20,000 or £30,000 at a moment's notice to further fresh plans for entrapping the public.

Between promoters and directors, there has sprung up an unholy alliance, which will hereafter, it is feared, militate strongly against the general body of shareholders. Except among first-class men who seek to join these various boards—and first-class men are not always strong enough to resist the temptation—a practice has been adopted of the promoter or promoters qualifying the directors, so that their names go forth to the public as guaranteeing the respectability of the undertaking, though they possess little or no pecuniary interest in it, and are protected against any liability in respect of it. This is un- doubtedly the most acceptable kind of "limited liability" as concerns the qualified director; but is it fair and straightforward, towards the great mass of the un- initiated public, who constitute the subscribing share- holders?

Indeed, we are rapidly approaching that era when it will be a condescension on the part of the aristocracy of wealth, to allow subscriptions to be received at all in sup- port of leviathan undertakings. Have we not seen it recently stated, that the whole of the capital has been subscribed towards two gigantic companies, the operations of which are to be almost universal? Surely this state of things cannot last much longer; it is the old chronic disorder of premium-hunting in its worst form; there are now professional directors, like professional pro- moters, who for fee and reward allow their names to be hawked about, ringing the changes on the boards of the different companies. These City company-mongers do not exhaust themselves without being adequately satis- fied for their labours; and though the fecundity of the "guinea-pig" race has wonderfully exhibited itself during the last twelve months, grades are becoming apparent in this, as in every other walk of life.

A director of first-class pretensions, takes part of the promotion-money or shares, claims his special privileges at his board, and a stipulated extent of patronage. He never condescends to look at a second-class project or prospectus, but acts like a celebrated promoter, who, when asked to father a scheme which involved hundreds of thousands, significantly bowed the applicant from his presence, saying he never dealt with anything under a million.

The second-class director holds himself in reserve for good companies, that float readily at a moderate premium; he too seeks special privileges, and a certain amount of patronage. If he possess a weakness—and second-class directors have their foibles—it is when he is asked to bolster up a failing adventure, in the hope that his name will give a stamp of respectability to others of a rather shady character. His reply is, " Get the shares to a premium, then I shall come in with *éclat;*" and, of course, he has his complete apportionment at the best quotation.

The third-class director — and his name is legion — does everything, and anything to secure position; aims at allotments, patronage, and the several waifs and strays, pertaining to a board-room—possibly a little commission on the printing and stationery, if there is not a very vigilant secretary—for he is desirous of making way in the world, and that by the shortest route. Unhappily he is too frequently only his own enemy, since not being brought within reach of the top branches of the great Pagoda-tree, he is unable to make those fortunate pulls at the fruit which his more elevated brethren obtain; and after getting heaps of worthless shares and scrip certificates, and incurring liabilities as plentiful as blackberries, he subsides into insignificance, and if pressed, unhesitatingly " skedaddles" to the Continent.

This picture is no exaggerated outline, of the position and character, of the leaders in the great game of speculation, that is now being played within a circuit of a quarter of a mile of the Royal Exchange, and which seems likely to be perpetuated. It has frequently been urged, when this matter has been discussed, that the public, learned in their own generation, are wise enough to take care of themselves. We hope it may be so; but notwithstanding the lessons of the past, we very seriously doubt it, and shall be only too pleased if we eventually discover our apprehensions to have been misplaced.

XI

THE STATE OF THE MONEY MARKET FROM A FRESH
POINT OF VIEW.

I REMEMBER well, when I was a tiny boy, the strange feeling of dread inspired by my father, who was a fund-holder, emphatically desiring me, as fathers can do, to look under the head of money market, and read to him the two or three first paragraphs respecting the state of the stocks. This command was usually made at break-fast-time, as I was the first to rush to the newsman when his short, sharp tinkle of our bell announced his arrival; and if I was deeply engaged in perusing the horrors of that frightful discovery, the murder of Maria Martin in the Red Barn, and the further particulars of the apprehension of Corder, taken, as I well recollect he was, while cooking eggs at his own fire-side, my annoyance was increased, because to wade, as I then thought, through a dreary column devoted to facts and prices, was an ordeal second only to that of returning to school after the customary month's vacation.

But although not immediately yielding with the best grace, yet I knew that if my father desired it, the most pleasant course was to comply, and get out of my misery with the least delay, since, notwithstanding he was an affectionate parent, there was not the slightest utility in endeavouring to evade his imperative request. Little did I dream at the time—now more than thirty years ago—that I should ever have been thrown so completely head-over-heels, as it were, into this maëlstrom of financial life, or that this same heavy, dreary column, would become the bread and cheese of my every-day existence, serving to support Paterfamilias, with a numerous family, whose wants and requirements are not of the most insignificant kind.

Well do I remember how greatly I used to wonder at the old gentleman being so solicitous about whether the Three per Cents. were up or down—whether Long Annuities had moved or not, and if any notice was taken of the next red-letter day at the Bank. To me it was wearisome in the extreme to have to plod through these miserable figures to satisfy paternal curiosity, particularly if, by a furtive glance of the eye, I could see on the next page, an interesting narrative of Mr. Green's balloon ascent from the royal property, Vauxhall, or the narrow escape of the Duke of Brunswick when he accompanied Mrs. Graham. Still the duty had to be done, and I accomplished it in the best spirit I was able, and being the youngest of a family of five, my inclinations on the subject were neither studied, nor respected.

In course of time, as I grew up, I became more accustomed to the quaint, crabbed phraseology of the markets, and finding that my father used occasionally to tell my mother, when the prices were going down through rumours of war, or political differences, that it was the right period to "buy in," I discovered that there was some pecuniary reason at the bottom of all these diurnal investigations. I did not fail to shortly put a few interrogations to my mother, and being slightly a favourite, I was informed of the nature and importance of the money market, the position and interest-bearing capacity of the funds, and promised, if I were a very good boy, a trip with my father to take his dividends.

Although no doubt my poor mother, a clever, sensible woman, gave me a clear, intelligible account in her own way of the Government connection with the Bank, the rise and progress of the Debt, and the difference between Consols paying three per cent. and the Long Annuities returning almost six, my mind was of too errant a cast to at once appreciate the information ; and when she told me that the neighbourhood of the money market was the Bank, the Royal Exchange, and the great lottery establishments, which loomed out in Cheapside and Cornhill, with their prominently emblazoned boards of Bish, Hazard, Goodluck, and the other singular names imported to give weight to their transactions, I became more confused than ever.

According to my notion, as I then saw by the best light I was able, the money market ought to have assumed an eminently practical appearance, and I expected, as I told her, to see when I went round the Bank, and the other localities, bank-notes, gold, and stock offering for sale, as you would see articles of merchandize exhibited in other trading places. She was not long, however, with the assistance of my father, in explaining that although this was not so in actual matter of fact, it really was the case in effect, through the intervention of bankers and brokers, who made it a special business to deal in these things. When I grew older, my father, to redeem the promise made on his behalf, took me with him to receive his dividends, and then much of the hazy film, which had previously covered my young and inexperienced eyes, was suddenly removed.

There through the ancient rotunda, the resort at that

time of a great body of the jobbers, I dragged my way with difficulty, following close to the " governor," and I soon became enlightened as to the manner in which some of the transactions of the country were conducted. The calling of the name from the books, the check and issue of the dividend warrants, their conversion into bank-notes and gold, and most of all, the apparently careless shovelling up of the heap of glittering coin placed before the clerks, riveted my attention, and from that date to the present, I have been a close observer of the course and current, of our principal financial operations.

From that point of view I will dismiss all considerations of the money-market, and now look at it from a different one. It will be understood, *in limine,* that I am now directly interested in the state and fluctuations of the rate of discount, in the position and change of the various investments and enterprises, not as an operator or dealer, but in the character of a daily chronicler of facts and events. I am therefore thrown into association with the leading bankers, the chief discount establishments, the principal money and stock-brokers ; in short, with almost every one who has anything to do with capital or finance.

With my matured light and experience, I should now as soon think of visiting the gorilla country or Japan, as reading a murder or a balloon ascent, in preference to at once diving into the financial columns of the press. I scarcely imagine I should be able to sleep at night, without I was well posted in the latest price of Consols, French Rentes, and knew the closest price of money, both at the Bank, and in Lombard Street.

What an avalanche of sorrow should I be immersed

in, if the Bank directors ever raised the *minimum*, and I was not acquainted with the circumstance! Surely I should never recover the shock, and it might probably terminate in a financial suicide. What are the best oratorical excitations of Mr. Gladstone and Mr. Disraeli if they are not associated with revenue and expenditure, fiscal and other alterations, producing an impression in Mincing or Bartholomew Lanes? And do I not loudly asseverate against their want of compression in dealing with facts and figures, so as to bring their information within manageable compass and ready comprehension? What I used to think an intolerable bore—what a great number of other people still think an intolerable bore— a City life, is to me now, a paradise of delight, and I move through its shifting scenes and its circles, much in the old-fashioned manner of a horse in a mill, who rarely leaves the centre of his operations save to take his rest and his corn, and does not seem after all much the worse for wear.

The only close stickers to the collar like myself are the money brokers of the present day—and when I say the money brokers, I mean those who are really money brokers, not the discount brokers, or those identified with general financial transactions, who do their business in ordinary course—but the type of the staid old school, whose very looks and appearance are capital itself, and whose simple word for £100,000 would be taken quite as readily as their signature or their cheque.

The body as a class, are not so numerous as they were; the two principal representatives of the firms who take the lead in this kind of business—and they rank in name according to the two first letters in the alphabet—B, perhaps, in point of importance in this instance, taking precedence of A—having brought nearly the whole of these particular operations into their own hands. The sober seriousness of both these active, intelligent gentlemen, the weightiness of their engagements being impressed upon their visages, the bustling progress of the one, with the alert walk of the other, indicating how fully they enter heart and soul into the nature of their calling. The knowledge that the house of one has been nearly a century occupied in the same absorbing pursuits, and that the firm of the other, can go back upwards of half a century in close relations with most of the great money firms, will at once account for the division of the business between them, in so far as relates to special departments.

Both occupy extremely important positions in their respective walks, and being like myself City pedestrians, through the nooks and corners surrounding the Royal Exchange, Birchin Lane, and other various outlets and inlets associated with monetary engagements, it seems to me in some respects a lost day, if I have not encountered either of them in my route. As they constitute the great "go-betweens" in the banking and discount community and the Stock Exchange, turning over frequently a half or three-quarters of a million a day, they in the course of conversation acquire a vast fund of intelligence, and by reason of their actual transactions, can trace the causes and effects of the several mutations in the money-market. These are the parties acting for such firms as Messrs. Glyn, Mills, and Co., Messrs. Overend, Gurney, and Co., the National Discount Company, the Joint-Stock Discount Company, and other large institutions having the command of the floating balances of the day, for use at the Stock Exchange, or among the bankers and brokers themselves.

If money is to be provided, in consequence of heavy sales of securities by the Government, or the Court of Chancery, and the bank-notes current in the market to meet the requisite demands run short, it is usually one, or both of these gentlemen, who have, by arrangement, to obtain loans by which the proper supply is secured. Sometimes, in similar transactions for the large Insurance Companies, or the Scotch Banks, the supply being restricted in the market, and the means of these individuals temporarily exhausted, applications have to be made to the Bank itself, and then the pressure being comparatively great, the quotation increases.

It may be fairly estimated that the chief of these establishments, enters into operations ranging over some five or six millions a week, the other at least four to five. As illustrating the importance of these engagements, it may be safely asserted that at the period of the Turkish Loan of 1862, when the enormous deposits were made on account of that transaction at Messrs. Glyn, Mills and Co., one of these money brokers dealt with nearly £2,000,000 in the course of a day, having to employ it, to the best advantage he could, in his several channels. Such an influx into the general market, naturally at once largely influenced the rate, and then it was, that the terms for short periods averaged about 1½ per cent. To use my friend's smart and practical expression in relation to such an extent of business, " It was indeed something like a day's work, and the commission represented a pretty penny."

Marvellous must be the sums passing through their hands from year to year, particularly in connection with establishments like Messrs. Mullens, Marshall and Daniell, Hitchens and Harrison, Lawrence, Pearce and Son, P.

Cazenove and Co., G. E. Seymour, Hill, Fawcett and Hill, and the other old-established, and leading Stock Exchange houses.

Let me suppose I am going my diurnal round. I am passing through Lombard Street between 11 and 12 a.m., I meet the great money broker B——; he is just coming out of one of the banks. I ask if there is anything fresh. He says he hardly knows. The market is not in condition yet, not having gone the whole of his circuit. Perhaps in half an hour or an hour, I encounter him again, either coming from "the house at the corner," or one of the discount companies. "Money, money, eh! what is it?" There is a good supply; he has been able to get large sums, and the rate he thinks ought to be quoted from day to day about 2 to 2½ per cent.

Later again, perhaps, I meet him with a blue bag containing securities, India bonds, Exchequer bills, and other first-class descriptions, the value of which if divided by ten, would, he graciously assures me, make either of us comfortable for life. The market meanwhile has fluctuated. There has been a diminished or increased supply, and the rate has varied in accordance with the wants of the moment.

Another day I meet him rushing, driving along: scarcely time to exchange a word. He is in and out, of banking houses, discount houses, stock brokers' offices; he pulls up people in the open thoroughfare; he exchanges a word and hurries on. I see him; he sees me; it is not convenient to speak to him, and knowing that I shall be in the same circle for several hours, I bide my time to obtain my information.

At length, in the afternoon, we fall across each other. I then discover, what I had previously anticipated from the course of events during the day, that great stringency had been experienced at the Stock Exchange through the calling in of loans, and that owing to this shortness of supply, he has been up to his chin in re-arranging his engagements, altering the rates, curtailing amounts in some quarters, and carrying them on in others.

Thus his daily avocation requires unremitting attention, and either for himself or his competitor in the same kind of business, little time is left for recreation, save what can be snatched from the end of Saturday to the beginning of Monday. But they work on steadily and well, and prosper, making position and profit in due proportion to their untiring exertions. I only hope that their successors—for the time must come when this constant wear and tear will have to be relinquished—may be as popular, and as deserving of support, and that their transactions may prove equally lucrative and extensive.

XII.

WHEN the Indian mutiny took place in 1857, and the power of British rule suffered, as was supposed, from the policy of "clemency Canning," the several securities connected with the three Presidencies experienced a decline which, it was feared, would prove severe and permanent. There was at the time, indeed, good reason for this apprehension, because, although few doubted the result of the struggle for supremacy, the cost of the war, and the expectation that it would not speedily terminate, prepared every one for new loans, and large deficits in the Government accounts. The mutiny spread, and the new loans and large deficits came in regular course, and had to be provided for; but notwithstanding the anxiety exhibited in connection with Indian indebtedness, the public gradually absorbed the stock, and having become apparently reconciled to the fact that India, doubtful as her past had been, also promised a future, took heart and kept themselves steeled against unnecessary alarm.

If, however, stocks were not for a lengthened period seriously depressed, Indian railway shares exhibited a very extensive fall, through the issues having taken place in rapid succession, and calls having been made without regard to the capacity of the market to bear them, in order to supply the demands of the Leadenhall Street Treasury. Loudly as the system was deprecated, and pernicious as its effects were at the moment upon Indian credit, the Home Government sanctioning the proceeding, it was carried out with a high hand, much to the annoyance of the great body of shareholders, many of whom saw nothing else before them but the destruction of themselves and their properties.

As is usual in all periods of gloom and despondency, the endeavour of the Indian authorities to exercise pressure was attributed to dishonourable motives; and it was asserted that their pertinacity in enforcing these payments was, in the first place, to obtain all the resources they could from every channel available, and in the next, to abrogate the contracts if there was the slightest approach to default. This suspicion, groundless as it eventually turned out to be, happily did not last long; and the Home authorities having at length, taken the superintendence of Indian affairs immediately under their control, favourable hopes were entertained of better administration, which, with modified taxation, would produce an enlarged revenue.

Before, however, this satisfactory state of things was arrived at, various changes ensued, which more or less affected the whole class of Indian securities, and caused them to fluctuate considerably ere they became consolidated into their present position, and exhibited the firmness which they now invariably manifest. Despite predictions to the contrary, the assertion that India had sunk irretrievably in a financial point of view, appeared at that juncture to be only too strongly borne out by the confused mass of statistics, dignified by the name of the Indian Balance-sheet. The approximate statements, as they were called, approached so closely to absolute Indian bankruptcy, that even when the mutiny was quelled, it was questioned in several quarters, whether the Presidencies had sufficient recuperative power to struggle against the weight of increased expenditure.

Then arose that cry of a future for India, which, both in and out of Parliament, did much to support the value of the debt, and encourage those who had embarked the savings of a lifetime in the great undertakings which, as a system of communication, had they been in full operation, would have assisted largely in repressing the Sepoy outbreak. Vain regrets were useless on this heavy score, but the fact could not fail to have been brought to mind, that railways for India had been advocated in public meetings, but neglected even before Mr. Auber retired from the India House secretaryship.

With the cry of a future for India came the accompanying necessity of a proper, and equitable adjustment of its finances, and to effect this, it was desirable to appoint an Indian Chancellor of the Exchequer, who should co-operate with the Supreme Council in Calcutta, in re-arranging the taxation, investigating the expenditure, and establishing, through the chief Presidential Government Bank, those financial conduit-pipes for the collection of revenue, which would bring it without delay to the fountain-head.

The late Mr. Wilson, the first occupant of the post, succeeded in a great degree, when he arrived out in Calcutta, in unravelling and simplifying the mass of conglomerated detail, which, as exhibited in the House of Commons by Sir C. Wood, perfectly defied inquiry. Although Mr. Wilson's balance-sheet, in one or two minor points, was not free from blemish, it exhibited a brighter picture of Indian finances and Indian resources, than the majority of the most sanguine dared to suppose. When that hard-worked functionary announced the probability of the revenue not only meeting the expenditure in a year or two, but of positively leaving a surplus, credulous people shook their heads, and, inclined to believe, as they were, in their favourite, thought he had been influenced by the rose-coloured estimates of his subordinates, and that he would subsequently have to recant.

But greater was their surprise, when death removed the first Indian Chancellor, to find that the second, the Rt. Hon. Samuel Laing, was even more satisfied than his predecessor, of the expansive power of local revenue, and the general resources of the country. This was almost too much for Sir C. Wood, who, chagrined at the success of Mr. Laing in a department where it was said he must fail, denounced in open debate the assumed figures of his *protégé*, and ungraciously attempted to disprove his sanguine estimates. No one could stand such a reproof as this, and certainly not a man of the mould of Mr. Laing; he, therefore, resigned, and left his work, so vigorously commenced, to be followed out by others.

Meanwhile, India and her resources never faltered— she struggled forward, and gradually disencumbered herself of her embarrassments, the revenue steadily increasing and rising, till at last it actually verified Mr. Laing's promise. Dispatched to perfect the plans inaugurated by Wilson, and further promoted by Laing, Sir Charles Trevelyan left for the seat of Government, and he in his budget has since confirmed, and in every way attested, the elasticity of Indian capacity to provide for Indian expenditure, and leave a surplus. Sir C. Wood has very wisely abstained from breaking a lance with this last Presidential Chancellor, and he seems now prepared to submit, inconvenient as it may be, to India having recovered her pecuniary *status* with much greater rapidity than he hoped.

India having thus resumed her former position, or being, under her present administration, in a decidedly superior condition to what she was when John Company possessed her management, the debt has become a much more appreciable property, and the shares of the railways have exhibited strength at an enhanced value. It has naturally been a work of time to get these securities into a better and firmer condition ; but there seems no reason to doubt, from what is passing, that they will maintain, if they do not rise beyond, their current quotations. They have, indeed—and there can be no doubt about it, though a financial writer has occasionally endeavoured to combat the fact—come largely into competition with Consols and English securities ; and whether we look at the India Five per Cents., the rupee paper, the debentures, or the list of the railway shares, the class of holders speak significantly of their character as pure and sound investments.

Endeavours at one time have been made, to dispute the validity of the contracts of the railways, with respect to the nature of the guarantee ; at another, Indian revenue, it has been said, may decrease, and then whence the source for the payment of dividends ? But these are merely the views of speculative operators, whose feelings are as jaundiced as the colour of the gold they would draw, if possible, from their dealings when disturbance is ruling in the markets, and when the public are prematurely frightened into selling.

The original guaranteed India Stock, the fixed capital of the old Leadenhall Company, to be paid off at a definite date, is held much in the same way as Bank Stock, and, with its certain annual return, rules at a full value. The India Five per Cent. Loan, the result of the money raised to liquidate part of the debt of the mutiny, and the Four per Cent. Debentures, terminable at a regular date, are supported at prices showing that the public have great confidence in them, and are prepared to hold them as a high-class marketable security. The late endeavour to convert them was one of those mistakes, which Sir C. Wood is so fond of committing in the shape of experiment; and if the character of the debentures existed upon his power, instead of resting safely, as they do, on Indian revenue and the sanction of the British Government, nothing was more calculated than this step to interfere with their stability.

The admission of the rupee paper for registration in England, was one of the wisest steps ever adopted. It was a financial operation of an important nature, and carried out at the suggestion of several of the Indian banks, was attended with advantage and considerable profit to those interested. Ranking as the three classes do, according to their rates of 4, 5, and $5\frac{1}{2}$ per cent., they command quotations, which it is imagined will be well supported. The railways, with the completion of capital, the speedy progress of works, and the returns which traffic indicate, must ultimately become good dividend-paying properties; and as they will in the majority of instances attain a *maximum* beyond the guarantee of 5 per cent., proprietors should be amply satisfied with prospects, and not seek to chop or change them for any other ephemeral security. Indian stocks and shares must be allowed to take a foremost stand among the best kinds of negotiable property of the day, since they possess a basis, that can only be destroyed by the decadence of the English Government itself, which will be near at hand when we lose our sway in British India.

XIII.

WHAT IS AND WHAT IS NOT AN INVESTMENT?—A FEW MINUTES WITH THE CACIQUE OF POYAIS.

IT is difficult to conceive in these days what is, and what is not, an investment. So multifarious is the nature of securities, and so very exceptional are the means brought to bear upon values, that any kind of stock or shares, though the lowest of the low in the rubbish market, should not be regarded as worthless, much less destroyed or utterly cast forth. Those who have passed through life in the neighbourhood of Capel Court, if they were not some two or three years ago prepared to admit the truth of this assertion, will not now dispute it, with the evidence of the fluctuations and mutations of 1863 before them.

Many even who have participated in the profits of the great rise which has been witnessed in foreign stocks, allow that they have followed what they considered an *ignis fatuus*, and are, now the excitement is passed, only too glad to find they have escaped with the slightest margin of prices in their favour. While many have gained, others, however, have lost, and numbers, who have for years and years pined over stocks which they held to be altogether valueless, have, when they saw the speculative movement in its early progress, been so pleased to find a market for dormant securities, that they have rushed in, and sold before prices attained anything like their late advance.

No one has seemed to fancy that quotations would take this course of steady improvement, and yet the current market has borne them on, till a fabulous elevation has been almost reached, and from which there appears to be no permanent retrogression. These depreciated securities, which certainly two years ago were not viewed as investments, have now become some of the best current; a fact solidly proved to those who purchased Mexican as a "lock up" at 26 and 28, and could have since realized, if they wished, at an improvement of nearly twenty per cent.

There is an old theory among the operators of the Stock Exchange, that the "rubbish" market should not be neglected; viz., that the waifs and strays, which occasionally float, should not be pitilessly ignored, but that selections should be made of them from time to time, and put away till circumstances favourable to their locality or character, shall again bring them into public favour. It is well known that the Dutch are the great buyers of these "unconsidered trifles," and that when there is no inquiry here for particular stocks, detached coupons, or assumed worthless shares, they command a price, even if it be most nominal, in Amsterdam, and can be dealt in by arrangement there.

This was the last known *locale* for business in the shares of the celebrated bubble the United States Bank, and long after poor Nicholas Biddle, the famous president of that establishment, had passed away, and his well-known agent, Mr. Jourdan, had fallen from his high estate, the shares were quoted for as many cents as they had previously represented dollars. If ever a new United States Bank were organized, and a proposal were made to allow subscriptions with a margin of priority, to possessors of old shares, the fathers of the tulip mania might, there is reason to believe, by right of present holding, send in the largest share of applications.

But among the most recent remarkable recovery in the prices of worthless, or supposed worthless securities, is that connected with the great country of Poyais. Till within the last eight or nine months, it was presumed that Poyasian bonds and land warrants, were thoroughly dead and forgotten. Students in history were of course aware that some excitement had been created, about forty years ago, by the Poyasian " swindle," as it was then not unfrequently designated, with which the name of Gregor MacGregor, otherwise styled Cacique of Poyais, was mixed up, and which, through the attempted loan and sale of land warrants, promoted emigration to the Mosquitia territory, which was described as a paradise of delights, but which was eventually found to be a land devastated by malaria, and infested with animals of prey, and venomous reptiles.

The grade of civilization attained, even within ten years, may be estimated by the circumstance that the last time the King of Mosquitia was seen in public at Bluefields, he was, on the authority of an American skipper, seated on a rum barrel, arrayed in an admiral's old cocked hat, with naval coat and sash, but no nether integuments, smoking at his leisure ! What his ancestors may have been, it will require little imagination to determine ; and these were the sort of rulers to whose tender mercies, the Cacique of Poyais proposed to entrust the care of his countrymen and their property.

No wonder, despite attempts to reorganize the undertaking, and to infuse fresh blood into the management, that the successive reports received of disasters, by sea

and land, to the vessels sent out, caused the whole affair
to be blown upon, and that the Cacique of Poyais and his
colleagues, suddenly sank into oblivion and disgrace.
The Poyais bond was the first to feel the severity of the
blow; it struggled, and struggled hard for vitality, but
the money advanced was gone, and in course of time it
died out.

Not so with the land grants; they were held to be
worth something, if ever so fractional, and representing
territory, should there be according to the Milesian philosophy, "only enough to turf a lark on," it might some
day or other produce a value. For a lengthened period
that value was *nil*, notwithstanding every now and then
a few transactions took place; if the price went up from
6*d*. per 1000 acres to 10*s*. or 15*s*., a sudden flood of
grants came forward, and soon swamped the market. At
one time or another projects have been talked of, for improving the whole area within the limits of Central
America, and since it has been said that Poyasian claims
would be admitted, the rumours have brought the grants
into more notice, and again the price has actively
fluctuated.

A few years ago a mixed commission was named in
Nicaragua or Honduras, which was deputed to investigate
a variety of claims against the general governments of
those countries, and then it was thought that certainly
these securities, if they ever possessed a chance of being
valuable, were approaching the important crisis. A sort
of indiscriminate demand arose for them; nobody actually
knew the basis of the rise, but everybody spoke with a
mysterious air, and talked of the prospects of a new El
Dorado.

Besides, it was further affirmed that our old friends

the Dutch were, not again in the Medway, but in the market; and they, it was gravely asserted, would not be buyers of this " rubbish" without something was afoot legitimately to improve its worth. At this date a great number of people got into these securities ; and old stagers, at last persuading themselves that there was something in reality in the grants and the price, £1 and £1 5s. per 1000 acres—no small extent of territory for the money—the quotations went up to £1 10s. and £2.

When parcels of the grants had been dealt in for a few months, and no further rise was attained, the fever began to cool, and little further having been heard of the mixed commission or its progress, sellers appeared, wishing to be relieved of what they purchased. The result was natural, a decline occurred, and, without any interval of moment succeeding, a reaction of 5s. and 10s. very speedily took place. Everybody who was in, wished they had got out, and, to add to the disappointment, the Dutch, it is said, were so bitten by what was alleged to be false information, that they had determined never more to negotiate the warrants. Here was a crushing blow to the future of Poyasian land grants ; it seemed as if they were doomed to complete extinction.

Two or three friends of mine had purchased largely, regarding the warrants as a sort of lottery ticket; if they turned up a prize, all well and good ; if, on the other hand, they remained a blank, they could afford to lose their money, and not be prejudiced by the sacrifice. Many others were in a similar condition, and though Poyais land grants drooped from the endeavours made to realize, and at length stagnated at the price of about 5s. permanently, for at least three or four years, there were no failures announced through speculation in this special security, and the current of business finally became altogether arrested.

One of these friends, who at that time had not the slightest idea that he would ever come to want, was subsequently, by a series of misfortunes, reduced to absolute poverty, and the last thing he attempted to part with, was his thoughtlessly purchased parcel of Poyais warrants. He tried to effect an immediate sale, but as everything else was dull, and Poyais grants were doubtful at any time, it was useless; and if he had been literally starving he could not have got a penny for them. In his emergency he went to another friend of mine to request a loan, and being a man of punctilious honour, he would not accept the amount without depositing security ; that security (the friend smiling as he received it) was this very parcel of Poyasians.

But the sequel has yet to come. A year or two passed, nothing more for the moment was heard about Poyais stock or warrants, and speculation continued sluggish— yea, as sluggish as the dark, dank stream of Lethe. My poor friend, he who deposited with the other friend the security, had failed to recover his position, and was still fighting with the troubles of the world through impoverished condition.

Singularly enough, when the tide turned and animation was again manifested in the low class foreign stocks, a sort of presentiment possessed me, that the old " blue and green" backed security would come into vogue, and if not to the same extent as formerly, at least sufficiently so to relieve in a substantial shape, the necessities of this poor fellow.

In one of my walks I met him, and told him so ; he could not, he said, believe it, the things were so thoroughly worthless, and out of date. I bade him be of good cheer, and assured him I felt convinced Poyais would rally, and make him a better man. He laughed incredulously, and, waving his hand, added, "Ah, that money's gone—it is sunk for ever!"

I keep my eye on Poyais, principally for my poor friend's sake, although I am myself somewhat interested; and month after month I ask among the second-class dealers and "little go" men, whether there is any price for land warrants.

Some smile at the notion of a price for such a security; others, who have a few, and cannot get rid of them, simply say that they wish the Cacique of Poyais and the King of the Mosquitia were at Hanover; and one, only one, dealer, promises to let me know if there is ever anything doing in them. He speaks more hopefully; he has a variety of friends in, who hold for a rise, and he thinks they will come out, after all, with a profit.

One morning, as I alight from the omnibus which brings me near the Royal Exchange, I am tapped on the shoulder by my friend in the "rubbish market," who says quietly and cautiously, "There is a move in Poyais; they have gone rapidly to 30s. per 1000 acres."

I ask if there be any reason. "None," he says, "that I can divine. New Grenada and Ecuador have advanced; they have land warrants attached to their debts, and perhaps it is sympathy with those descriptions."

"Perhaps it is," I rejoin, and request that he will let me know the price late in the day. He says he will. Meanwhile I write off to my poor friend and tell him of the prospect of change, advising a speedy appearance, in time to take advantage of his good fortune.

The same night the price goes to 40s., and the final

quotation is, to use the customary phrase, 40s. to 50s. There must, I fully understand, have been some activity in the market, for as I leave the City for home, late, I hear a jubilant spirit—an outsider—as he holds confidential converse with a lamp-post, and slaps an imaginary friend on the back, wish luck to " the Ca—Ca—Cacique of Poy —Poyais, and the K—Ki—King of the Can—Cannibal Is —I—lands."

My poor friend arrives in the morning, but not quite soon enough to secure the top price, for up to 50s. Poyais go, and as soon as they touch it they recede to 40s. Like all people, when they see the value of their negotiable property rising, he hesitates to sell, and thinks, naturally enough, the price may still advance further. He, however, takes counsel of one or two intimates, who show him how desirable it is that he should seize the golden opportunity ; and the chief of these being a broker, he resigns himself to his hands, and in the course of the day leaves town a much richer and happier man than he entered it.

The sum obtained was ample, considering the many thousand of land grants he possessed, to liquidate numerous small pressing liabilities, and leave something for his future wants, till he could turn himself round and struggle once more into position. Never have I before seen so strikingly exemplified the indirect advantage, gained, as it were, from a miscellaneous adventure. My friend regarded it as a sort of providential intervention on his behalf, and it certainly has assisted, more than any other partial aid received, to bring him out of his embarrassments. After this short recital I think the majority of us may put the question—" What is, and what is not an investment ?"

XIV.

IF ever a speculative saturnalia has been witnessed in almost defunct and depreciated stocks, it has occurred within hail of the Bank of England during the last six months. That huge, imposing monitor, with all its financial knowledge and skill, has been unable to repress the mania, and is compelled to remain the passive beholder of its vagaries. It is curious to trace the order of operation in these foreign securities, and to notice upon what slight grounds business at first takes place, which, maturing with activity, leads to the strong inflation invariably preceding a collapse. The history of these things, if looked into, especially in detail, presents circumstances and facts not only instructive and amusing, but which show the deep passion created for Stock Exchange gambling when once it sets in. Nothing can more strongly illustrate this than the late operations in Turkish Consolidés, Greek and Spanish passives and certificates.

It would be a visit well worth the trouble of any West-end lounger to go into the City, and see how these things are done. It would scarcely be imagined that within a stone's throw of the Royal Exchange, millions, in figures, are hourly changing hands, with much less noise and excitement than that which prevails at Tattersall's on settling days. True, there is a certain hurry-scurry down Bartholomew Lane; the weird and eager looks of many of the speculators in Throgmorton Street denote at once that some interesting activity is afoot, and the thickening crowd in Lothbury, with the various small groups debating prices, indicate the existence of some kind of dealing; but the actual course of affairs could never be divined, until made the subject of investigation under the tutelage of some initiated friend.

Perhaps as a speculation in every sense of the word, the introduction of the Turkish Kaimés or Consolidés has been the most successful of any known, since the appearance of Ottoman securities upon the European money-market. At one time they were so depreciated as to be hardly negotiable in the Exchange bazaar at Constantinople, and being part of the internal debt, it was never supposed that they could recover until the institution of the Imperial State Bank should bring about a financial reformation. But in a lucky moment two or three English and Parisian operators hit on the experiment of importing a quantity to this country, not as a sound or *bonâ fide* security, but as a questionable commodity, which, bought at one price, might sell at another, and leave a fair margin of profit.

The experiment was made, the endeavour succeeded, but for a time the Consolidé as a security was far from popular. Prejudice ran high against it, for the dividend on former issues had not always been paid, but had, from time to time, been postponed and added to the principal. It was admitted that the interest was six per cent., payable in the celebrated *Medji d'or*, or about 18s. to the pound sterling, but then it was argued that Turkish finance was weak, and without an assignment of special securities, the imperial treasury would be only too glad, if necessity required it, to shirk the responsibility if it interfered with the punctual performance of obligations in other directions. Thus for many months the price suffered the blight of a damaged reputation; and this was magnified by the holders of other Turkish securities, who dreaded the competition of the cheaper stock, and the ardour exhibited in pushing it in the market.

The chief difficulty was to get the quotation above 35. First brought forward at about 29 and 30, the value before long advanced to 32, but between this point and 35 there was a temporary stand. Fresh issues, it was said, could be made ; and the arrival of different parcels, led to the inference that their manufacture would be indefinitely prolonged. Fluctuation among the dealers quickly followed. But the original importers did not flinch; they had engaged in the traffic, and having tasted a handsome profit, were prepared, in the words of Nathan Meyer Rothschild, "to support their market." And support it they did, with such confidence that although when the bonds themselves were delivered, they were received with a shout of derision—*badinage,* powerful as it was, did not interfere with their stability.

Tattooed all over with Turkish characters, and surmounted with the emblazoned crescent of the Osmanli, they were so different from any other current class of security, that the public—the timid public, many of whom had bought without in reality knowing what they were purchasing—fancied they had been victimized. Eventually, however, the feeling of doubt diminished, investments became frequent, and from 35 they gradually but steadily made their way to 40. From this period Turkish Consolidés have maintained a position, not unchequered by variation, but still tending upward; and the favourable accounts of the forthcoming budget, which nevertheless remain to be realized, assist to support their value. They have been quoted as high as 56; on the whole an advance of no less, in round numbers, than 24 per cent., compared with the price at which they were ushered into the London market.

Without attempting to decide upon their merits as an investment—for time alone can ascertain that point—it must be allowed that they have been a fruitful source of profit to the Anglo-French and German operators, who possessed confidence enough to make them the centre of their transactions. But, as in all similar adventures, the original parties have long since retired from the field. They had the good sense to sell out when the quotations ranged from 40 to 45, believing that they had secured the greatest part of the rise. Having made, as it is strongly asserted they have, at least £200,000 from this stroke of business, they have been content to let their other colleagues in the Exchange take the remainder of the advance, wisely thinking that the price may be carried too high, and that if a reaction should take place, it will probably prove disastrous.

And now a few words on Greek securities. Owing to the indebtedness of the State, amounting to several millions, these were never dealt in, and hardly even thought of, until the dethronement of Otho. From that time they came into favour with the speculators, who pretended to anticipate great prosperity from the development of the country under a new and beneficent rule; as if the errors of a quarter of a century could be rectified in one or two years. Surely this must have been the hope of men who, concluding engagements in the Five per Cents. at 8½ and 9—the quotation immediately after the outbreak of the Revolution—have since been prepared to give 40 for the same security. Admit that the circumstances of the country are greatly altered, where, after all, is the foundation for this very important improvement? Perhaps the best solution is the old one,—the existence of a speculative *furore*.

Ask those who evince such faith in the future of Greece on what grounds they base their expectations, and they tell you that the debt is to be settled on a one per cent. basis; there is also to be a National Bank,—nothing now can be done without a bank,—and a system of railways and irrigation-works, will complete the programme of financial prosperity. Without doubt this looks well upon paper. But why do men shut their eyes to the struggle that must be made, to accomplish this long course of pecuniary recuperation? *Caveat emptor* was never more applicable than in this case; and though we are quite ready to go along with those who believe in the regeneration of Greece, still it must not be imagined that, under the happiest auspices, there will be a speedy return to financial regularity. Certainly the Greeks themselves are not so sanguine of general peace and plenty as many of our English capitalists. That their debt would be settled at the date of the Greek Kalends had passed into a proverb. Recent events show more favourable prospects, but they have yet to be completely realized.

Of all the movements that have taken place recently at the Stock Exchange, perhaps the most legitimate is the advance in Spanish passives and Spanish certificates. Not that this is to be attributed to any real desire on the part of the Court of Madrid, to mete out justice to the

foreign debtor, or to the unsullied character of the hands
into which a part of the negotiation has fallen. It is
simply the consequence of the improved appearance of
the country, the satisfactory increase in the revenue, and
the necessity of the financial authorities adopting an
honest policy, in order to secure the introduction of
capital for territorial improvements. Through the disgraceful conduct of Spain to her foreign creditors, the
quotations of any new securities have long been excluded
from the European Bourses, and being thus prevented
from availing herself of the advantages of railways, and
other public works, she will be compelled before long to
adopt measures to restore her credit.

The national property set apart for the liquidation of
the passive debt, has never been properly applied. The
balance has largely accumulated, and if regularly dealt
with, the stock should be redeemed at a much more
elevated price than at present. But although these
circumstances have been well known, it required a
speculative epoch to give the price an efficient impetus.
This it has received, and the quotation has now been
carried 10 or 12 per cent. in advance. If the thing be
not overdone by "time bargaining," and if the old
stagers be not too precipitate in their action, a favourable issue may be attained. But diplomacy will be
necessary, and the next, or the succeeding Cortes, may
have to sit their term, before the end is accomplished.

The indication furnished by the enhanced price offered
at the monthly biddings at Madrid, is evidence that the
pressure from without is being felt. Advantage will be
taken of this, and the seed sown must eventually bear
good fruit. The certificate question is another matter of
moment. Whether an adjustment will precede the

Spanish settlement, or only follow it, is a matter of trifling consequence; it must come, although *ad interim*, frequent variations may be expected. When those things shall have been brought to a satisfactory conclusion, Castilian honour will no longer be a by-word or reproach, and, with the assistance of local improvements, the glory of old Spain may be revived.

The practical lesson to be deduced from what has been advanced is, that depreciated investments may at particular seasons be obtained at cheap, and moderate prices—that by a current of speculation, their value may be taken up far above their intrinsic worth, and that when the mania subsides, a ruinous reaction is probable.* On entering into business of this description, it is advisable that individuals should purchase only as much as they can conveniently hold, without risk to themselves, or to the parties with whom they deal; for in speculating, *i.e.*, buying for the rise, or selling for the 'fall, they may "be cut to pieces," or ruined by a sudden revulsion.

* Since this paper first appeared in print, the course of fluctuation has produced panic, and many failures have taken place.

XV.

IT is not every one who can recollect the great days of speculation in produce—when quicksilver netted in the course of a few months, hundreds of thousands of pounds to the fortunate holders; when indigo, cochineal, and tallow, were subsequently articles in which gambling, on a proportionate scale to some of the transactions in the funds, was carried out; and when business in Mincing Lane was conducted, as was invariably the case in the winter months, by candle-light. Individuals who can remember these events, which, in the shape of retrospection stretch back more than half a century, will probably associate with some of the movements high names, such as might include the elder Rothschild, the leviathan leader as he then was in almost everything, old Jeremiah Harman, Mr. Richard Thornton, James Wilkinson, the eccentric Mr. Nicholson, James Cooke, and a few other of the lesser magnates, who at that period occupied positions in commercial circles, and were, either for themselves, or for their principals, closely mixed up with such gigantic operations.

Perhaps the tallow speculation was the most desperate of any that occurred in those days, owing to the constant fluctuations in price, and the ultimate depreciation. Many individuals made large losses at the time who were supposed to be wealthy, but who were eventually weakened very considerably by these unfortunate transactions. The Baltic Coffee House (not where it stands now at the extreme corner of Theadneedle Street, but when it was situate opposite the Royal Exchange, on the site now occupied by the Telegraph Company), was the centre of this special branch of business, and at that date the settlements were watched with as much fear and anxiety, as any of the recent heavy adjustments of accounts in foreign securities. It was never known at the time what were the real nature of the losses or the gains, and it remained for after investigations into two or three special mercantile disasters, to show how these were apportioned, and which firms in reality bore the brunt of the sacrifice.

The quicksilver speculation was confined to a few hands; perhaps it may be said to have been organized by two heads—*arcades ambo,* and these fortunate individuals, knowing the soundness of their information as to supply and demand, never allowed the public the chance to participate, but perseveringly continued their transactions till they secured the whole stock, and then dealt with the price as they pleased. The adventuring in indigo and cochineal, was in a great degree originated by James Wilkinson, who in the course of his early career was one of the leading men in the produce markets, and the large profits then obtained by his principals, secured him a reputation, and a business, which unfortunately were not supported, when a second and third series of similar transactions came to be finally arranged.

The last attempt to bring cochineal to an approximate fair value, when it was unreasonably depressed, succeeded to a limited extent, but there was not the stamina among the parties engaged to maintain the price, and consequently the movement was cut short by a premature collapse : and never since can there be said to have arisen any important engagements, in what was once so favourable a medium for a little speculation.

The tea speculation which suddenly sprang up at the time of the great war with China, about the year 1840-41, was another of those mercantile phrenzies which, commencing on a legitimate basis, was afterwards stimulated by enlarged transactions, till prices were carried to an undue height, leaving many of the operators penniless, and others deeply embarrassed. It was not enough then to believe that partial scarcity would ensue, but because the Chinese showed a determined resistance, it was predicted with confidence, that supplies would altogether cease. Company's congous—the brand of East India Company's import—were soon made the Consols of the tea market, and the price of that description was regarded as the barometer of business; the rise and fall being eagerly noted by every individual interested.

Through the excitement following reports of total annihilation of the British forces, and of the poisoning process asserted to be adopted in the preparation of new teas, the quotation in the space of ten or twelve months, was run up from 11d. to 3s. 6d. per lb. ; and in the meanwhile, on the arrival of every China mail, variations ranging from 3d. to 6d., and even 9d. per lb., ensued in the course of twenty-four hours. Mincing Lane was never before so crowded, even by " outsiders ;" not only were the brokers and the agents deeply engaged for themselves and their friends, but private capitalists, stock-exchange brokers, and a large number of the general public, were incited to take a few chests of Company's congou. Business was transacted there in the morning. Later in the day it was continued on 'Change. There was a regular closing price for Congou consols; and if any special news arrived, fresh operations were conducted with vigour at Garraway's, Tom's, or any of the neighbouring coffee-houses.

But this state of things did not last for ever. The speculation after the period of a year or more seemed enfeebled, through the exhaustion of the means of many of the parties engaged in it, and the strong fact at the same time being evident, that though shipments were occasionally arrested, the stock of tea was never in reality seriously diminished, prices gradually receded, leaving those who had purchased at the extreme quotations, either to liquidate "heavy differences on their contracts," or "to take up the leaf," and realize its worth at their leisure.

Some large amounts of money were made by independent parties; but the tea-brokers, as a body, were the most successful in their arrangements. The majority refrained from speculation, confining themselves to the receipt of their commissions, and from this source alone, three or four houses secured the most princely returns. Failures and compositions were not uncommon towards the fag end of the movement, and many were compelled to " waddle " as lame ducks in the neighbourhood of the Commercial Sale Rooms; like others who had previously, and have since, " waddled " from the precincts of Bartholomew Lane.

Since that date the greatest speculation in produce has been in cotton, through Southern secession and the blockade by the North of the ports of Charleston, and New Orleans. From the earliest outbreak of hostilities it was imagined that the price of cotton would be considerably enhanced, but few were prepared for so great or continued an improvement. Immediately after the election of President Lincoln, and when the first glimpses of a rupture were clearly perceived, many showed a disposition to purchase the staple, reckoning on an advance of 2d. or 3d. per lb. This, it was believed, might prove the extent of the rise, and on these figures were based, what were considered by some, very sanguine expectations.

Hovering between hope and fear—hope that the improvement would be attained and realized—fear lest secession should be nipped in the bud and prices recoil, the operators paused as the advance proceeded, and when from 6d. to 9d. had been reached and supported, and the price was going towards 1s., fresh confidence produced fresh buyers, and the foundation of the market became firmer than ever. Liverpool, the great seat of the cotton market—the transactions occurring in London being altogether secondary and unimportant—has always sustained a high reputation for its speculative tendencies, and therefore when internecine hostilities in America were actively commenced, it was at once evident much scope was presented for these transactions. It was also apparent that the financial facilities available through the accumulation of capital from stagnation in trade, would enable the brokers and others to pursue their operations with unrestricted energy ; and this has since turned out to be the case, to the profit of nearly all, while in particular instances fabulous fortunes have been secured.

Most parties, especially during the last six or nine months, who could scrape money or credit together, it is said, have gone into cotton more or less extensively as they have found it convenient, and as the rise from the lowest point has been gradually progressing, until a *maximum* figure of 25d. or 26d. per lb. has been reached ; and the immediate fluctuations having been comparatively insignificant, no serious drawback has been experienced to occasion general panic or decline. About midway in the rise was when the greatest apprehension prevailed, because if then by any stroke of luck the federal forces had " squelched " the rebellion in forty days, according to the vain boast of Mr. Seward, intelligence of this kind would have exercised a fatal effect upon prices. The strength of the advance occurred speedily after the miserable retreat at Bull's Run, and the discovery of the total inefficiency of the Northern generals to control their forces. As the chances of war have fluctuated, partial variations in value have naturally succeeded, but the market, as a market, has never permanently lost its position.

The speculation in cotton, at present, has been a speculation in which most of the operators have taken profits ; for floating with rising prices, they have either gone the whole length of their tether, or have retired when they were satisfied with the margin of gain presented. It is seldom in speculations of this character, or in those connected with general securities, that such an important advance is maintained. Dealings in these markets ordinarily require the most delicate manipulation to avoid getting in too late, or when in, to wait the proper period for advantageous sale. The constant oscillation in quotations, a sudden rise or a sudden fall, is as likely, when an individual is operating either in produce or stocks, to leave him with a loss to pay, as a profit to receive ; and therefore the vigilance necessary, with the constant attendance on the skirts of the brokers and jobbers, is hardly worth the anxiety they entail.

But it has not been so in the cotton speculation. At the same time it would not be prudent to assume that because there has been this extraordinary advance (more than double the original average quotations), many persons have been fortunate to run with, and attain, the whole current of the rise. Large sums have been obtained from this source, and instances of £50,000, £80,000, £100,000, and even £200,000 and £300,000, are alleged to be known, as the extent of wealth realized by firms and individuals, from their speculation in the staple ; but these form, in all probability, the exception, and not the rule.

As already indicated, the first improvement of 2d. and 3d. per lb. was succeeded by a pause ; then afterwards when the price went beyond 1s. up to 1s. 6d., a good deal of caution was manifested for fear the thing should be overdone, and it was not till stocks became reduced, and exports were in reality made to New York for manufacturing purposes there, that the extreme quotations were so generally upheld. And there appears even now little immediate prospect of any visible alteration. The cotton speculation, as a movement, as far as advance is concerned, may, except under peculiar circumstances, be considered to have reached nearly its culminating point, and it would be exceedingly dangerous to enter into it unless the South speedily recovered their lost ground, and re-established themselves firmly against the North. On the other hand, looking at the difficulties which surround President Lincoln and his government, it would be puerile to predict when a lower range of prices may be anticipated ; for if the South cannot be subdued, the war may be indefinitely protracted, and whence are adequate supplies to be had to relieve the great and universal cotton dearth ?

Various are the anecdotes current, in proof of the enormous returns made by adventurous operators in cotton, during the past eighteen months or two years. Cotton carriages are now, it is said, as common in Liverpool, as railway broughams were in London, at the period of the railway share mania ; men with shattered and broken fortunes have, through hazardous enterprise, retrieved their positions, and again fret their hour upon 'Change with every appearance of full fledged *millionaires ;* and all this through King Cotton, in one sense deposed, but in another completely triumphant.

XVI.

THERE was a period, about five-and-twenty or thirty years ago, when American credit, and American securities, took a position among British capitalists which promised to give the inhabitants of those States great facilities as borrowers of money. It was, of course, antecedent to the explosion of the United States Bank, and previous to the discovery of the trickery and fraud perpetrated by the astute Nicholas Biddle and his accomplished colleagues, with the view of supporting that doubtful and rickety institution. Nevertheless, meanwhile, through the assistance of trusty agents, attracted by the promises of huge commissions, and large margins in price, several well-known London establishments requiring employment for their resources, did not hesitate to enter into engagements to adopt a variety of American issues, both in the shape of State stocks, and the bonds and debentures of a number of the railway companies just then struggling into existence.

To ensure a ready negotiation of these supposed valuable securities, which in almost every instance carried a rate of interest equal to 6 per cent., the loan-mongers and brokers introduced contracts for the purchase of iron and railway material, so that the extra " dead weight," of a second commission induced many persons, who would not otherwise have ventured in them, to take a portion of the risk incident to a fresh business arrangement. The progress the contractors made in floating stocks, shares, and bonds, encouraged the manufacture of new classes, and consequently the appetite of the public was gratified by competitors, over the length and breadth of the Union, who, if they did not find first-class establishments here ready to enter into their arrangements, speedily obtained access to second and third rate houses, which, tempted by the success of some of their neighbours, could not resist the profits that were said to arise from this kind of business.

The staid peculiarity of Lombard Street was even for a while carried away by the excitement, and bankers and others in that locality, who had formerly looked only to Consols and Exchequer Bills as the kind of negotiable property on which to make advances, filled their boxes with American scrip, and American promises to pay, allured by the seeming advantage of the rate of interest, and the price at which they were held. During the time this financial game was proceeding, our 'cute Yankee cousins were constructing their public works, and principally their lines of railway, the banks were also organized. These schemes, by one special channel or another, aided to maintain the existing fashion, till the great crisis of 1835-36 arrived, when the true extent of transatlantic indebtedness, and the worth of the paper which America had circulated throughout the world, became properly ascertained.

When the grand collapse occurred, its influence permeating all banking circles, it was speedily discovered that the Britisher was not companionless in his misfortunes, for the Parisian, and the Hollander, were alike sacrificed—since they in their turn, not having allowed the golden opportunity for participation to pass, experienced difficulty from the inability of States and companies to fulfil their engagements, even where they had sufficient honesty to recognize their liabilities. Then arose the doctrine of repudiation, which, forming a most convenient though discreditable mode of avoiding payment, did more than anything else to destroy the *prestige* of the States as borrowers, and the character of their merchants and citizens as trustworthy people.

At the same period, and nearly as possible at the same date, the United States Bank, with its diminished capital, and enormously large liabilities, succumbed, and in its fall brought a succession of disasters, from which there was no recovery for years. In the various investigations which followed this break-down of State, bank, and railway responsibilities, circumstances transpired to show that if the Yankees were too willing borrowers, offering any terms rather than not obtaining the money, English and other capitalists, had in special cases been but too facile lenders, thinking that they had secured a good bargain, with sufficient guarantee for its due enforcement. Their great mistake in this respect was only rendered apparent when the law courts of the Union failed to administer justice, and when the disgraceful proceedings of those, who should have preserved their country's financial honour, provoked the caustic satire of the writer of " Peter Plymley."

The shock thus given to American finance, and American credit, has never yet been repaired. Years have intervened, and endeavours have been made at one epoch and another, to secure assistance in the European money markets when assistance has been required. But never have these attempts been successful in the manner that they should have been, looking at the great resources of the country, the aptitude of the people for its development, and their untiring energy. United States Stocks—those based on the security of the Union—have occasionally been popular at a price ; some of the Southern State Stocks, like Virginia, have also been supported, and two or three of the long arterial railways : but whenever it has been desired to give a stimulus to American credit or .American enterprise, the gaunt spectre of repudiation has appeared to damp the ardour of the public, or the individuals, who sought prematurely to encourage the movement.

But the second blow from which the railway interest of the United States suffered, was the revelations elicited in the Schuyler fraud, the explosion of the Ohio Trust Company, and the liquidations which succeeded those memorable events. The extravagant expenditure on the lines, the doubtful accounts presented, the depth of indebtedness, owing to the issue of first, second, and third mortgage bonds, and the eventual suspensions of dividends, entailed another panic, from the effects of which even some of our prominent statesmen did not escape—the honoured Richard Cobden himself having in a pecuniary sense been compromised. The character and credit of the Americans again were seriously damaged by acts of flagrant jobbery, which placed men in an unfortunate position in these undertakings. Wholly incompetent persons were appointed to manage them, with salaries out of all proportion to their deserts, and this at so critical a juncture in the existence of the works, that it was, in fact, a question whether they would not have to be altogether stopped.

The third, and in all probability the final blow, to American securities, will prove to be the war between the

contending factions of North and South.   Each party has
already experienced its ruinous effects, from the drain to
maintain standing armies in the field, and to provide for
the requisite expenditure.   If the South have had to submit to exorbitant rates to obtain moderate amounts of
capital and supplies, the North have had to appeal to forced
loans, and this not always with success.   The currency of
the South has naturally become depreciated, and has circulated only in those quarters where its value is looked
upon, more as a symbol of money in the midst of a great
national struggle, than as something of worth ; and in the
North the free issue of greenbacks, has produced such a
revolution in exchange and quotations, that the Federal
debt will, before long, represent an enormous total.

   With labour disturbed, and manufacturing industry
utterly paralyzed, there can be no other result than utter
financial ruin, which will sooner or later accrue.   Take
place when it may, and the end cannot be far off, the crash
will be most fearful to contemplate, and the North and
South alike will, if possible, be plunged still deeper into
fiscal disorganization and mercantile embarrassment.
What hope can there be in the next decade, for America
or her securities, even when she in reality possesses a
chance of emerging from such a " slough of despond ?"
Financial regulations have not burdened the North for the
last eighteen months ; favour has been accorded and
licenses voted to the Secretary of the Treasury, to do
what ?   To increase the debt by every means in his power,
and by every strategy he could devise—not with the ultimate view of redemption, but to obtain ready money, in
whatever shape he could or on any terms he was able, to
pay the army, to feed needy Government officials, and to
keep up a semblance of solvency.   With all these resorts

to Treasury issues, to advances on loan notes, to greenbacks, and to postage currency, the stream of finance is
drifting to one end—absolute and inevitable bankruptcy.

The excitement of the situation, the lust of conquest,
may maintain the Treasury and its resources so long as
there is the military chest to supply; but as soon as the
charm of war—if there be a charm in bloodshed—shall
subside, we must be prepared for the worst, for it will
then be very speedily realized. Even the most sober-
minded of our English merchants and capitalists, have been
looking ahead and arranging accordingly. They have sold
out their securities for what they would fetch; they have
narrowed their mercantile engagements to within the most
confined limits; and they state unhesitatingly, that they
equally distrust both North and South, as to the strict performance of any engagements that they may discover
hereafter inconvenient to bear. In fact, the revival of
the doctrine of repudiation will, it is believed, be witnessed, not in single or isolated cases, but in a wholesale
form; and the very tone of resentment adopted towards
England and Englishmen, is presumed to be the precursor
of that change, which if it shall not seek revenge in open
hostilities, may effect its covert purpose in a less dignified
way.

Of course, it is highly probable that some of the
American railway stocks and shares, may turn out good
speculations, so far as a rise or fall in prices is concerned,
and it is also extremely likely that combined operations
may occasion a temporary inflation, in order if possible to
trap the unwary; but the day of popularity for American
securities, as *bona fide* securities, has passed, and the public
will exercise a sound and healthy discretion, by hesitating
to invest in any description, however tempting the quota-

tion, or however *couleur de rose* any of the reports may seem. British losses by American stocks and shares, may already be reckoned to have reached millions ; and it is very desirable, much though it may be deplored by New York operators, and New York agents, whose aim is commission and brokerage, that this system of plundering the English should be for ever arrested.

XVII.

Post tenebras lux. "It is one thing to be in difficulties,
another thing to get out of them." So thought Eneas
Pinchbeck, when he sat in moody reverie by his quiet fire-
side, after his good spouse, Mrs. Pinchbeck, and all the
little Pinchbecks, had retired to rest. Alas! staid and
steady Pinchbeck, he was an unhappy man; every line in
his features bespoke, in the plainest possible manner, his
heavy sorrow; for he was getting deeply into debt. His
once flourishing business in the grocery trade, in the little
village where he resided, was fast dwindling to decay,
under the combined influence of railway improvements
and metropolitan competition.

The principal inn, for the last six months, had been
closed, in consequence of the "Red Rover" being off the
road; the surveyor had quitted the locality, for a more
advantageous residence at the neighbouring market town;
the clergyman obtained his supplies from Sweet and Cheap
in London, their circular advising him of the precise state
of the markets, and the low rate of their commissions;
and the only remaining customer, the exciseman, was one
with whom he could have readily dispensed, since he was,
to all intents and purposes, what is familiarly termed "a

* It is scarcely necessary to say that this sketch was written before the
new bankruptcy law came into force.

long credit." Pinchbeck, through this melancholy metamorphosis, found his receipts far from approaching payments in full, and from the vast weight of accumulating
difficulties wished a release.

As already notified, staid and steady P. was a
married man, and possessed in the agreeable and long-
suffering Mrs. P. a most affectionate wife, and unre-
mittingly attentive mother. For six successive years she
had, with most praiseworthy punctuality, never failed to
present him with an offering from that mysterious kingdom of babydom known as the "parsley-bed;" and he
acknowledged, faithfully and lovingly, the high honour
conferred upon his house and limited resources. For six
successive years, Mr. Pinchbeck had been graciously introduced, to the monthly nurse, the blue satin pincushion,
emblazoned in flowing characters with "Welcome, little
stranger!" and the rickety stump four-poster, in the
back parlour, with the accompanying one rush-bottomed
chair, and the worst set of fire-irons. All this he had
borne, and could bear, with becoming resignation; but
the late adverse change in circumstances, now foreshadowed
dark and dire distress. So, with his prospective misery,
of a large family, declining business, and an uncertain
future, no great abundance of comfort existed for contem-
plation by a melancholy mind.

Eneas, nevertheless, endeavoured to solace himself,
and in fitful moodiness resorted to the companion of his
halcyon days—his pipe. Puff, puff, puff; as the curling
smoke rose, and enwreathed with its fragrant odour his
depressed countenance, suggestive reflections followed.
He silently interrogated himself concerning the interior of
places—receptacles for the indebted—called Whitecross
Street, and the Queen's Bench. He was acquainted with

the precincts of the county jail, the governor having been supplied with grocery. Were governors, in general, so kind and complacent ? Probably not. Again ensued another train of thought. What sort of people in appearance, were the representatives of those captivating gentlemen, John Doe and Richard Roe. Lately, inquiries had twice or thrice been made on their behalf respecting his whereabouts, and the cash-box contained indubitable proofs of their kind intentions towards him.

While thus deeply cogitating upon his concerns, Eneas seized, as a temporary relief, an old newspaper lying by his side. The last thing he thought of was the probability of escape from his embarrassments, but he readily dived into its contents to interrupt the current of his meditations. It was, however, perfectly useless. He eyed the first column of advertisements ; they were attractive. Several vessels were about to sail to America, and one to the Indies ; others to Australia and New Zealand. Eneas was strongly tempted ; a trip to foreign climes would certainly not endanger his health ; a berth among gold diggers or savages, would be preferable to his present condition. But, ah ! the great drawback—Mrs. P. and the little P's. A pencil to take the terms of freight and passage-money, although lifted, was soon cast aside, as his heart instinctively wandered back to his home, and his family.

In silent and dogged humour, he turned to the list of bankrupts. There he imagined he already saw his own name recorded: "Eneas Pinchbeck, grocer, Swannington, Essex. Mr. Commissioner Snap, Basinghall Street, Tuesday, June 28, and Thursday, July 6. Hector Twigg, official assignee ; Sprig and Hook, solicitors." Oh, horror of horrors ! he had once proved a debt under an estate in

the London Court of Basinghall Street; he had once seen
Mr. Snap in his judicial robes; and he had at the same
time encountered the astute and vigilant Hector Twig, and
he was certain he entertained not the least desire, to make
a legal acquaintance with Messrs. Sprig and Hook.
Without further consideration he was about casting the
paper from him, when his eye caught the heading of an
announcement: " To persons in difficulties." " Nothing
can suit my case better than that," ejaculated Eneas,
recovering breath. " Crumbs of comfort may yet be
spared me."

The advertisement he had alighted upon was one of no
ordinary character. It stated, with great pretension and
confidence, how one Mr. Tobias Debit did for people in
difficulties, what they could not well do for themselves,
viz.:—arrange their books, see their creditors, and, if
possible, make honourable terms of compromise. More-
over, it intimated that the process of bankruptcy and insolvency, intricate as it might appear to the young and
uninformed, could be well familiarized to those, who had
the least suspicion of being compelled to avail themselves
of the statutes regulating the affairs of unfortunate debtors;
and finally concluded by advising all persons in that condition to hasten to a special interview, of course not for
the advertiser's, but for their own personal benefit.

" There is still hope," said Eneas, when he had concluded a perusal of the paragraph. " To-morrow, if I'm
spared, will I see this cunning man in figures." With
that single observation, the impression to which it gave
rise being deep rooted, he made his way to bed, and
Pinchbeck slept sounder and better that night than he
had done for many nights before. The next morning
found him in town, with the address of Mr. Debit care-

fully deposited in his waistcoat pocket, the especial casket provided for the treasure he had so opportunely discovered.

It was in one of those small squares situated in the northern and eastern suburban districts, where stunted lilac trees, and dark, dingy, privet hedges, arranged within a prescribed circle of forty feet, strongly guarded by iron palisades, render the spot cheerful and salubrious, that Mr. Tobias Debit dwelt. It was a very small square, with very small houses ; but every establishment presented unequivocal symptoms of being engaged in a large way of business ; the doors ornamented with extravagant addresses, seeming to vie with each other in displaying the brightest brass plate, knocker, or bell handle. In fact, the place was nothing better than a colony of cottages, made subservient to the operations of trade.

Hither our friend Eneas directed his steps. He hesitatingly, as he proceeded, fumbled for the address ; it was there all right, legibly written : " Mr. Tobias Debit, Arbitrator and Accountant, No. 12, Fairlight Square." Poor P., through the nervousness occasioned by the excitement of the journey, had entered at the wrong end of the horseshoe range of buildings delighting in that euphonious description, and discovered that he was in close proximity to No. 24. At length, however, No. 12 is arrived at, and looking there he beheld, as he hoped, his haven of rest.

The cottage of Mr. Debit was one of the most neatly arranged in the square, the small white marble slab on the door designating the occupier's profession, being only equalled by the unexceptionable condition of the steps leading thereto. Flowers, not of the choicest kind, but well selected, were displayed in the windows, and a musk

plant sent forth its odour on one side, while a gay scarlet
fuchsia was exhibited on the other. All this seemed to
speak soothingly to the perturbed spirit of Eneas, and
after a cursory survey, a subdued rat-tat with the cherub
face of the knocker, brought him another step nearer to
the presence of his expected friend.

"Is Mr. Debit at home?" was the mild inquiry of
Mr. P., shaking from head to foot, as though he had committed some enormous crime.

"Yes, sir," said a curly-headed urchin, about eight or
nine years of age ; adding, "if it's on business," almost
divining Pinchbeck's errand from his appearance, "he
can be seen immediately."

Eneas nodded assent, and was forthwith introduced to
the front parlour, evidently dedicated to the purposes of
a counting-house. The arrangement of papers, carefully
fastened with red tape, and the few tin boxes, with initials
and dates, proclaimed the business carried on. Everything was in order, and the very stumps of the pens in
the old, black, oblong inkstand seemed to enjoy their
position, notwithstanding the quill had departed long ago,
and they were, as schoolboys say, "deep in the pith."
Eneas could not help noticing the calm tranquillity of the
place, and in the fulness of his feelings almost involuntarily exclaimed, "I know I shall get relief."

"I hope so, sir ; I hope so," said a smooth-faced little
man, dressed in shabby black, with a stiff white neckcloth,
who emerged from behind a screen, much in the same
manner as a change would be effected in a pantomime.
"Is it to be by bankruptcy, sir ; insolvency, sir ; or a
composition ?"

Eneas turned and made an obeisance.

"My name is Debit, sir," said the small gentleman,

continuing the colloquy, and cheerfully rubbing his hands; "I believe you require my services;" and thus, with mutual explanations, an introduction took place. "If by bankruptcy, sir," continued Mr. Debit with great volubility, as the conversation was resumed, "If by bankruptcy, sir, you ought not to pay a large dividend; if by insolvency, sir, no assets are now recognized as the means of speedy relief; and if by compromise—compromise, indeed—ah! that may be easily settled. If a man can compromise, he ought never to fail; for in that case he can put off the evil day by payments at six, nine, and twelve months."

Eneas scarcely comprehended the import of this harrangue, and without further delay gave Mr. Debit to understand that he was but little acquainted with the general laws of debtor and creditor, further than the payment of every claim, if possible, to the uttermost farthing, and his perfect ignorance of the *minutiæ* of bankruptcy or insolvency practice.

Whereupon Mr. Debit proposed to look quietly into the case. That was what Eneas wished, and paper and ink were soon in requisition, to work out and solve accurately the difficult problem of Mr. P.'s mercantile and financial position. Although the particulars were less complex than might have been imagined, and the assets presented much more favourable prospects than Eneas could, at first, persuade himself to believe, he was eventually satisfied that his affairs were not in a condition so deplorable as he had anticipated.

And remember, good reader, that Mr. Pinchbeck is not the first individual who has viewed with greater despondency than necessary, the actual situation of his pecuniary engagements. According to Mr. Debit's estimate, and he was ready to stake his reputation upon its veracity, if the figures furnished were correct, there was a good fifteen shillings in the pound ; a sum that any reasonable body of creditors would accept, satisfied as they must, no doubt, be, of the integrity of Pinchbeck's career. An offer, consequently, of that amount, with liberty to carry out a full investigation, if it were thought essential, was considered by Mr. Debit the proper course to pursue ; and he requested permission to communicate the proposal in the ordinary form.

But Pinchbeck, although partially satisfied, was somewhat daunted. The notion of his inability to discharge the full claims of his creditors, and the disgrace attending a composition, seemed to hang heavily upon his conscience.

" Why be downhearted, my dear sir ?" said Debit, in a remarkably kind and soothing manner ; " you are not the only person I have carried through difficulties. Indeed, your case is one much more favourable than the majority ; and with assets such as yours, few would even think of pulling up."

" But," said Eneas, with apparent suspicion, " if they should refuse the offer ?"

" Oh, come, that's too good," rejoined Debit ; " refuse our offer !"

" Yes, if they refuse our offer."

" Well, then," said Debit, with great solemnity, and as if he meant it, " we will go at once into the *Gazette*."

" Go into the *Gazette* !" shrieked Pinchbeck, in agony, " and be immediately ruined—never ! I cannot do that. What would become of Rhoda, and the dear children ?"

" Yes, it must be," continued Debit ; " we will go into the *Gazette* ;" and he expressed himself as if that operation were a species of pleasant pastime. " I never knew that remedy fail when a decent composition was slighted. The position you stand in is, fortunately, very different from a host of instances I could mention. Why, bless my heart !" continued the little man, his face assuming a very luminous and jocular appearance, " there would be no courts of bankruptcy, or insolvency ; professional advocates, lawyers, and accountants would starve, if the standard of morality presented by your teaching were kept at that elevated point. I recollect, my dear sir," he proceeded, as he pointed to a large roll of papers lying upon his table, regularly endorsed, " I recollect the great firm of Wiggins, Whiffin, and Co., general merchants and importers ; they did me the especial honour to consult me on their affairs. Drew out their balance-sheet with care and punctuality ; it showed enormous debts and large accommodation transactions ; the stock had run down to a low figure ; book debts and general assets limited : called the creditors together. There was a great meeting ; explanations required ; entered into lengthened statements. Offered 3s. 4d. in the pound—indignantly refused ; went to 4s.—contemptuously declined. Took an adjournment, and again gave their accounts consideration ; adhered to the second proposal, and suggested payments of 2s. at three months, 1s. at six months, and 1s. at nine months. And then came another difficulty—' What security ?' Could not give any, not even for the last instalment. Creditors thereupon became obdurate— threatened bankruptcy. Replied immediately that we were sorry so prejudicial a course should be hinted at, but, if it would at all facilitate the object, we would directly sign a declaration of insolvency. Ah, ah !" said the little man, as he chuckled and tapped his knuckles, knowingly, with a ruler, "that brought them to their senses. 'What would bankruptcy produce ?' inquired an old gentleman, averse to litigation and official assignee's commission. 'Perhaps 2s.; perhaps less.' He was against it; and being one of the principal claimants, he turned the tide of wrath. 'The estate would require management, tender management, and was Basinghall Street the place for that ?' He, with a few sentences such as these, snubbed the representatives of those who advocated the *Gazette,* and we came off victorious with our composition."

"And of course the firm liquidated as arranged," said Pinchbeck.

"Not at all, of course, my dear sir," rejoined Debit; "they paid the first two instalments, but there was a trifling hitch with the third, which was settled somehow, though it is not necessary to disclose all the secrets of the prison-house. It matters little, however, for they did eventually go into the *Gazette,* pass, and obtained a satisfactory certificate, notwithstanding the doubtful nature of their trading. They are now once more in business, with fresh capital and augmented connections, and their operations are as extensive as ever. So, you see, my dear sir, your lapse in credit, even if you should fail, will not involve such consequences as those I have described."

With much persuasion Eneas at last allowed Mr. T. Debit to take the initiatory step of sounding his creditors, on the promise that he would adopt no active measures for calling a meeting. Debit was quite prepared to make this concession, because he felt satisfied, by the information he had extracted from Pinchbeck, that the arrangement would prove one of the easiest that had ever fallen into his hands.

A few days were only required to issue the circulars, with a statement, and the answers were of the most satisfactory description.   Many extolled the character of Pinchbeck for probity and straightforward dealing; volunteered support while he was "getting through;" and he suddenly discovered that his position, notwithstanding his misfortunes, was far better than any estimate he could have ventured to form.   Instead, therefore, of sinking under his dreamy despondency, he was encouraged to greater exertion, and having paid the fifteen shillings in the pound, was also enabled, some three or four years after, through increased success, to clear off the remaining balance of the twenty shillings.   *Post tenebras lux.*

XVIII.

ONE would scarcely suppose in these degenerate days, that our forefathers possessed the opportunity of making more money, and probably through means as steady and legitimate, as we of the nineteenth century. Yet so it would seem, and those who take the trouble to consult the chronicles of old will find, if they have a mind to carry out the investigation, that we are perfectly correct in making this assertion. It is true that jobbing contractors were in existence then, that prices advanced and receded, that the public were ever alive to looking after themselves, and that where there was presumed to be a royal road to wealth, the route was not neglected. But while this was the case, and every means was then sought as now to move forward in the pursuit of riches, much less competition existed in the struggle, and the sources for the employment of capital were certainly not so hazardous.

It is not essential, in elucidating the theory we have had the temerity to start, to go back as far as the period of the good old "Domesday Book," or Stow's "History of London;" we shall be quite content to descend to a much less ancient, though, at the same time, an equally potential authority, viz., that plain-sailing, and, some persons think, dull publication, the authorized lists of the Stock Exchange; and we think we shall be able to show, that within the last fifty years, the medium for investments has so increased that while they exhibit a much wider field for operating and dealing, the returns are of a decidedly more illusory character. Putting out of the question, as we shall in the consideration of this topic, the extravagance of the age, the questionable means resorted to in every circle to augment resources, and the distress that, in nine cases out of ten, results from the want of success in attaining this desired end, a simple appeal to what may almost be described as dry statistical fact will prove the truth of these observations.

Of course, in forming such a contrast, allowance must be made for exceptional cases—instances in which fortunes have been secured by what are popularly known as lucky hits—and for those where special transactions, and special knowledge, have led to the realization of objects in connection with popular inventions, with the development of which the art of money-making is so closely allied. At the same time it must be remembered that in arriving at the conclusions adduced, the views must be treated as comparative, and in the ratio of the progress of population and wealth, the latter principally produced by the success of commerce, and not from those engagements which seem to be understood, and appreciated as investments.

If we turn to the pages of the lists published so far back as the date we have mentioned, it will be discovered that the securities existing for negotiation were, the English funds, the Annuities, a few foreign stocks, gas, bridge, and dock shares, Bank and India stock, and a small array of miscellaneous companies hardly worth special enumeration. But if these classes were limited, and the greater portion of money was placed in them, the rises and falls were not of that spasmodic character which is now their characteristic, nor was there that extent of gambling,

which unfortunately appears to increase with our growth
both in capital and resources. There was, with the steady
improvement that occurred immediately after the peace,
an augmentation in prices which sensibly enriched those
who had purchased at low values, and though inter-
mediately the great Cochrane conspiracy had taken place,
the mischievous results of that affair were speedily frus-
trated, by the exposure and punishment of the principal
delinquents, and speculation was not generally of a rife or
rampant character. To use a trite but well-recognized
expression, it was then more the age of "money grub-
bing," and if our tastes were not so delicate or refined,
they did not require to be stimulated with the excitement
now apparently necessary to support position, even should
it terminate in bankruptcy, or temporary expatriation to
Boulogne.

Between 1815 and 1825 we passed the fixed limits of
business as steady investors, and opportunities were subsequently afforded to speculators, with the increased facilities afforded by the joint-stock banks, and the foreign loans
so rapidly and extensively introduced, for active gambling;
and from that date forward we have never returned to the
old condition, despite the penalty paid about every ten
years for the national madness, which first produces a
mania, and subsequently a panic. From 1825 to 1835
intervened the epoch which saw almost the last of the
bubble mining companies, and the Spanish American loans,
and which changed the shifting scene of operations to the
United States; and, notwithstanding that this fresh phase
in the great game of speculation terminated in 1837, the
lessons of the past were evidently altogether forgotten,
and the forfeit incurred was even heavier than that
which had liquidated the claims of 1826.

But as the country grew, and the population spread, the list of investments also increased ; and if they were not so profitable as the experience of the previous generation could testify, they presented an infinitely greater variety of almost every conceivable character. As the length of the list increased, the losses seemed periodically to become greater; and though the argument, in some respects, holds good that the money merely changes hands, still the filtration of it through the various channels causes enormous distress and sacrifice. In the next decade, bringing us down to 1845, sprung up the railway mania, which strengthened in the course of three years, when, from progressive improvement in the system, it became developed into " the rushing madness of a nation," and that again entailed its misery and loss in the years of sorrow, 1847 and 1848. This period, more than any other, swelled out the catalogue of securities ; and from a small slip of paper, as originally issued, the daily railway list has now become one of such magnitude, that it is something really imposing to investigate.

We have since had our little Californian and Australian gold mining speculation, and we are now passing through our new banking and miscellaneous mania—the latter being sure to produce its fruit in good time. But for the purposes of the present occasion, it will only be requisite to cast an eye over the Stock Exchange list to observe the contrast that has already been referred to. It is particularly instructive as showing the maze of securities that exist, the bewildering aspect they present to the steady and legitimate investor—for that race has not quite died out, though it is in a fair way of being extinguished—and the difficulty of being satisfied with what you are supposed have purchased.

Excluded from consideration in this notice is the English list, comprising English and Indian securities, recently increased by the detail of the rupee paper and the 5 and 4 per cent. debts ; and the foreign list, which contains every debt, from the colonies of Central America to those of Morocco. We strictly confine ourselves to English railways, foreign railways, American securities and railways, British and foreign mines, banks and miscellaneous. Here is a category for capitalists and speculators to gloat over. The vision is puzzled by the mass of names and the description of the property. It is almost a positive relief to cast aside the paper. Please, kind reader, take it in hand and look at it. Between eighty and ninety ordinary railway shares and stocks, about one hundred and fifty different classes of preference shares, fifty lines leased at fixed rentals, twelve or fourteen debenture stocks, nearly as many lines in the British possessions, twenty-four Indian railway debentures, forty foreign lines, with obligations, and plenty of colonial government securities. The American securities present a good list, and the British mines and foreign mines are also numerous. The banks average between sixty and seventy, a great number altogether new, and the miscellaneous undertakings slightly more.

Can it be a question of surprise then, that fluctuations when they take place in the round of these securities so greatly prejudice the pockets of the public, or create the serious extent of loss frequently mentioned. The great wonder is from the overwhelming mass of securities, that quotations are as well supported as they are, considering in many instances the limit to dividends, while a large number make no return at all. It would be a great boon to the public if these lists were shortened or condensed.

The labour, with a little consultation among the Committee of the Stock Exchange, would not be insurmountable, and in a better arranged and less detailed form, the railway and miscellaneous share list would prove much more attractive. A number of the undertakings, indeed, of second and third class character, in which transactions now seldom or never take place, might be, if necessary, altogether omitted, and transferred to the weekly publication.

XIX.

AT HOME ON THE CINDER HEAP.—THE MYSTERIOUSLY BURIED
" TALENT."

On the route between Kingsland and Hackney, a neighbourhood recently improved by buildings of every description, winds a slow sluggish canal, flanked on either
side by straggling tenements of a doubtful and unsubstantial character, intersected occasionally with tumble-
down wharves and land sidings, available for the barge
and lugger traffic employed in the business conducted on
this spot. The property at many points, if property it
can be called, presents to the passer-by a very discouraging
appearance, and notwithstanding two or three suburban
coal merchants and lime dressers have bestowed labour in
devising the necessary room to carry out operations, the
special district, as a whole, exhibits strong evidence of a
struggle against inevitable decay. New thoroughfares
and streets exist, filled with carcases of unfinished houses
—the work of those enterprising explorers who cover with
bricks and mortar every nook they can secure—and which,
cutting through green fields and market gardens, not a
dozen years ago the grounds of recreation and delight of
the rising generation, indicate the provision essential for
the ever-increasing population of the great metropolis.
These roads and inlets for the most part diverge from the
path of the dark stream, which glides lazily along in its
own course through its dull and dreamy way, leaving on
its sombre borders shattered wrecks of many old establish-

ments, which but for numerous contrivances in battered and besmeared wood, grey irregular stone, and clamped iron, must long before this have dropped piecemeal to ruins.

More than one gas company overshadows the banks with tall black chimneys, huge gasometers, and coke ovens; soap manufacturers use the water of the canal, and there no doubt run off their refuse; ice-wells are located near, and many itinerant trades seem to be pursued, which would receive no support in other places. In the spring and summer time, the few trees that stand skirting its banks give out a little freshness, and the attempts made at some of the smaller habitations to get up a garden, increase the exhibition of vegetation; but the greatest amount of colour presented is in the form of the yellow blossom of the stone-crop, everywhere, here and there espied upon the wall, and the pale purple of the stunted lilacs which have thrust their heads through broken fences, or overgrown the surrounding palings. Through autumn and winter the spot is bleak and extremely dreary. There is ample room and verge enough, for the north-easterly winds to give full vent to their feelings. In the course of this two or three mile circuit, plenty of sharp angles abound, round which rude Boreas can exercise his gusty whistling propensities, and attack travellers from the front or behind, in the most unceremonious manner.

If the weather be dry and in good condition, there is a very fair chance of being blown off your feet into the canal; if the elements should be, on the other hand, perverse, and rain descend, good rifle boots, knickerbockers, and a mackintosh, will scarcely be sufficient to escape the mud and damp. In deep winter, if the season be hard, and I have known it so hard that the canal has been frozen over for days together, a little more rough life exists ; for the stream, since Bunker's Pond has been filled in, has become the arena for skating and sliding, and hither the masses from Bethnal Green, with troops of men of the Kiddy Harris class, and boys, whose training will not especially fit them for the higher grades of society, hie to disport themselves in all the gracefulness of one-leg evolutions, bumps, trips, and side falls. In full sunshine alone is the locality bearable, and then it must be very strong sunshine to enable the place to look pleasant, or the illusion as you make the route will be speedily dissipated. The latest, best, and greatest improvement has been the erection of the above-ground telegraph communication, which with its elevated garish green and white poles running the length of the water, diminishes in a degree the apparent absence of marked civilized tone and propriety.

To see this place in all its grandeur of desolate magnificence, a visit should be made at night time, as near as possible to the midnight hour. Scudding rapidly through this route, as I frequently have in a cab returning home, I have had the opportunity of viewing it under all aspects and in all seasons, and I have certainly been very much struck with the effects produced at night-fall. The spot is naturally dull and sombre, but its loneliness is intensified as the evening advances. Between ten and eleven o'clock the little activity that was noticeable in the neighbourhood has become exhausted ; the low glimmer of candles seen in windows quickly fades away, and the gaslight on the two or three bridges which cross the canal, although in so close proximity to great gas institutions, beam feebly and sullenly as if they were never properly supplied. The large black chimneys rear their heads against the sky, the dark rotund forms of the coke ovens loom out upon the water, and intermittingly through their doors flash out streaks of light, which for an instant dance in shadow and then disappear. Large gasometers rise in portly proportions, and o'ertower everything in their neighbourhood—like huge caldrons which might be supposed to have been used for culinary purposes by the sons of Anak, and looking grisly and hoar with their long iron riveted sides, and their many beltings of hard-cased metal. Dwarf whitewashed walls run not far beneath, from the centre of which dart out the fires of the lime-burners who are now at work, and whose comparatively pigmy forms may be occasionally seen, flitting backwards and forwards in attendance to their duties. Sufficient light is visible from a stray flickering gas-lamp to show the slow turgid motion of the stream, and the black tarred body of a brick barge, or perhaps the lighter hull of an oil-cake lugger, with sepia-coloured flapping sails, constitutes the remaining outlines of a picture which is not frequently met with.

In this as in other desolate places eccentric characters are to be encountered, and it has formed at one time or another the locality for eccentric abodes. Some of these eccentric people have thrown off their eccentricity, and have moved into more civilized spheres ; but this has not proved the case with them all, and several remain carrying their peculiarities to the highest pitch of extravagance. In the old days, it may be remembered, there was the celebrated wooden tenement which, placed on wheels in the Kingsland Road, was the subject of conversation for years, the inhabitant being a person who was said to contemplate establishing a freehold right on the site, but whether he did or not I cannot precisely recollect. I have, however, a clear remembrance of investigating the premises myself, and being surprised that in that hut, cribbed, cabined, and confined as it was, a man alleged to be far removed from want could endeavour to bring up a wife and children. My astonishment in this respect subsequently cooled, when a few years later in my peregrinations I discovered a greater wonder than the tenant of the wooden four-wheeled house at Kingsland. This individual—a man of fortune and good intellect—owned, so the story went, some ground in one of the cross streets running through the back of the Hackney Road, and taking it into his head to purchase a travelling van, had it placed there, and leaving a comfortable abode, made the vehicle a permanent retreat. Day or night he was seldom seen; when he was, it was only for a moment or so, and to seek his supplies he always sallied forth in the dark. The regular stream of smoke from his dingy iron chimney was the sole evidence to his neighbours that he continued alive. From his mode of habit and life, although he was not uncivil or disobliging, he became the scoff of the children, and the back and the sides of his dwelling were literally made a cinder heap, all refuse and rubbish being thrown there by the immediate population.

Things went in this fashion for years; the old gentleman, meanwhile, was accumulating money and valuables, having, it was alleged, a great taste for diamonds, which it was believed were deposited with his bankers, for he was shrewd enough to avoid the risk of robbery or murder; till at last a strange sensation was created one morning by the appearance of a well-dressed female, who entered the caravan, and appeared to be received with all possible politeness. If an earthquake had assaulted the neighbourhood more complete consternation could not have been created. The notion of a creditable woman allowing herself to be seen in that place with that old man, and without an associate, shocked the decorum of every one. The visits, few at first, gradually increased, and then it was noticed that the old gentleman became less unsociable, and a little more visible. He discarded his former attire, dressed in a cleanlier style, and placed outside his window —a sure sign of rising hope—boxes of mignonette! The "strange lady," for that was the title by which she was called by the neighbours, continued to be seen in and out of the vehicle near the cinder heap, but no great change took place in the appearance of the residence, except that the row of flowers increased, and shortly included variegated balsams and Tom Thumb geraniums.

Suddenly a further alteration appeared, painters were employed, the sides of the caravan were pumiced down, and they were engaged for three whole days, in renovating this singular habitation in panels of green picked out with white. The single window in the establishment was now ornamented with a neat short blind, supported by a small bright brass rod; and, as if with the view of making everything extremely complete, a small full-faced lion-head knocker and a bell-pull were added to the highly-varnished door. With this repainting, repanelling, and extra decoration, the caravan appeared more like one of those used by the proprietors of country exhibitions, than the dark, sombre object of former years, and of course it was at once supposed that a marriage had been arranged, or, perhaps, was finally concluded. The old gentleman steadily improved in his habits; first mounted a stick, then exhibited a guard chain, and finally a massive bunch of seals. Still the strange lady came and went; they were not much seen together; but occasionally the old gentleman, out of gallantry, would escort her to the top of the street, till she was clear of the vicinity, and fairly on her road to

town, being perhaps apprehensive that she might be interrogated or molested by the inhabitants.

At last the poor old fellow—for, though he was not
very advanced in years, he showed symptoms of premature
decay—was seized with illness, and then the female came
and remained. There was no blinking the question longer.
They were man and wife, and had been so for some time.
Surmounting her scruples after the improvements in the
habitation, she took up her abode permanently, and lived
there in apparent comfort for a considerable period.
Eventually, even this residence was abandoned, and
another in a substantial house, the property of the old
gentleman, was sought, more congenial to his improved
taste and convenience. By steadfast attention and per-
suasive ministering, this good creature restored her partner
to society, not perhaps to the rank he should have moved
in, but certainly raised him from the grovelling position
in which he had been plunged for nearly a quarter of a
century.

Little ever transpired respecting the cause which seemed
to have blighted his early days, and on this topic he always
preserved strict silence. Some said it was a cross in
love; others that he had been deceived by professed friends
when he first entered his mercantile career; but nothing
very tangible could ever be elicited. He was exceedingly
well related, his brothers and nephews holding good commercial positions, and had he possessed the will or the
energy to have broken his cold reserve, and pushed into
the world, would, from his peculiar knowledge and ability
—for he had not neglected self-culture even at the cinder
heap—have made some figure in financial circles. Both
himself and his wife have departed; but not before they
were able to show how much he appreciated a restoration

to actual civilization, from which he had been so long an
outcast.

I journeyed over to the old spot the other day, and the
site formerly occupied by the caravan and the cinder heap is
covered with cottages.   The neighbourhood is still poor,
and apparently struggling against hard fate.   Some of the
doors are half painted, and being dirty from rough usage,
still give a woe-begone appearance to the place.   Improvements there are in other directions, and the contrast
consequently is doubly striking, manifestly to the disadvantage of this suburban Slough of Despond.

XX

THE FINANCIAL SIGNS OF THE TIMES.

THERE is little or no warning now ever given by the actual state of the money market previously to the occurrence of a financial disturbance. In former days, when the public were not so alert as they are now, symptoms of impending change were more freely prognosticated. It was perhaps then less a matter of guess-work than it is at this period, in consequence of the steady influx of gold from America and Australia, which, in the course of a few weeks, if it accumulate in the Bank, speedily alters the appearance of the general money and discount markets. When, however, an internal and an external drain set in together, a change in the other direction is as quickly wrought, much to the surprise of those who fancied there was to be continued abundance, with every species of facility.

Plentiful harvests, with average prospects for trade, should always exercise an influential effect in connection with the circulation of capital and its employment; and surplus capital may always be used with advantage, in promoting sound enterprise, and developing cosmopolitan undertakings, if the outlay be kept within due bounds, and the arrangement for its liquidation adjusted in proportion to the supposed growth of the wealth of the country. But when very sanguine estimates are made of the capacity of the public to support companies, and these are formed on a scale out of all comparison with those estimates, favourable as they may be, it will not appear surprising that sooner or later a disruption takes place, which not only interferes with the progress of those of acknowledged character and public utility, but also breaks up those which have no foundation of success, causing great sacrifice and disappointment.

It does not matter whether it be a railway, a banking, or a miscellaneous mania, the consequences are invariably the same; and though some curious and devious course in working out the final result may be taken, it comes to the old point at last, leaving trade impaired, confidence shaken, and the Stock Exchange department gorged with a mass of unsaleable securities and scrip.

When the principal Continental cities have been engaged in a round game of speculation, they are always sure first to feel the effects of the collapse, simply because, whether the revulsion be occasioned by political events or a monetary stringency, the circle of operations among them is comparatively narrow or insignificant. Speculation in every sense of the word has been recently more than ever confined to London and Paris, and probably was more active in the great English metropolis than the French, for though the ramifications have partially extended to the other side of the Channel, they have not affected business or financial relations in an important degree. The weight of these engagements thrown upon the English money market, which certainly is the central pivot of the financial transactions of the entire world, always occasions disquietude when it reaches a heavy total, and induces the Bank, and the various auxiliaries, to prepare for any contingency that may arise, so as to protect themselves and the public.

If, as in days gone by, the drain be external, prompt measures must be resorted to ; if internal, the alarm is not so great, for the bullion may before long return ; but if these conjoint causes come into simultaneous operation, there is then little hope left that any remedial steps can be adopted, save the stepping in of the Government, as was done in 1847 and 1857. From the difference in the action of the Bank of England and the Bank of France, notwithstanding that the best relations are maintained between them, a struggle every now and then arises for supremacy of control over bullion ; the Bank of France, if deficient, by a bold stroke endeavouring to secure £2,000,000 or £3,000,000 through actual purchase. Conducted, as these transactions may be, with every effort to preserve secrecy, the fact very soon transpires, and immediately up goes the rate of the Bank of England. So long as the Bank of France takes bullion, unless it be through special arrangement, the Bank of England is compelled to advance the rate until the remittances cease and the rectification of the foreign exchanges, as it is termed, brings bullion back again from Paris and the other subsidiary markets. The same sort of action takes place in Paris likewise, when an outflow of specie ensues for the silk or the grain crops, and also if silver or gold be suddenly required thence or from London for St. Petersburg.

Latterly the French gold demand has been to forward supplies to Mexico, while the absorption for local improvements has at the same time been extremely important. Though M. Fould has not had the courage to admit it, the Treasury shows a large deficit, which will have to be replenished by a loan. The apprehension created by that operation has increased the difficulty noticeable in the

Parisian money market. Here, in London, the public have been surfeited with companies of every variety and denomination. The successful harvest has caused a large supply of sovereigns to be sent into the provinces, where they are still in circulation, and will probably remain some time longer. During the time that capital is being swallowed by these numerous undertakings, and temporarily withdrawn through the harvest requirements, the Bank of France resorts to its old policy, and purchases at any risk or cost whatever gold it can, so that American or Australian supplies are immediately cleared away.

We are likewise peculiarly situated in another point of view—for if we have left off sending gold remittances or goods to America to pay for cotton, we have to liquidate similar engagements in India and Egypt, and thus an additional strain is created. This strain tells with great effect, occurring as it does in the later months of the year, and, considerable at any period through the payments for produce in China and the East, the liabilities for cotton have enormously augmented the total. Besides, it seems almost certain that if peace were restored in America to-morrow, the prospects of the advantageous results of the extension of cotton cultivation in India and Egypt are so encouraging that they would still be developed ; and although full competition with American classes would not be anticipated, operations could be conducted with profit, even at a large reduction in current prices.

With these causes in operation, no other result than a rise in the rate of discount could be expected, and it has come and has passed, unaccompanied by any of the more serious consequences which usually intervene when the stringency is general. It is wonderful what an effect is produced by the changing of £2,000,000 from England to France, and *vice versâ*, and through the enormous character of our general financial transactions, though they may not be permanently disturbed, some suffering must be occasioned in a few particular branches from the enhancement of the rates.

XXI.

WHENEVER any temporary excitement arises at the Stock Exchange, it is curious to notice the groups of busy operators lounging near the Bank, in the neighbourhood of Cornhill, at the entrance of Capel Court, near Hercules Passage, or in the front of the Royal Exchange. Be the weather fine or wet, there they are in anxious congregation, discussing the prospects of the favourite investments of the hour, and the various fluctuations are noted with the most eager attention; the rise or fall of a quarter to a half per cent. enriching some, while the same mutations in an equal proportion impoverish others. The *aura sacra fames* would indeed seem to be strong as ever, and watching the revivals of character in the course of the changes for the last fifteen or twenty years, many of the outside dealers, though they have frequently courted Fortune's smile, and have encountered in return only her frown, still pursue their career with an ardour which is truly marvellous.

Keen eyes can trace the features of Jew and Gentile among these motley assemblies, who have haunted the neighbourhood from generation to generation, and who, by occasional slices of luck, appear likely to secure a position, but never ultimately to realize it. But the tendency is ever the same, and they embody in personal illustration the never-ending task of Sisyphus. If in the

days gone by the great attraction of speculative prices
was centered in the shares of the Churnett Valley, the
Trent Valley, or some of the other valley-routes which
were mapped out, but several never thoroughly projected,
and North Staffordshire shares, with Oxford and Worcester, absorbed the chief fluctuations which were then
presented, precedence can now be claimed for the long-
neglected Greek stock, Turkish kaimes, or Spanish
passives, each in turn taking as wide a circle in price as
any of those far-famed railway securities.

Where the second and third class speculators come
from, or go to, is a problem almost as difficult to solve, as
that furnished by Charles Dickens in connection with
post-boys and dead donkeys. That they live, move, and
have a being, there is not the least manner of doubt; that
they are to be seen, actively engaged in business, between
the hours of 11 a.m. and 3 p.m. is well attested by their
appearance and position in the purlieus named; but to
what points they all retire when the shades of evening
draw in, and how they dispose of themselves when the
great game of speculation is over, or has become exhausted, taxes the ingenuity of the most observant.

To talk of the operations inside the house having been
large, the transactions outside the house recently, particularly those associated with these small securities, must have
been of great magnitude, and money cannot fail to have
been made by the more adventurous, if they have had
confidence sufficient to follow the course of the market, in
taking Greek kaimes, Mexican, or Spanish passives, to the
middle, or highest points of the market. The business
proper in foreign securities, has become one huge speculation, and, first fed by moderate transactions, these have
increased, until now, such is the volume of engagements,

that it is difficult to estimate to what extent they may be carried.

The rage will continue until these several stocks, are either placed on a better footing, through the progress of events in those various countries, or a collapse shall be brought about by failures, when startling revelations will be made of the unstable bases upon which many of these transactions have been conducted, and then will succeed the customary reaction, creating heaviness, accompanied by a revulsion in prices. The effect upon the horde of petty operators outside the house, so soon as any change of this character ensues, will be remarkable. The bright hats, the smart ties, the new coats, the cable chains, and the bulbous pins, will gradually 'tone down, or altogether disappear ; and the spirit of seediness quickly make himself visible, in the shape of tight-fitting and close-buttoned garments, greasy *chapeaux*, and the absence of Paris gloves.

My friend of yesterday, who, full of vigorous hope, rushes up to me impetuously, and asks me what I think of Turkish Consolidés, Greek or Spanish passives, and who, of course, believes that they will go higher—because the wish is father to the thought—has seen his ups and downs in this line before. He has had years of experience, it is a mania with him, and therefore he is prepared, for present ease and comfort, to take the ultimate risk. He went through the fever of 1824-25, when Real del Monte shares touched 300 pm., though afterwards, in succeeding years, they sold at 5s. per share. In the railway period of 1847-48 he was again in complete swing, and possessed at the end of the period, sufficient scrip and shares of defunct schemes to paper his rooms, as a memorial of his folly. And now again, though an old man, fresh in visage and quick-sighted, he is with the same spirits, and unflagging zeal, rushing in with the new school, believing that if he lost then, he may now gain, and ultimately retire with a competency.

The lessons of the past, he candidly confesses, have had but little weight or influence with him; he has speculated all his life, and he thinks he is too far advanced in years to dispense with the excitement. Originally he came from a Dutch family, who, either as bankers or merchants, made gigantic fortunes; and he is the sole representative of the patriarchal tree, who may properly be said to have tasted poverty in any form. Perhaps, however, his cup of bitterness has never been filled to the brim, or he might have sought some other and more ennobling calling; but having managed to hang about, and run in and out of the counting-houses of his former friends, and now wealthy associates, though frequently as near as possible coming to grief, he has escaped the penalty attaching to the mishaps of many of his regular comrades, who, if once "knocked out of time," never had the chance of recovering their position. He will probably again live through this foreign stock mania, and after making a little money, find it run as rapidly through his fingers as he did before; perchance he may this time lose everything, break down, and have to vanish altogether from the scene of his operations, like better and greater men. And mind, it is only a very serious shock such as this, even if this did accomplish the object, that would take him into other paths for a livelihood, though his opportunities for a change have been, and still continue to be, numerous.

The other gay birds of plumage will, after a short period, become birds of passage; a strong migration will set in, principally to the provinces and outlying districts, and some will take refuge in prisons. The few that remain will consist of the seasoned, and casehardened individuals, who can either run the gauntlet of a small amount of indebtedness, or eke out a dreary subsistence until some new fashion in speculation shall be introduced. In a celebrated case years ago, heard before Mr. Commissioner Holroyd, a question turned upon the identity of certain securities, in which the members of a family were interested under an old estate. The point was raised, and evidence brought forward to show, that the bankrupt had been interested in a particular description of Spanish American stock. One witness, a highly respectable tradesman, was called to prove his knowledge of some transactions at the particular time; and when questioned admitted that he had been "a speculator on the Royal Exchange" (at that time the outside operators occupied that place as their chief post of dealing); and in answer to the interrogatories of Mr. Edwin James, added that he was "a speculator in the complete sense of the word, for he had everything to gain and nothing to lose;" but he soon got tired of the harassing life, and after incurring numerous liabilities, at length returned to his settled avocation, regretting he had ever, even in the height of the furore of 1825, neglected it.

XXXII.

An analysis of the formation, and organization, of the various joint-stock companies during the last two years, if it could be satisfactorily framed, would prove a most instructive lesson, for the study of the statistician, and the information of the public. It would be agreed on all hands that, from their multifarious and miscellaneous character, the crop of undertakings more approaches in extent, and general amount of liability, the mania of 1824-1825, while surrounding circumstances at the same time lead to the inference, that the encouraging aspect of our trading relations has deluded those who have entered into the arena of speculation, with the belief that all is resting on a stable, and well-adjusted foundation.

The days of " Prosperity Robinson," as the Chancellor of the Exchequer was then termed, from the glowing accounts he periodically gave of the progress of trade and finance, appear, according to the records of history, very much like our own at the present juncture; and if Mr. Gladstone's last budget be accepted in contrast, it must be admitted that his extraordinary surplus spoke volumes in favour of the success of commerce, even in the midst of a cotton famine, and Lancashire distress.

For two years at least, have the investing public been inundated with companies of every hue and description, and though the fever has never reached any very particular height, save in exceptional cases, it has been of so continuous a character as to render it difficult to repress its progress, without interfering with the development of many utilitarian industrial, and mercantile enterprises. The endeavour to found one or two new banks was accomplished without much difficulty; and after this was effected the competitive system was adopted, extending the number, which at first it was supposed would be restricted to five or six, to at least five-and-twenty. There was ample field for a few establishments of this kind to test the principle of limited liability; but now the number has so fearfully increased, further competition will be established, and in the course of a year or two, if not before, we shall see the effect of it both in London, and in the provinces.

Next to banking enterprises the most popular, and well-sustained projects, have been the Credit and Financial Companies, but these have been supported because it seems they are following out in full integrity, the promises made by the directors in their prospectus, to eschew speculation, and irregular operations. Adopting the Credit Mobilier principle in form, they have avoided its worst features, and if the respective boards and their managers, can be induced to pursue a legitimate course throughout their career, the dividends payable, if not outrageously high, will probably be sufficient to satisfy the great majority of proprietors. It would not, however, be desirable to see the number of such institutions carried beyond their present limits, since it is quite evident that those existing, can absorb all the business likely to be presented to their notice.

The hotel movement is one that will require more time than has at present elapsed to indicate what will probably be its issue. Taking past experience as a guide for the future, the dividends paid, it is known, have been good and well-supported. This may continue to be the case in those companies where remunerative businesses have been purchased, and where the management is invested in individuals who have previously superintended such establishments. Where mischief may ensue will be with hotels, projected and located in spots, which will have to attract a business to them, the difficulty in these instances being to surmount the necessarily large preliminary outlay. Hotels in fashionable quarters will, no doubt, pay, but the rate of expenditure for maintenance and management will be excessive ; and therefore, on the whole, too sanguine an estimate of the average returns should not be formed. These three kinds of enterprise form the distinct varieties of " limited liability " projects which the present mania has introduced. They were as a class more or less required, and the speculation of the period has supplied recognized wants. Indeed the activity of organization has gone much further, and produced a redundancy, the consequences of which will, in a measure, be hereafter found embarrassing.

Of the miscellaneous projects—and this list includes a fabulous amount of liability,—it must candidly be confessed that their titles and purposes, appear to shadow forth little chance of general prosperity. Whether as manufacturing companies, trading companies, or land companies, the elements are not sufficiently striking to lead to the conclusion that profits will in the aggregate, allow a return for the capital employed. Special exceptions there may be in favour of India Tea Companies, the prospects of which generally, if well-managed, are encouragingly spoken of, but in any instance where the seat of superintendence is far removed from the vigilance of the directors, strict discipline and economy, must be combined, to ensure thoroughly advantageous results. A mass of companies, although commenced in regular course, and reaching the honour of a premium in the market for shares, very frequently progress not a step further. The directors find they will not work; the shares are insufficiently subscribed, and probably before the list is closed a hitch occurs with the promoters. Each of these causes separately, or the whole conjointly, are frequently enough to make many of the schemes drop through, and consequently after having lived a few weeks in "all the panoply of state," they eventually sink into insignificance, and are never again met with, save under the dread category " in liquidation." Hundreds and hundreds of companies, which have been announced in a preliminary manner, have been either withdrawn in the earliest stage, or allowed to float quietly down the stream, and ebb themselves out, by the directors paying the expenses, and submitting to the first loss as the least, and therefore all prospective engagements on their account are at an end. The total to be deducted in this respect will be considerable, and the weight of calls proportionately lightened when they come to show their full effect.

The question of "call" payments is, nevertheless, a serious one, and it will be found so if any pressure should exist, when the larger number of them falls due. It must be remembered that we have been encouraging banks, and financial and credit establishments, all of which require large amounts of capital to carry out their operations. The hotel subscriptions have been important, and the sums will be quickly called, and freely expended. At the period of the railway mania, the average of calls was about £1 10s. or £2 each. At the present date, in the case of banks and financial companies, they are £3 to £5 each, and will be secured with every possible celerity, despite the state of the money market, or any of its ultimate contingencies. Instead of a pressure mitigating "calls," it generally assists to increase them, as the directors then take alarm lest they should not obtain their capital, and adopt every means to ensure their collection. If the pressure be augmented by this additional strain it naturally works vicious consequences, and then speedily follows the panic cry, producing the panic penalty. The grand climacteric in this respect may arrive sooner than anticipated. No unsound symptoms as yet present themselves, except the excess of speculation in all kinds of stocks and shares; but this has been weeded out latterly, through the exhaustion in prices, and the indisposition of the brokers and jobbers to encourage a revival of speculation.

From the clouds which are gathering in many quarters, it is strongly imagined that the spring will be a time of financial trial, and if our gold supplies shall be as quickly taken up as they arrive, it will be many months before there is a return to moderate, or low rates of discount. Predictions are now freely uttered that the revulsion about to take place will approach, if it does not exceed, in severity, the great company crash of 1825. Should it not extend to commercial walks and injure trade, so much the better for those engaged in legitimate mercantile pursuits.

XXIII.

THE PERIODICAL PAYMENT OF DIVIDENDS.

THERE are two things of which it is said the British lion, the trusty representative of *perfide Albion,* is proverbially fond, namely, his dinner and his dividends. The ordinary routine of the latter institution, time honoured in its observance, is substantially shadowed forth by the periodical return of those semi-annual cycles when the *pièce de résistance* is a good handful of crisp, crumpling banknotes, or a heavy cheque upon some establishment in Lombard Street, the denominational proceeds of which, assist to make the recipient comfortable for the remaining five months of the year.

No doubt much wisdom exists in the smart saying, attributed to Lord Eldon, about the "elegant simplicity of the Three per Cents.;" and often have we been tempted to believe that the Iron Duke, when setting forth his renowned axiom of "a high rate of interest," usually denoting "inordinate risk," had at some period of his life paid for experience by entering into adventures, the concoctors of which promised, but failed to return, excessive profits. It is not unreasonable to suppose that the authors of each of these maxims had, in their day, once tried their hands at a little financiering; and if they did, and were not successful, the loss was theirs and the gain the public's, from the golden precepts they left for the benefit of the nation at large. If this were in reality the case, and the effect subsequently was to keep their accumulations wholly in the British Threes, India Stock, and the other well-constituted home funds, they exhibited much prudence and sound common sense, and their heirs and assigns can have had little reason to regret the fact.

It would, if possible, be interesting to discover, if either of these sagacious personages did ever touch doubtful securities—whether New River shares, in the original form, had any attractions for their money, or whether Real del Monte shares, the rage of the old 1823-24 mania, swallowed up any portion of their wealth. The old style of the sturdy and cautious school is perpetuated in the hosts of dividend-seekers at the Bank in January, April, July, and October, who have the principal of their money deposited and employed in the several stocks, funds, and annuities, represented by the National Debt of about £800,000,000. It is impossible to imagine to what gigantic proportions, this source of our country's greatness would have attained, had not some £500,000,000 to £600,000,000 been diverted to railways, banks, and other joint-stock undertakings, which have been developed, and, after various mutations, have become thoroughly successful, since the days when Lord Eldon and the Duke of Wellington uttered their important warnings.

It is not so very long since the payment of the last July dividends, which was, as usual, accomplished with ease and facility, the result of which was apparent in the rise that took place in Consols, Reduced and New. The period of the July dividends is a great date for effecting re-investments, and last year they were made on a considerable scale. The very weather itself had been seasonable for the operation; first, through the encouraging heat

for the harvest, inspiring hope in the future; and
secondly, through a disposition, towards the close of
the summer, to be adequately provided against adverse
contingencies.

To carry out the simile, it was precisely the weather
when John Bull, rising early, and looking out of the
window, would call for his boots, and having consulted
Mrs. Bull concerning family ways and means, and finding
all straight and correct, take his course to town and place
his running balance out to advantage. With his hands
in his breeches-pockets—the pockets of those capacious
yellow-corded smalls—the hue of his growing corn—
containing his cheques and notes in that identical brick-
colour bag, which has seen such service—he comes up to
buy stock, and stock he will have, though the price may
rise, and Mr. Golightly, his broker, may endeavour to
tempt him with other preferential securities.

This staunch old patron of the British Threes is not
singular in his unfailing appreciation of the Debt, and
being supported by hundreds of thousands of his fellow-
mortals—hale, hearty trustees, mature spinsters, timid
minors, and the huge host of auxiliary or helping powers,
that beset every Chancellor of the Exchequer in his dealings with that mammoth liability, deemed alike a blessing
and a curse by posterity—there is no prospect at present
on this side the Atlantic, if there may be on the other,
of a sponge being applied to the national slate, to wipe
out foul indebtedness, and make a clean beginning.

What a pleasant sound it is to hear a friend say, "I'm
going to take my dividends," no matter whether it be in
Bank Stock, Consols, Reduced or Indian Fives, or whether
the amount be large or small. Dividends in any, and in
every case—even under a bankruptcy or a trusteeship—

for though under the latter categories they tell a double story of something lost and something recovered, inspire confidence and self-respect. To be in a position to receive a dividend in Basinghall Street you must have been able to give credit, and if you have been sacrificed, either in a trading connection or by friendship, in these days of moral obliquity, only thank your stars that there is a dividend to take at all; but further let us hope that it is a good one. From high prosperity we have descended to bankruptcy, but it arises through the consideration of the euphonious expression " dividends," which carries a weighty meaning with it, solacing to most people and dispiriting to few. Even the poor creature who has been ruined by blind confidence in a leviathan firm, which, toppling over, reduces him to the alternative of seeking the indulgence of his creditors, says, with an honest sigh, " Well, it might have been worse; there is the dividend from the large debt I shall have to prove for; they will have to take it, and share it between them."

Railway dividends were always expected to be great, and the prophecies of ten and fifteen per cent. lines in the days of George and Robert Stephenson were freely ventured. What was to be the return from the Oxford, Worcester, and Wolverhampton; what the payment of the North Staffordshire Company; and what were the nature of the pledges, by the highest authorities, in relation to the Manchester, Buxton, and Matlock route? Why, these companies were to be second to none in point of traffic and dividend capacity, and their several boards were sought and coquetted with, as if they possessed the certain prizes of the great network of the iron way throughout the United Kingdom! The miserable failures that these particular lines have since become, through the conjoint influence of competition, the battle of the gauges, and the system of amalgamation, is now well-known. Compared with the delusive expectations held out, but which, it must be in fairness said, scarcely at the time appeared exaggerated, they are now little better· than wrecked properties, and notwithstanding they have since, more or less, been incorporated with neighbouring powerful companies, old shareholders, if many exist, will not fail to make a painful contrast of the past with the present.

The dividends of the railways showed immediate diminution from the date of the portentous warning uttered by Mr. George Carr Glyn when he announced, as chairman of the London and North-Western Railway Company, that that great undertaking could be considered no longer a ten per cent. line. Some boards and managements struggled to maintain high rates of dividends, and imposing balance sheets; but subsequent inquiries showed the questionable artifices adopted to deceive the proprietors, and never since has a permanent recovery been established. Capital accounts have been closed, economy has been strictly enforced, Parliamentary contests avoided, territorial aggressions abandoned, popular chairmen evicted, and their chief opponents selected to succeed them, while railway property, as railway property, has not in the aggregate been greatly benefited, though its general administration may now be considered sounder and better than ever. Railway shares with their present dividends are not an unstable investment, though, without some extraordinary improvements occur in management, and a further reduction takes place in expenditure, the total of revenue, save in exceptional instances, will not largely increase.

Perhaps the best dividend paying securities of the age are the shares of the Joint Stock Banks. It was never supposed, however, that they would attain their present *maximum*, and agreeably surprised must be most of the directors and managers, to find themselves allied with such remunerative undertakings. A great deal of the success of these establishments must be attributed to the high and honourable conduct of the respective boards, and to the diligence and perseverance of such men as Gilbart, Pollard, and Scrimgeour. Nevertheless, had not the public supported, and materially assisted to develop the principle, the London and Westminster Bank might have remained in its nook in Lothbury, the London Joint Stock within its confined premises in Princes Street, and the Union Bank of London would never have been compelled to remove from Moorgate Street.

It has yet to be seen whether the new institutions started upon the foundation of "limited liability" will be equally prosperous. Some years, of course, must necessarily elapse, before their permanent success can be considered assured. But if a judgment is to be formed, of what is supposed to be their prospects, from the value of the shares in the market, then it must be confessed the opinion entertained is favourable indeed. It would be preposterous to presume that the price is at all regulated now, by the amount, or the character, of the business transacted. Purchases in these shares have been made as investments, not for the dividend to be paid this or next year, but for the rates of distribution anticipated some four or five years hence. May the sanguine aspirations of every one be gratified. May the old Joint Stock Banks pay as good dividends as ever, and may the new

Joint Stock Banks, through sound management and extended financial connection, run closely to, if they cannot outstrip, their predecessors. May all the readers of this paper have dividends to take, and may they find them steadily augment as every half-year expires.

XXIV.

THE Stock Exchange has recently undergone a panic second to none witnessed there the last few years. The approach of a collapse like that which has been experienced will not, however, have taken many persons by surprise. For the last three months it has been quite evident that the markets have been overweighted; first by the enormous number of new schemes introduced, and secondly, by the dangerous character of the transactions entered into by the host of petty operators who have here been able to obtain credit to gamble in foreign stocks. These two causes combined have, more or less, conspired to occasion this reaction which has so prejudicially affected quotations. Everybody—even the most sanguine of the speculators themselves—must have been quite aware that the alteration would, sooner or later, take place; and although many have arranged for the emergency, it was difficult to decide, looking at the splendid result of the harvest and the general supply of money, at what period, and under what circumstances a revulsion would, in reality, occur.

It turns out that the question of peace or war with Russia on the arrangement of the Polish difficulty, the exports of specie to pay for cotton, are the points which have tested the state of the markets for general securities; but more especially those in which the late great current of time bargains has been sustained, and the fever-height of premium fluctuation has been encouraged. Although, of course, regret must be felt for individual losses or for any failures that may arise through the fall in the several stocks and shares, still the beneficial effect that will be exercised, not only in the neighbourhood of Capel Court and Bartholomew Lane, but throughout the country itself, will fully compensate for any such temporary inconvenience or sacrifice.

Since the panic, which lasted but a few days, the state of business has become more tranquil, the fluctuations in prices are less, and the excessive fall has been arrested; but, nevertheless, the unhealthy symptoms are so prominent, that it will be requisite for the brokers and dealers who have the command of several of these markets, to show great vigilance in superintending the conduct of future engagements, or we shall speedily have a recurrence of the wild scenes of confusion just passed through. One event that has taken place has in a measure, perhaps, checked the further decline for the moment, viz., presenting closing of accounts; and it has afforded numbers the desired opportunity, seeing the danger and the risk by which they have been surrounded, of bringing the operations of their clients to a conclusion. They have, no doubt, acted very wisely, and may, if further retrogression follows, save themselves through this course from extremely heavy losses; a large proportion of the speculators, including foreigners, who, so long as profits are to be received, will accept them, but who, immediately a balance appears on the other side, either make an ordinary default or levant altogether. It must be remembered that a great deal of the business in the course of the last twelve months has been in Greek,

Turkish Consolidés, Spanish, and Mexican. These have constituted the stock-in-trade of the high and low, the rich and poor, among the fraternity visiting the precincts of 'Change, and the temporary nooks and alleys in which those secret and mystical transactions are carried on.   It would not be difficult to indicate where the speculative Lords and M.P.'s might have been found during that period, for if they were not company-mongering, they readily entered into financial dissipation by buying a few thousand Kajmés or Greeks for the rise.   The termination of the session, and hurried departures for the Continent, have sent these birds of passage on their way in other directions, and consequently the markets have been left with the fag-end of the multitude to support them, prices meanwhile having been carried to a most dangerous height.

It was not to be supposed they could be sustained at this dizzy pinnacle, and therefore the first slight sand crack in the foundation has brought the whole fabric tumbling about the ears of those interested, naturally much to their chagrin and disappointment.   Tracing the current of prices, and noting the effect of the fall of one security upon the other, will show to the meanest comprehension the close identity of the movement.   It is necessary, in order to exhibit the progress of this special reaction, to intimate that though Consols and railway shares were in a slight manner affected by the drop in values when it was first apparent, they soon recovered their equilibrium— a circumstance proving that as investing and permanent securities their position could not long be compromised. The earliest decline was in Spanish Passives and Spanish Certificates, the hopes of the Anglo-French party of a speedy settlement of these claims having subsided.   The quotation having temporarily drooped was again buoyed up by the attempted strength of the Dutch and French operators to carry forward; but these principally consisting of third and fourth-rate individuals, they could not well succeed. Turkish Consolidés, after attaining the high quotation of 55 to 56, have never since presented a very healthy appearance. The first-class houses who were fortunate enough to introduce them, and who carried the price from 29 to 38 or 40, had the sound sense to retire when that advance was reached. Latterly the small speculators have also taken these up; and having succeeded in forcing the price to the greater elevation, were content to pay enormous rates of "continuation," in anticipation of the value going to 60. Faith in the accomplishment of this object was placed in the speedy promulgation of the Ottoman Budget, which it was averred would show the most startling progress; but though it has lately appeared it has not had the effect of supporting their value.

Greek stock and Greek coupons advanced to a price beyond all precedent, in the first place, through the quiet and peaceable conduct of the revolution; and, in the second place, in consequence of the selection of Prince William of Denmark to rule the future destinies of that monarchy. But a successive improvement in value— from 8 and 9 to 40 in the one case, and from 0, or in reality nothing, to 20 in the other—was largely anticipating the probable advantages of any such change, and a tension in prices of this character could scarcely fail to be accompanied some day by a significant relapse. Mexican, the other foreign stock which has principally suffered in the general *melée*, valuable in itself, taking its arrears as representing something of revenue and resources existing in the country, has been the centre of operations by weak and timid dealers. The sudden advance through favourable reports which ensued in this stock failed to be supported, and the consequence was rapid reaction, followed by subsequent depression.

Was it not probable, then, taking such a condition ot business into consideration—with the chief supports withdrawn from prices, the influence of events by which the rise had been governed, to use a Stock Exchange term " discounted," and the individuals who had in most instances inaugurated the movement standing aloof and shaking their heads in apprehension,—was it not probable, we repeat, to expect this crisis ? We unhesitatingly reply it was ; and the public and the members of the house ought to be thankful that the fall and the loss, great as they have been, have not proved more disastrous. The eminently cautious and prudent operators have only just retired in time to escape the difficulties which it may be well feared are now but in their incipient stage of commencement. The Rothschilds, the Sterns, the Oppenheims, the Bischoffheims, the Cohens, and the large houses are out, leaving the brunt of the burden to the foreign speculative tailors, the pill and ointment manufacturers, and similar celebrities, who, having made money by the legitimate and honest pursuits of trade, seem inclined to risk their position and capital by the more adventurous course of Stock Exchange dealing.

The depreciation in the stock of the Confederate Loan, and which has in some degree increased the excitement lately manifested, was a panic fact *sui generis*, occasioned by direct events, which would at any time have created a strong decline. This loan has not from its early introduction been largely speculated in, owing to its hazardous character ; and notwithstanding the Liverpool and Man chester people were partially inclined to encourage it when first placed upon the market, it has latterly ceased to occupy attention except on the arrival of the respective American mails. This stock, to use a current phrase known in the neighbourhood of Capel Court, has gone out of fashion, but it may hereafter rally again when least expected. We have still to wait patiently, to watch what may be the result of the late wholesale speculation in many of the low-priced stocks and doubtful shares ; and we are quite prepared to encounter further discouraging changes.

XXV.

I CANDIDLY confess I never liked proceedings in bankruptcy. And yet, nevertheless, I was a great deal occupied at one time under the old smoky sombre roof, that still exists in Basinghall Street. If, however, I did not relish the work, or the painful revelations, I there experienced, many of my friendships, and those of a permanent nature, have been contracted through that connexion. If in one sense the administration of the law of Dr. and Cr. had few charms for me, still there were relations in the immediate neighbourhood which lightened the labour, and imparted a kind of grim enjoyment to what would have otherwise been a most unthankful office. My parents, to use a simile of the great departed Hood, were not kangaroos, and therefore in seeking a profession for their child, it was not necessary that they should make him a short-hand writer; I, however, following the bent of my own inclinations, in early years became one; and it was in the Bankruptcy Courts that I brought into use my knowledge of a comparatively occult art.

During the few years that the Courts of Basinghall Street were my home, I saw several changes supposed to be improvements, but none ever proved successful, or were acknowledged by the public to have met the requirements of the financial or commercial community in dealing with indebted estates. All that has ever occurred, and has been suggested, appears to have tended simply in one direction—viz., expensive variations in the general form of bankruptcy judicature, without in the least improving its efficiency. Increased salaries, increased retiring allowances, less occupation for the higher offices, and the performance of duty by deputies for the lower functionaries, have, in fact, constituted the sum total of the amendments and consolidations so frequently effected, much, probably, to the satisfaction of the officials themselves, but certainly not to the practitioners in the Courts, or to their clients, who have to prove debts and realize dividends.

Indeed, whenever any of these alterations take place, although much parade is made about them, and they are said to be specially for the benefit of the mercantile interests, the advantages proposed for the behoof of the commercial world are invariably curtailed, or frequently shelved altogether, in the amalgamation of the clauses when the respective Bills have passed Parliament. Like many other systems and things, which have recently suffered from the high steam pressure of existing legislation, bankruptcy, as practised and administered in Basinghall Street, has decidedly seen its best days.

In saying thus much of the past and present of bankruptcy proceedings, it must be allowed that these Courts have, in a degree, run to seed, through the facilities afforded out of doors to private arrangements with debtors, in consequence of the almost universal adoption of the plan of inspectorship, framed on the principle of bankruptcy administration. Thus, while the machinery of the law of Dr. and Cr. has been made available to effect a liquidation of these estates privately, the direct operation of the Act has been avoided, chiefly with the view of preventing publicity, or the unpleasant exposure that might arise from protracted investigation.

The effect of bankruptcy has been regarded too much in the light of a disgrace rather than as an endeavour to relieve those who have fallen through misfortune, and hence the apparent sensitiveness of the commercial world to its arrangement; more apparent, however, than real, since, under the guise of private adjustment, some of the worst preferences and doubtful transactions that ever occurred have been concealed. It has been said that through inspectorships, assets can be more readily collected, questions of trading settled, and dividends distributed, with much greater celerity than under bankruptcy. This may be true in special instances, but, as a rule, the argument is entirely incorrect. Many persons assert that under private arrangements the amount of dividend can be increased. There may have been truth in this when the officials of the Courts strained every nerve to work assets to augment their own emoluments; but latterly, through the stringency of enactments, and the vigilance of the public themselves, they have not the chance of using the licence they formerly possessed, while, in other respects, the new law exhibits greater facilities.

Dating back as far as the old list of Commissioners, that mode of transacting bankruptcy was open to some objection; when the next alteration occurred, appointing official assignees, and remodelling the financial and dividend system, there were faults discoverable in the development of the scheme. The succeeding change of amalgamating bankruptcy and insolvency turned out, as it was predicted it would, a most astounding blunder ; and even the method of the classification of certificates, sanctioned though it was by high authority, never secured that popularity to which it was considered entitled. The latest alteration of the law was, perhaps, the most ill-advised that could have been adopted. High-class merchants seek its assistance less than ever, because of the renewal of the alliance between bankruptcy and insolvency ; the " white-washing" process is so complete, through the assistance of the Crown Solicitor, that the attendance in the purlieus of Basinghall Street is worse than even it ever was, and vies with the most degraded days of the entrance to the old Insolvent Court. Estates are now sent into bankruptcy more as a punishment to the debtor for fraudulent or reckless, than a *locus penitentiæ*, for unfortunate trading. In former periods a banker or a merchant would submit to the process ; and if he made a clean breast of it, presented a creditable balance-sheet, and his assets exhibited a fair dividend, he left the place without any serious detriment to character. Now, however, it is very different ; good or bad as any such estate may be, every endeavour will be made to keep it out of bankruptcy, for fear the contagious touch of the Court should either damage the future prospects of the debtor, or dissipate the little remaining property.

I speak with some experience on the topic, for bankruptcy practice has been so much mixed up with my career that I have seen it in operation under two or three systems. I have seen also, apart from bankruptcy, how inspectorships have ruled the day in the great commercial crises of 1847-48, and 1857-58, where the first commercial and legal authorities in the land have preferred the

arrangements conducted through the one, to the anticipated failure of the other. I have, in fact, scraped the
acquaintance of an ex-governor of a Bank of England
during the time he was doing Basinghall Street penance,
and was subsequently busily engaged when the great
banker Chambers closed his affairs after his long struggle
against his assignees in Chancery. John Wright, the
banker of Covent Garden, I remember well, and the
whole intricacies of his estate, which spread large losses
among his creditors, and brought to ruin a house that
was transacting a noble business. These are experiences
that showed the working of the Act as it then stood; and
though it was not in every respect perfect, it was far
preferable to what it is at present.

Later there was the marvellous case of Madame
Vestris, the ladye of Wyche Street, but who, with all
her gaiety and *abandon*, could not find forbearing creditors. Then came the period of bankruptcy and insolvency
amalgamation, when my Lord Huntingtower—the long
lord, as he was familiarly called—first became bankrupt,
and afterwards, in due course, an insolvent; when Charles
Mathews played the same dual characters, and, from the
vivid descriptions of his misfortunes before the Court,
showed, as far as the bill-discounting fraternity were
concerned, that he was "more sinned against than sin-
ning." Indeed, it is much to be questioned if he ever
brought down heartier peals of laughter on the mimic
stage, than did he when he was recounting the story of
his career in discounting before the supposed prosaic
auditories in the rooms of Commissioners Holroyd and
Fonblanque.

But although rare instances of investigations like these
relieved the monotony of the business, they proved more

than ever the disadvantage of insolvency being worked in the same Courts and at the same time with bankruptcy. A happy severance was ultimately made, and it was hoped for ever. Great, however, was the surprise when the last new measure was introduced, to find it re-import this detrimental alliance, accompanied by jobbery in appointments, of the most flagrant description. The voice of the public formally protested against it, and the same serious remonstrance is once more raised.

If the necessity existed then, it more than ever exists now, for the Court of Bankruptcy requires to be rescued from its present state of social and moral degradation. Never could I have supposed that it would have sunk so low; for notwithstanding the constant chopping and changing in the law for the last twenty-five or thirty years, the sole benefit which seems to have ensued, is the gradual ascent in the scale of salaries to officials, and the increase in the weight of charge upon the Consolidated Fund.

Whenever an alteration of the law is proposed, the convenience of the commercial classes is only studied in a secondary sense. To barristers and lawyers is confided the drafting of the measure, who never can appreciate the true wants of the mercantile community in such a case. Perhaps two advocates there are in bankruptcy, each able in himself, though one may be allowed to have had more experience than the other, who could separately, or in conjunction with the assistance of the one Commissioner best qualified for the task, frame such a general Bankruptcy Act as would meet the requirements of all classes, and afford satisfaction under the administration of a law, where now nothing but disappointment is exhibited.

These special gentlemen would be eminently suited to the task, because mixing with, and representing as they do, certain branches of business, if their own practical minds were not clear on many points, they could appeal to, or seek the advice of authorities, well capable of solving any apparent difficulties. Besides, they have had the advantage of attending the greater number of the meetings of creditors in the great crises of 1847-48, and 1857-58, and ascertaining the views of those who actually evaded the process of Basinghall Street, in consequence of its ever alleged unsuitableness to the exigencies of the period.

The Court of Bankruptcy should be upheld with dignity, and its law, if based on justice and equity, rigidly enforced ; not only with the view of protecting the creditor, but also for giving the debtor a release from his liabilities, if his case be one of unavoidable misfortune. It has, however, through the last fatal alteration, become none other than a " bear garden" of the worst description ; the authority of its proceedings is constantly sneered at, and direct connexion with the institution is scarcely held to be respectable.

XXVI.

A SHARP axiom adopted by one of the old school of operators—a Ricardo, it is generally believed—always embodied the philosophy of his speculations in the curt sentence of " Cut a loss, and let a profit run." Wise will most of the brokers and operators have proved in their generation, if they shall have been cautious enough to follow this advice, and sought to make it available during the last two or three months. During the spring and summer of 1863 they had sufficient opportunity, if they followed the stream, either in foreign stocks or the best of the miscellaneous companies, to secure profits ; and if, accepting the precept of the shrewd thinker already mentioned, they have retired when reaction in its first phase became apparent, they will now, in the midst of the existing monetary stringency, have no cause to regret it, and in the exercise of prudence they will be able to await the advent of brighter and better times.

The class of outside dealers in stocks and shares have been quite prepared for the change, and although the fall may have affected them more or less, the premonitory warnings given have induced them to beware of going beyond their depth, even when appearances were the most favourable. This effect has been produced by constantly calling their attention to the very hazardous game that was being played. It has caused them to pause, and

has relieved them from the serious results of the engagements into which they in all probability have entered.
The speculation, carried forward as it was with reckless
avidity, gave way just in time to damp the ardour of
those principally supporting the movement, and having
since decreased with every half-monthly account, there is
no prospect of revival, with money at 6 and 7 per cent.
at the Bank and in the open market, and the probability
of a financial crisis in Paris.

Every one can well picture the sombre view of affairs
there, through the rapid decline in the stock of bullion;
and the apprehensions excited by the sensitive condition
of the Bourses of Frankfort, Vienna, and Berlin indicate
that no further tension of an extraordinary character
would be required to produce a revulsion the effects of
which would startle Europe. England might from the
inherent soundness of her position escape, in a great
degree, the worst consequences of such a blow; but she
has now become so thoroughly mixed up in Continental
business of every class, being the great reservoir from
which the different markets draw, that it would be impossible to avoid heavy losses. For the next few months we
shall be in a very equivocal situation, and it may fairly be
supposed that stagnation will prevail, because, although
the supply of money is good, it is nevertheless so dear
that many branches of trade will be depressed, and
bankers and brokers will not, under any circumstances,
make advances except upon the most tangible security.

It is all very well to look at the rate of 6 and 7 per
cent. for first-class paper, and to say that it is not
unreasonably high. These quotations do not, of course,
immediately affect high mercantile firms unless they are
in a very unsound position; but if that be the case, any

advance will soon stop their career, and the sooner the crash the better. But in treating of dear money and its effects it is necessary perhaps to look a little further. Second-class establishments—many of which are the thews and sinews of our ever-striving industry—feel it severely ; 6 and 7 per cent. to their superiors, is 8 and 10 per cent. to them, and when the third class are reached it is not even 10 or 12 per cent. to them, but the high rates act as a positive prohibition against obtaining money at all. Through these unseen channels it is that the advances in the quotations of discount work such discouraging influence, and if they are to be maintained, as it seems likely they will, the *Gazette* eventually must present evidence of the mischief.

A panic in Paris, an event we are not unprepared for, with similar appearances at St. Petersburg and Vienna, would show that things were approaching a crisis, such as many have thought for some time, has been impending. The palliatives resorted to by the Bank of France will, however, first be applied to the fullest extent, and no stone will be left unturned to secure it a supply of bullion. But these just now appear to be of little avail; so persistent is the outflow to Mexico and Italy. Those grand campaigns of the Emperor bring not only glory, but also a large margin of expenditure, which will have to be provided for through a loan or some other financial manœuvre. The days of the popularity of Mexican stock, when the quotations suddenly vaulted to 48, should have been seized as the juncture for concluding that loan which, if it had not entirely, would have partially relieved the French Government from its embarrassment, and supplied funds to have enabled the Treasury to pay its way.

Now it is exceedingly doubtful whether a loan, either for France or Mexico, would be successful, with the Fould ministry in its existing uncertain position, and the political feeling of Paris not altogether in favour of the Emperor. The budget has appeared, " cooked " to make things pleasant, but the figures, well marshalled as they are, fail to satisfy either England or France, the *deficit* being much larger than has been admitted. But the star of Napoleon, ever in the ascendant, will get him over the difficulty, if the term of his destiny is not yet expired, and if Europe is to be temporarily saved from another very general convulsion.

The most satisfactory feature for the moment in financial concerns, is that the Bank of England has not deemed it essential to increase the rate. This would seem to carry the impression, that the directors are not in the least alarmed for the future, and believe that a restoration to a natural equilibrium may shortly be accomplished. The directors themselves, seeing the anomalous state of the bullion market, are not prepared unhesitatingly to enforce an advance, unless it be imperatively necessary; and since they imagine they can in a degree cope with the evil, perhaps they are right in the mode they adopt. Although they have not raised the *minimum*, they have done the next thing to it, which will probably prove as effective. If parcels of paper are furnished to them for negotiation, and they imagine that they are to facilitate transactions in cotton, or to purchase bullion for export, they at once fix a special price, an additional 1 per cent., and the parties who propose to do business may complete the operation, or seek accommodation elsewhere. The highest rate the Bank has recently charged in exceptional engagements has been 9 per cent., but it would not stop at that point, if customers appeared inclined to take money at any cost.

Everywhere, when you ask the question, " How is money ?" the reply is invariably the same, " There is plenty of it, and the majority of the dealers have full balances. No scarcity exists; it is merely a question of price." And so it will continue till the efflux of bullion has become stronger, and then, when the drain has gone further, the strain will be felt ; and then it will be very astounding if some disruption of credit does not take place. The balance of trade is evidently greatly against us, both in India and Egypt; and until the amount is liquidated, no cessation of the draft of specie will be experienced. If France shall be sufficiently fortunate in righting herself, the severity of the efflux will be mitigated, but it will not then be entirely relieved. No solution of the difficulty is likely to be obtained until something transpires with respect to the prospects of the next season's supply. Meanwhile, a reduction in the price of the staple would have some influence to keep in check the irregular business which has arisen, not alone in Liverpool, but also in Manchester, and other of the Lancashire districts. It is to be hoped that the present financial pressure may pass over without entailing disastrous consequences, and that the current rates of discount will not advance higher. If, however, this should be the case, we cannot, even when the favourable reaction ensues, expect to have moderate terms for money till we have made some progress into 1864.

XXVII.

HE always was, and always will be—I think, to the day of his death—a great enigma. Even then I question, unless a confidential nurse worm out his secrets, if any discovery is likely to be made; and you may depend upon it, to a woman alone will be surrendered the history of a career which has comprised most eventful times, ex- citing scenes, and checkered experiences. Whenever I encounter him, and it is now at rare intervals, he flashes across my path like a meteor, and I look with mute astonishment at a man, who, though nearly three-quarters of a century has rolled over his head, scarcely seems to grow old, and who is nearly as active as when I first fell into his society twenty-five years ago.

Where he came from, what were his antecedents, or how his required resources have been supplied, no one could now satisfactorily answer; and few would perhaps care to inquire; but there he is, a living exemplar of what a sound constitution may go through, notwithstand- ing the uncertain vicissitudes of a speculative life, and its various disappointments. Most of his old associates, and former cronies have passed away—those who were deeply concerned in his extensive Portuguese and Spanish trans- actions, and his reminiscences of the Carbonnells, Mendi- zabels, and Da Silvas, would be of the most interesting character if they could be elicited; but probably they might revive unpleasant memories, and therefore it will be better to leave this blank to be supplied at a future date.

A marvel of self-reliance and persevering industry, he has never seemed actually poor; and though no question can be entertained that his means have latterly diminished, the studied endeavour to maintain a personal appearance was never more strongly manifested, even among the more advanced of the new school of the present day.

How he first reached the great metropolis has never transpired. He might have been imported from Cuba; from the Spanish main; from the coast of Riff; from Algeria; or from Madrid or Lisbon. Possessing a good knowledge of languages, a presentable exterior, and favourable address, he appeared at the moment when the Spanish American loans first made a success, and becoming acquainted with the clique, who pushed those contracts to an encouraging issue, he, as many other operators have since and before, made the first few hundred pounds which led him to adopt this kind of doubtful business. Claiming himself, it is believed, very high foreign connexions, he, with his little capital, worked himself into what was then good society—or the society of those who, like himself, had speculated, and speculated with effect, in the securities then current. Foreigners were greater favourites then than they are now; the English had not at that date lost so largely, as they have since, by the various specious foreign investments brought forward, neither had they suffered so much in their domestic circles, from closer association with many of these worthies. Availing himself of the impression he created, this gentleman made apparently rapid progress, not only in wealth, but

in position.   He could speak glibly enough French,
Italian, and Portuguese, play the guitar and other
instruments with effect, and managed most adroitly,
to get introduced to every distinguished *emigré* who
visited these shores, becoming without delay, one of
his most ardent admirers.   This facilitated the object
he had in view, affectionate *liasons* with ladies, and
assaults upon the pockets and resources of their parents
and relations.   People were made easy prey in those
days, and he used his talents with great advantage.

The Count D——, as he was called, though most
individuals within the range of two hundred yards of
the Royal Exchange held this title to be a mere
sobriquet, flirted so successfully on the skirts of society,
as it then existed in the neighbourhood of the Squares,
Bedford Square, Russell Square, and Brunswick
Square—for Belgravia was unknown, and Tyburnia
occupied no space in the Court Guide—that though he
was met everywhere, received invitations and accepted
them, none knew anything further of him, than that
he had large City connexions, frequented 'Change and
the coffee-houses, and talked vaguely of the large slices
he could obtain of every good thing that came out.
And no doubt some truth existed in the statement
he made, for his assurance was of a remarkable nature,
and on the strength of even a slight acquaintance he
would presume to volunteer his advice and assistance ;
and through his suave manners, and captivating address,
he was not unfrequently successful.   His greatest *coups*
were said to have been made in the Spanish American
Loans of 1824-25, when prices on small subscriptions
ran high, and the gambling in the several descriptions
was of a very fierce character.   He at that time

gave out he had netted something like £200,000 or
£300,000, but those who knew him well, and his habitual
custom of boasting, placed those figures nearer £20,000
or £30,000, allowing thus a large margin for an approxi-
mation to truth. He started his carriage and pair, took
a house at Kensington, visited Almack's, and was a
violent supporter of Lord Dudley Stuart and the Polish
cause, the appeal in behalf of which invariably terminated
in a grand Ball, either in Guildhall, or at the Mansion
House.

But the Count D—— did not flourish long after his
supposed resources became known; he mixed more than
ever in society, and became more than ever intrusive;
but his jet hair, his aquiline nose, his burning dark eyes,
and his neatly brushed whiskers and moustache, proved
so attractive in several quarters, that husbands became
jealous of their wives, brothers had to vindicate the
honour of sisters, and the issue at length was, his
gradual expulsion from the very circles, which originally
petted, and called him into notice. Well-grounded suspicions existed for thus dealing with so general a favourite, and the disappearance shortly after of the *fiancée* of
one of his most cherished friends, who was traced to
Paris with him, furnished sufficient proof of his guilt
in one case, while equally grave allegations were made
in others.

Thrown out of his old channels of success, he still
made his appearance in the City, but not so constantly
as before. He spent part of his time in France, where
the lady sojourned, being cast off by her friends; and
when he came to London it was principally to follow out
his stock operations. But many of his old associates
suspected their man; a taint had attached to him, and

they were now extremely vigilant. The lapse in honour
in private society, might, they shrewdly suspected, be
succeeded by non-observance of engagements in business
if necessity permitted, or convenience rendered it desirable. The times were also less favourable for speculation ; and the tide of prosperity wearing out, the Count,
having sacrificed his popularity, wore out with it, and
having steadily receded from his former prominent station,
it was not long before he found himself almost deserted.
He retired then to France with the last vestige of his
property, and for some few years avoided public appearance.

The first time he ever fell across my path was while
the " Pillar contest " with the elder Rothschild was in
the height of discussion. I had gone on 'Change to see
the leviathan capitalist leave amidst the congratulations
of his friends, after the ruffianly assault upon him by
the person, who endeavoured to occupy his post under
the old quadrangle, when my notice was directed to a
tall, gentlemanly-looking foreigner, with full whiskers
and moustache, who was evidently hurrying away. He
seemed wholly unacquainted with the history of the scene
going forward; but catching the eye of a friend who
was with me, he gave him a rapid recognition, and
pressed into the crowd. My friend seeing that I was
struck with the style and bearing of the man—for he
was dressed in a tight-fitting blue military suit, frogged
most elaborately about the breast—narrated to me the
salient facts now thrown into shape.

The Count D——, for that is the name by which he will
be known in these pages, though I may some day give more of
his inner life, had not visited England for several years; but
a fresh current of speculation setting in, he could not resist

the temptation of returning to London to take part in it, and to ascertain, if it were possible to retrieve a position. Reckoning on the chances of the majority of his old friends and associates, especially those whom he had duped and deceived, having either retired or died, he was prepared to enter into a class of transactions of a less pretentious character, trusting that if his presence were recognized, any who had known him would not take the trouble to hound him down, and leaving to good fortune the risk of being able to make acquaintances among the new school of operators. He was greatly disturbed by having unavoidably encountered my friend, who knew the whole of his previous career, and who seemed to have started up as a wraith before him. Having seen the Count in his new guise, and having heard the remarkable particulars of his early gaiety, when he was the companion of rank and fashion, it was not likely that I should forget him, and if he was to be an attendant in City walks, or a lounger round 'Change, it was almost pretty certain I should frequently meet him. The new speculation that had arisen was in Spanish and Portuguese; the Carlists were ravaging Spain, and the Miguelites were struggling against Don Pedro; to increase the excitement, and give a momentary turn to affairs, the advantages of asphaltum for paving and miscellaneous purposes had been discovered, and several companies were formed; so that those who did not care to transact business in stocks, could relieve the monotony by dealing in shares.

The Count did not show frequently at first, but gradually his presence became more regular. He was still the gentlemanly, upright man, but his tone of manner, from previous description, had greatly sobered down. He was between forty-eight and fifty, and though he had rather increased in bulk, it was generally allowed that he was extremely handsome, with a delicate profile. He again speculated largely, and, in a degree, with success; he made a round of acquaintances, among parties who did not closely inquire into antecedents; his agreeable manners, and his profusion of anecdote enrapturing his hearers. But he was never seen in private houses; he shone in coffee-houses after dining, behind the green blinds of Tom's, when the subscription-room faced Cornhill, or the North and South American, or the Jamaica.

When he left the City, he sought none of his old familiar places, but avoided them as he would had they been plague-spots; his haunts were the *restaurants* in Leicester Square, the cigar divans in the same neighbourhood, and late at night, Soho Square, Coventry Street, and the Haymarket. In these quarters he might be noticed loitering about from place to place, without any studied pursuit in the shape of pleasure, the exhaustion of time being the supposed principal object in view. Two things must, however, be said in his favour—he drank very little, the lightest Spanish or French wines, and smoked less. His poor and neglected paramour was buried in small apartments, in a back street, where he occasionally deigned to visit her; he, in fact, seemed to be an observer of men of pleasure, rather than one mixed up in the gaieties visible in those localities, in days not far removed from the riotous proceedings of "Tom and Jerry."

His round of operations was continuous. He never appeared to endeavour to rise again to his old *status*. The heart for that seemed to have left the man, and he was perhaps wise enough in not encouraging the probable return to such scenes, and further, possibly, risk the chance of a fresh *dénouement*. Like most great speculators, and I have seen some shoals of them in my time, when they make a false step, they sink at once from their position; and although they drop into the same kind of life, it is on a lower scale, and among men who have either through broken honour or misfortune, forfeited their rank in the upper circle. They constitute, if I may so speak, the second grade of speculators, who without much money, just appear at every convenient opportunity, to take part in the transactions of the day or the hour, and if they succeed, battle as they can to make a place in the circle in which they move.

The late Count D—— was now Count D—— no more; he cast away without the least remorse his title, and gladly took the simple form of Monsieur D——, by which he was accepted, and his acquaintance sought and cultivated. Many of his former companions recognized in the new comer the Count of eight or ten years preceding, but they troubled themselves little with his engagements; they only met him as he was passing through some of the thoroughfares near 'Change and down Bartholomew Lane, and wondering perhaps that he had the temerity to re-appear, merely shrugged their shoulders and went on. Although he was vastly proud he could bear this, since it served his purpose, and prevented any more embarrassing annoyance. On one occasion, as I subsequently learned, a rather stronger demonstration was nearly made, but fortunately his assailant retracted, or perhaps the results to both parties would have been exceedingly disagreeable.

A friend of Monsieur D——, who, like himself, having been in difficulties, had descended from his high estate, possessed in the manner that is usually obtained among this fraternity, a full, true, and particular detail of his (D——'s) former career. In a quarrel, through an irregularity in the settlement of some of their transactions, the friend in a fever-heat from wine, quietly reminded him that he was not prepared to be " swindled in the manner that Monsieur D—— had swindled his original patron, the great W——, nor need he attempt it." The whole life of the Count seemed to glide before him, if credence may be given to the statements of those who were present. The manner in which he jumped to his feet and seized his antagonist by the throat, showed the effects of the remark, while the next moment, gleaming in his hand (drawn from beneath a carefully plaited shirt) was a small dagger of polished steel. This *rencontre,* occurring in a public room, two or three of the visitors interfered, and just in time to prevent serious consequences. The aggressor, in language, admitted that he was wrong, without explaining in precise words what had passed. The Count, or Monsieur D——, expressed himself satisfied, observing coolly, though many doubted the sincerity of his avowal, that he was always prepared to protect, and, if necessary, avenge a lady's honour, " even to death." Although by this impudent assurance he threw the visitors off the scent of the real cause of the dispute, still T——, who had allowed his temper to get the better of his discretion, did not fail to set himself right with those about him, after Monsieur D—— had taken his departure.

It was now remarked, however, that Monsieur D—— quietly avoided T—— ; they dealt in the same sort of securities ; they were always in proximity to each other in the area of the Royal Exchange, or near the Rotunda at the Bank; but further than the careless shake of the head, which is supposed to signify a great deal, when it in reality signifies nothing, there was not the slightest cordiality between them. T—— said little, he had been a defaulter, and could not be received by the upper school; but Monsieur D—— was a defaulter in honour, as well as in pounds, shillings, and pence. Mr. T—— was not the gay, hilarious fellow that Monsieur D—— was, neither could he be equally certain in securing the notice of the small company in which they mixed; but if he were not as well able to be as amusing as Monsieur D——, one important thing was, that he was certainly more punctual on the account day. The story of the Count D——, his previous history, and the suspicions entertained of his straightforward character for business, now became generally ventilated; and accustomed as these individuals were to encounter shady reputations, Monsieur D—— fancied, and not without good ground, that his character was gradually going, like some of the shares and scrips in which he operated, to a discount.

Curiously enough the great rage for Spanish and Portuguese Stocks was subsiding, and Claridge's Asphaltum Company (with the noble captain who introduced the scheme) became over-shadowed by the Seyssel Asphaltum Company, the Trinidad Bituminous Asphaltum, and the ten or dozen other similar projects which then made their appearance. We have lived through the days of these undertakings, and the pavements which were laid down with the expectation of being gradually extended, are now regarded as curiosities; we have gone through the Metropolitan wood-paving era with similar mischance; and now it is iron that is to give us not only railways, but also common roadways and footways. With the Spanish

and Portuguese crash, and the grand Asphaltum crash, a
large number of the principal outside operators went at
once to the wall.   But the great Count D——, or the
more recently, modest Monsieur D——, scarcely waited
for the ordinary form of quittance, as recognized among
his companions, but quietly levanted, taking on this occasion the wife of another friend, to whose pecuniary interests he had paid the most assiduous attention.

For years subsequently he never again returned to this
country.   I ascertained that he was traced as having gone
to Germany, and thence to Mexico; but in what pursuit or
profession I could not discover.   Whenever any little
speculative excitement turned up I was always looking
for the Count D——.   The railway mania came and went,
and though it was a period which was not well suited to
his tastes, being a foreigner, he might have made money
if he had dared to show himself again in his old precincts.
But although I sometimes thought he was dead, I had a
kind of presentiment he would return, and that when he
was least expected.   He must be an old man if he did
re-appear; and I occasionally, in a dreamy, loose sort of
manner, pictured to myself what he would resemble.

I still thought he would be tall and erect—grey in
every sense of the word, with a close crop, or the full
appendage of beard and moustache.   Had he been sen-
tenced abroad for any misdeeds, reduced to the degraded
position of a *forçat*, I should have nevertheless anticipated
that he would display his old dashing military bearing,
and that his features would retain marked traces of their
original beauty.   Perhaps the most disagreeable part of
the portraiture that came to my mind, was the restless-
ness of the eye, the quiver of the lip when under excitement, and the depressed brow when he was angered.

During the time of the Australian and Californian gold mining mania, I felt assured that if the Count D—— was alive, the excitement of this "little-go" movement would draw him forth from his retreat, unless he were so well placed as to be above every inducement to speculate. Nor was I much mistaken. His appearance, however, was under very different circumstances, and in a very different position to what I could have imagined. So singular, indeed, was the metamorphosis, and so paralyzing the effect upon myself, that I thought it could be no other than a dream; and if I had not been a person of thoroughly good stamina, I might have given way under the shock. Attending as I did many of those meetings when share issues were proposed, I saw numbers of the old speculators who have for years hovered about 'Change, and the purlieus of the adjoining courts and alleys, because the smallness of the responsibility, encouraged by the £1 share system, gave them opportunities for mustering in force.

At one of these assemblies, the undertaking in this case was for prosecuting mining on the East coast of Central America, a discussion had taken place upon the resources of the property, and upon the individuals it was proposed to send out to manage it. I need hardly say, the chairman gave a very glowing description of the one, and spoke in high terms of the qualifications of the others. The property, as a property, had, according to his view, been procured for an insignificant amount, and the proposed managers and superintendents were all gentlemen of enlarged experience, who would no doubt speedily develop its resources. Herr R—— had been engaged in the silver mines of Bohemia, and contemplated bringing to working power some new principle of extracting silver; Mons. D——— had just returned from Peru, with high credentials, having been for years engaged on the mines in the neighbourhood of Cerro. The name did not strike me for the instant, but on the introduction of these appointed officials, there stood before my astonished vision the Count D——— of early days; tall and erect; grey, with full beard and moustache; and still imposing and handsome. Our eyes met; I dropped my pencil, and was mute; a simple *sacrè* escaped the closed teeth of my old friend; and looking once more at his fine form, now heightened by the display of a bright Genoa velvet waistcoat, I felt giddy and faint, and left the room.

From what I subsequently heard, Mons. D———, with his German colleague, passed the ordeal extremely well. The chairman congratulated the proprietors upon having secured the services of two such eminent practical mineralogists and metallurgists; and added, that he had every reason to believe, a few months would put them, by the aid of these scientific gentlemen, in the receipt of large dividends. I knew nothing of the German or his "surroundings," and therefore could not attempt to prophesy concerning him; with respect to Mons. D———, I feared that he, old as he was, would either compromise his position, or fail in the performance of promised duties. The Company went forward; the expedition was despatched; and the arrival out of the *employés* with the materials, was the only satisfactory intelligence gained for many months. Then slowly but surely, by every succeeding packet, came the news of the difficult nature of working the property, the failure of the reduction works, and eventually the death of the German professor, and the sudden flight of Mons. D———.

I now felt sure his career was ended; that he would seek Peru or Mexico, and there terminate the remainder of his days in quiet solitude; but no, it was only a few years afterwards that he again passed across the scene of his former exploits, though it seems, not to make any length-ened visit. I never could have supposed he would have deemed it prudent to seek a residence in England, much less show himself in the great metropolis. I rather fancied he would have sought his old occupation among the mining population either in the locality of Cerro, or Real del Monte, varying it probably with *pulque* drinking, or gambling, and then, when these resources failed him, aspiring to be captain of a band of muleteers, or the gay head of some obscure *venta*, where plans of assassination were blended with cock-fighting, and other Spanish-American pastimes.

I, however, was doomed to disappointment; for it was only about eighteen months ago I was waiting, with my trusty assistant, Hart, to secure a conveyance to the West, to put in an appearance at a place we wished to visit late at night, when my attention was attracted by a host of passengers alighting from a south-western omnibus, near the Duke of Wellington's statue, close to the Royal Exchange. The character of the baggage, dark leather portmanteaus, heavily labelled, and tightly bound, indi-cated foreign travel, and exposure to rough weather. Some of the wayfarers alighted, and hurriedly selected their portables, calling cabs, into which they thrust them-selves, and drove away.

One tall individual, whose features were concealed beneath a slouch felt hat, and whose form was enveloped in a dark blue travelling poncho, after taking his trunk and placing it in a vehicle, seemed to linger near the spot.

His companion was a female, evidently of Spanish or South American extraction, and a fine youth, whose olive countenance and dark black hair, almost bespoke the country of his birth. These the stranger placed with his luggage in the roomy four-wheeler; then sauntering back again, and raising his *sombrero*, at the same time throwing aside the broad folds of his travelling garb, the clear moonlight fell upon his face, and I beheld before me the Count D——, wrapt, as it were, in a melancholy reverie.

I stepped aside, if possible, to avoid recognition, and was fortunate enough to escape his glance. He paced up and down for a few moments; he scanned the Bank, the neighbouring buildings, and then, with one hand pressed to his forehead, muttered, returning to those whom he had temporarily left, "*Sacrè, sacrè!* how all is changed." An instant afterwards he had given directions to the driver, and that foreign living freight was borne away northward.

Shall I ever, I sometimes muse to myself, see the Count D—— again? His age, his lengthened travels, and his previous vicissitudes, almost preclude the probability. If he be still alive, it is not unlikely, but I should think he will scarcely seek business circles. The dark history of his career will, I fear, never be completely revealed, though some glimpses of it have been unfolded in this short narrative.

XXVIII.

THE FATAL FACILITY OF STORY-TELLING.

IT sometimes happens that individuals unwittingly speak the truth. Unfortunately, however, it is not now the universal practice to observe this healthy characteristic of conscience in daily business, for if it were so, it is highly probable there would be less deceit and double-dealing, even among financiers, and others who should decidedly set a high and bright example. The old school in many departments seems, as a body, to be fading out, and is being succeeded by others, who appear to have one purpose alone to serve, and who do not hesitate to take advantage of every opportunity that is presented, to push their own interests, even at the risk of sacrificing their best and dearest friends.

The complete incarnation of selfishness, as exhibited in almost every walk of life, is one of the principal motive powers of the new school, but whether it will in the long run be found enduring, the experience of a few more years will perhaps decide. The leaven of personal interest and personal convenience, is eating fast into the constitution, commercial and financial, and though this is probably produced chiefly by the business competition, of which every one, more or less, is now the victim, it crops out so offensively occasionally, that it is difficult to repress the indignation felt when it is intrusively presented.

This, when it is attended, as is almost invariably the case, by the twin graces of affectation and conceit, is thoroughly annoying, because through the flimsy gauze of appearance you trace the existence of the real cancer, and are not, perhaps, in a position at the moment to cauterise, or cut it out. But wherever it is found, in whatever shape, or under whatever guise, a lasting service will be done to the public and posterity, by the " operating " fraternity, if they will only practise a little of the healing art, by using their best endeavours, first to subdue the evil by moderate remedies, and if those fail, then to resort to extreme measures to eradicate it altogether.

How much better would the world be if, through the encouragement of friendly relations one with another, the circle of the year were thus impelled. Instead of that constant struggling, that intense antagonism, existing among all grades and all classes, to supersede their fellows, a return would be accomplished to those halcyon days, when the hurry and scurry of business life was unaccompanied by the present fashion of intriguing against, whispering away, and "damning with faint praise," everything and everybody.

When I first commenced this little anecdote, which will be discovered to hinge upon the fatal facility of storytelling, I never intended to attempt moralizing, but I was led away by the fact that truth is now so scarce a commodity, as to warrant the belief that the stock of it is getting very low in the general market, without any great prospect of its being replenished. When this valuable article shall have entirely disappeared, the specious substitute introduced, will speedily show its value by the entire absence of the ring, and colour of the proper metal. Receive this, kind reader, as an unintentional digression, a sort of stage "aside" between you and me, before proceeding further.

While it sometimes happens that individuals unwittingly speak the truth, others unwittingly tell stories. This was proved in an especial instance many years ago of an old banker-broker, who when he died cut up worth a plum at least; but in his life-time, though shrewd and calculating, was always turning the joke against himself. Notwithstanding it occasionally made him ludicrous in the eyes of his friends, he was of that agreeable and cheerful disposition as to be prepared to accept a *faux pas* of the kind, and make little bother about it.

The individual shall be nameless; but he was a great man; one who could count his hundreds of thousands, and yet not run to the end of his financial tether. He was not bad-hearted, for a variety of charitable acts which, performed by stealth, eventually became discovered, unmistakeably showed that his was not altogether a selfish career, though it must be acknowledged he possessed a quick eye for business. In his own circle, in the midst of the money world, among the nabobs of New Court, the Stock Exchange, or the precincts of Lombard Street, it was very difficult to get the best of him, and his alacrity in realizing securities if necessary to discount, what he would denominate a fine batch of bills with bankers' endorsements, if the market got in Threadneedle Street phraseology, "tight," indicated his rare perception of the time to apply the screw.

Though not a "hard calculator," in the worst sense of the term, he was to all intents and purposes, sufficiently alive to transactions which would present a fair share of profit, and he contrived, as most people usually do, to make the best terms he could, and avoid if possible the least individual responsibility.

It was at one of these especial periods when he accomplished a remarkable *coup*, for prospectively imagining that there would be a pressure in the money-market, he sold large parcels of stock at high prices, and having in the first place secured a profit, in the second he was enabled to lay out the proceeds, at extreme rates of discount in Lombard Street and elsewhere.

When the rates of discount advanced, and touched a point showing that it was likely the pressure would increase, a sharp and decisive panic immediately followed in stocks and shares of every description. Failures were taking place at the Stock Exchange in rapid succession, but one declaration was marked by features of the most dishonourable character. The defaulter levanted, having before he made his escape heavily fleeced some of the prominent members of the house.

Our friend the banker-broker, in conversation with his intimate acquaintances, dipping his hands deeply in his trowsers' pockets, boasted of the large quantities of Bank Stock, Consols, Reduced and Exchange Bills, which he had sold to go into the discount market, and make more profitable use of his capital: £100,000 of this, £200,000 of that, and £50,000 of the other, he said he thought would show that he had "slipped his securities" in time, not only to avoid loss, but to give him a better market in another direction. To prove further that he was not overstating his position, he pulled from his pockets a batch of first-class bills, —bankers' endorsements—nothing less, crying exultingly, "Here, these are what I call investments, to run off at three and four months; all at 6 per cent."

His acquaintances congratulated him, and the conversation was continued, when one broker rushing past, the simple inquiry was, "How stand prices?"

"Oh," replied the almost breathless runner, "don't ask me about prices ; have you heard the news?"

"No—no," responded every voice, "what is it?"

"Well, the hammer has just gone against Le G——; and it appears he has bolted, having converted all his securities into cash. Four or five of the best men are let in, the delinquent having had the audacity to take stock against his cheques till the last moment."

Each man stares at the other, the banker-broker included, and the latter says, after a slight pause, "Gentlemen, I hope we can all say, as I can say for myself—*poor, but honest.*"

"Come, that will never do," rejoins one of the party, "two lies in three words is an excess of perfection in ordinary composition. You must amend your style of speech as you are now upon the horns of a dilemma."

The banker-broker laughs as he retracts, asks his friends to believe that while he admits the impeachment of being rich, there is also some spice of honesty left in his dealings, and walks off to the house to ascertain more authentic accounts of the operations of the runaway, and the losses of his victims. His friends shortly scatter, and spread the anecdote which fully illustrates the fatal facility of story-telling.

THE NEW *versus* THE OLD SCHOOL.

Every period of speculation brings out some new phase in the arrangements connected with it, and the rage for limited liability companies has therefore not been sin-

gular in again producing change. The scrip and certificate days of the old mining epoch, were succeeded by the
letter of allotment system of the railway mania, and now
the much dreaded deed of settlement, has been once more
superseded by the articles of association, which every one
is informed he can consult, but which few ever take the
trouble to look into, save for special motives.

In the midst of these periods arise new agencies and
new individuals, through which these schemes are promoted, and by whose activity and perseverance they
become finally launched. Proceeding with the work on
the principle that the labourer is worthy of his hire, they
endeavour to protect themselves by bargaining for a considerable fee, or proportion of profit, if the undertaking be
a success; on the other hand they have to submit to
a sacrifice of outlay, if they fail to ensure satisfactory
share subscriptions. Promoters, as a class, have latterly
much increased, the large gains of the few who were early
in the field, having tempted many who could not better
occupy their time, to turn if possible any City, or other
available relations they possessed to advantage.

But as promoters have increased, the chances of success have become more doubtful, because the public in
the first place have raised their voice against the principle,
and in the next, the companies have themselves so rapidly
multiplied, that the preponderance of imitative schemes
has damaged the prospects of those which were in reality
required.

In the summer of last year, 1863, when much activity
existed in company formation, when, to use a geological
phrase, the stratification was rather deep, and it was difficult to float any but high class enterprises, two friends
met within five minutes' walk of the Stock Exchange; one

an old city *habitué*, the other a recently imported fledgling from the West.

The old City habitué is attired in a modest suit, steady and respectable in appearance, but he walks with a firm step, and looks everybody in the face. The young gentleman from the West End approaches, he is in bright attire from head to foot, rounded off with a magenta tie and pea-green gloves. They salute each other, and a conversation ensues, much in this fashion.

Old City habitué.—Good morning, friend; what brings you into this neighbourhood among the whirl of City people? I imagined you were deeply employed in chambers with musty books, and all the associations of a student's life.

Young Gentleman from the West.—Ah! so I was; but I have temporarily cut that, to visit the Civic Tom Tiddler's ground, and assist in picking up the gold, if not the silver. Here am I, with good friends and relatives east of Temple Bar, and I don't see why I should not make use of them. I shall show in a very different character presently; (whispering confidentially) I have turned promoter, taken offices, and am coming out in thorough good style. Lots of 'appointments for the week to see tip-top fellows to join boards. I shall want four or five secretaries, if you have any poor friends; and I am sure to bring out a Bank.

Old City habitué.—Glad to hear of your favourable prospects. Hope they are not delusive; but pray take a word of advice, as I know you will, from me. Your costume is a little too fast for City life; tone down the colour of your coat, whatever may be the nature of your introduction, lynx-eyed directors will not believe in them; change above all things your neck-tie and gloves, and let neither be too bright, nor too new. By these means, you will avoid the suspicion that you intend a swindle.

Young Gentleman from the West. — Thanks, thanks; I am glad I have met you before seeing P——, the banker, who has taken up my grand Continental scheme, which will accommodate the whole of Europe with financial facilities, and who is quite predisposed in favour of it, because it will not interfere in the slightest degree with his own London business. (Communicating at length the details.) Don't you think *that* will be sure to go?

Old City habitué (smiling incredulously at his friend). —Yes, perhaps it will. Everything of the kind, however, runs on so smoothly in conversation, and sometimes when in print it even reads better; but the issue of any scheme can be more completely solved when you have got your prospectus in order, the chief directors secured, and your own arrangements settled for promotion fees, etc.

Young Gentleman from the West.—Oh! ah! yes; but that can all be easily settled. The scheme; I want your opinion of that. Don't you think it will be supported?

Old City habitué.—Yes, the scheme: that is all very well in its way; but I have heard of two similar undertakings already, and, if I mistake not, they are making rapid progress towards completion. Don't delay, because in these days it is not so much the soundness of the project, as it is the circumstance of being *first* before the world that ensures success.

Young Gentleman from the West.—Ah! yes, thanks; but I thought nobody else had any notion of my scheme —the title so clear, so complete, the plan so comprehensive—surely it has struck no other mind.

Old City habitué.—Not struck any other mind?

Pshaw!—nonsense! Perhaps scarcely in its details and general organization. I tell you, I know of two other projects now afloat, the parties associated with which are running a race against each other, to get directions adjusted and officers appointed, so that they may at once come out. Your grand Continental scheme will have very little chance, if you have not made some progress, more than the mere arrangement of title, and the general plan of business.

[Three gentlemen pass at this moment, deeply engaged in conversation, and hurrying forward as if in haste to keep a special engagement.]

Old City habitué.—You know them, of course ?

Young Gentleman from the West.—No; certainly not; never saw them, I think, before in my life.

Old City habitué.—Well, then, if you do not, I will tell you who they are: the three greatest promoters of the present day. If they have not been successful in every instance, they have in several. Earlier in the field than yourself, they have not been idle, and now are probably engaged in forwarding one of your own pet schemes.

Young Gentleman from the West. — How can they know my pet schemes ? I have hardly divulged them to any one.

Old City habitué.—Perhaps not; but since they possess a " manufactory " for companies, I would almost be bound to say that if you could secure the list of all they have in course of preparation, or propose to supply, you will find all that you may assume to be direct wants are provided for.

Young Gentlemen from the West (nervously). — You really don't think that is the case, do you?

Old City habitué.—Yes. You see I speak pretty freely for your benefit. These three special gentlemen —and there are other cliques like them—have got the ground, and perfectly occupy it. Their "manufactory" is at ————. They possess a board-room nicely furnished, good auxiliary offices for themselves, and decent rooms for one or two clerks. Their library of reference is probably the London Directory, the Banking Almanack, the Hotel and Licensed Victuallers' Guide, the Book of Roads, and the Insurance Register. Files of the daily papers, to watch advertisements, and catch ideas from any fresh prospectus issued, constitute their stock of periodical literature, and in this they revel to their hearts' content. They have planned many banks, failed in some, and brought others to bear, and have many others on hand, cut and dry to order. When banking schemes do not show sufficient vitality, they readily turn their attention to the organization of hotels, and in this they have occasionally been successful. Assurance and Insurance Companies have obtained assistance when it was necessary to be supplied, and even mining properties have been "manipulated" when directors could not be immediately procured through other channels.

Young Gentleman from the West.— Then they must transact a very important amount of business.

Old City habitué.—Most decidedly; and consequently competition with them is almost out of the question. You may risk not only labour but money for nothing, and, despite your connections, come off after all second best. Besides the risk and liability, the immediate expense is equally proportional. If they cannot always be original in their enterprises, they may follow suit, and become imitative. If shares are not well subscribed, they can, through the exercise of a little ingenuity, get the list filled, and perhaps bear the brunt of the responsibility. Shares that in reality do not float at first, will with a little coaxing, come to the surface subsequently, and after all in the end produce a respectable premium.

Young Gentleman from the West.—But I did not know that all this trouble and labour was entailed in carrying out these things. I thought that you selected a project (one not before started), arranged to select a board, your friends of course readily joining, got the solicitor to secure the legal formalities, and the broker to place the shares, which on the basis of a sound scheme ought to go up.

Old City habitué.—You see, my good friend, you have reckoned without your host; and it is perfectly plain that unless a more than ordinary share of fortune attends you, there will be great risk without compensating profit. But try your hand, and when we meet again, you will be able to furnish me with a little of your own experience.

The old City *habitué* and the young gentleman from the West separate, and do not meet again for some two or three months. Meanwhile new companies have appeared by the score; but although they include every conceivable kind of project, good, bad, and indifferent, none emanate from the particular channel in which the newly-fledged promoter proposed to concentrate his energies; and the names of the solicitors and others he had confidentially communicated failed to appear in the various prospectuses.

At length, in the dull days of the autumn, the old City *habitué* meets once more his friend the young gentleman from the West; and finding him leaning against the railings of the Bank of England, and eyeing the

portly proportions of the building, says, rallying him—
" Well, I never suspected you of that—certainly, an
attempt on the Bank itself was the last thing I thought
any respectable friend of mine capable of, and glad am I
to have arrived in time to prevent it."

Young Gentleman from the West.—Oh! don't think
I've come to that yet, though, perhaps, after my sore
annoyances, I might be tempted to do anything. To
my mind, it seems about as difficult a thing to get up a
company, as to break into the Bank.

Old City habitué.—Then you find what I told you was
not altogether untrue. I hope, if you have wasted any
time, you have not wasted much money over it, because
I'm afraid your returns will be inconsiderable.

Young Gentleman from the West.—I have, I am sorry
to say, not only wasted time, but also money, and, I
fear, with very little success. Except that which may
hereafter arise from satisfactory introductions, and making
a few additional acquaintances, I see no prospect of
return. But you, my good friend—you that spoke of
appearance, and of toning down dress (pointing to a
heavy gold guard-chain which the old City *habitué* has
recently displayed), you seem now altogether upon the
other tack.

Old City habitué.—Of that more hereafter. What I told
you was, that, as a fresh importation to City life, you
must not make so great a show, or perhaps it might be
fancied you intended a swindle. For myself, I have been
a dweller in these circles for fifteen or twenty years;
any occasional change in me like that you notice, does not
excite the least surprise, since it is reasonably presumed,
if it be not true, that I have swindled many already
(laughs heartily). But, *badinage* apart, what are your

failures, that you look so crestfallen and disheartened ?

Young Gentleman from the West.—Not less than five all such promising, *bona fide* schemes, that it seemed impossible they could go to the wall. Yet they did, and in one or two instances have since become anticipated, or absorbed, by less important projects. My grand Continental, a broad and expansive notion, soon went by the board when the competitors named by yourself were announced.

Old City habitué.—Yes, I thought of you, too, on seeing those flaming prospectuses, with long lists of English, as well as continental, directors; but if they interfered with your project, there is some satisfaction in knowing that neither of them has been a thoroughly legitimate success.

Young Gentleman from the West.—Then I tried Hamburg and the Hanseatic towns, and on submitting the plans to my friends, every one prophesied a favourable issue. I worked hard at the preliminaries, thought I had secured directors ; but when I endeavoured to fix them, they sheered off on the plea of responsibility. The solicitors promised everything, and did little or next to nothing ; and when we came to complete registration, discovered, to our disgust, a similar institution, with a similar title, was there before us.

Old City habitué.—It does seem hard indeed, that such remarkable perseverance has been so ill rewarded.

Young Gentleman from the West.—But this is not all. I have accommodated myself to the moving current of the times. I have not only endeavoured to start distinct projects ; but when these would not take, and I have learnt that competitive schemes were in the field, I have offered terms of amalgamation, which have been rejected simply because I would not qualify directors, accept the greatest share of promoters' liabilities, and participate in the least share of the fees.

Old City habitué.—And I should say, by this time, you are heartily sick of the business ?

Young Gentleman from the West.—A few more visits, and I shall shake off the City's dust from my feet, never to return to it for a like purpose. I may honour the Bank with a call, if it should ever be my good luck to marry, and the friends of my wife make a settlement, or if by any strange mischance I should be a residuary legatee ; but I swear by all the patron saints in the calendar, that I will never seek its purlieus on a similar errand to that in which I have been lately engaged, much less waste life and substance in its pursuit.

Old City habitué.—Then, in truth, I suppose you have, like myself, come to the conclusion that company promotion, except under special circumstances, accompanied by extraordinary facilities, may simply be designated phantasmagoria.

Young Gentleman from the West. — Yes; and phantasmagoria of the worst description ; for, without you are prepared to promise everything, and perform little or nothing, to cajole directors, wheedle subscribers, and take care to secure a regular agreement for your fees, the generosity of those by whom you may be surrounded is so great, that at the last moment you may be " thrown over," to suit the convenience of unprincipled parties, and left to obtain redress how and where you can. No, no—back to the books, back to the reading-chair in chambers, and grind away again, I will, at the law— trusting that, with the woolsack in view, though I shall never attain it, I may at least make a respectable professional man.

The friends then separate. The old City *habitué* crosses the road, and passes into the Gresham Club, where he is speedily absorbed in digesting the contents of a pint of Amontillado and the evening paper. The young gentleman from the West seeks a cab, and is soon deposited in snug rooms near the Temple, where he has invited a few companions to join him.

DRAWING UPON THE IMAGINATION.

The effect of contrast is not always immediately discernible. Something that may be hurriedly said, when subsequently reflected upon, will occasionally present itself in a new light, and it is frequently a matter of ease to mould it into form. Many clever things, uttered in a moment of surprise, even if not so complete as they would be afterwards, if put into shape, are lost through the indolence of those whose remembrance, if lightly taxed, might greatly increase the resources of our social conversation, and impart at intervals a little brilliancy, where otherwise the most unmitigated dulness prevails. To get people up to the mark for these sallies is a work of time, especially among those who would be frightened outright at the semblance of a joke; but a course of gentle training would accomplish much good, and lead to the expansion of genial feeling, which, when moderately combined with business, greatly smooths the rugged path through which many have to wade, of contracts, orders, and commissions, and makes a morning's toil pass off like play.

The one thing needful to be avoided, in this kind of what may not be inappropriately described as commercial rattle, is the verging on the offensive or personal. It was the principal fault of the old wits, that they never hesitated to blurt out whatever they had to say, at the cost of friendship or the closest ties, so that their shaft flew straight home. If it created pain, nothing was thought of the consequences, provided the pointedness of the joke was preserved. Like the hilarious traveller, who once entering a customer's premises, and seeing a highly ornamented, and highly emblazoned gauze blind in the window, with " ———— and Co." upon it, asked, in a bland and supercilious manner, "*if the Co. was the blind, or the blind was the Co.,*" never anticipated his mistake, till the irate principal sent him reeling on the other side of the pavement. Through well-merited chastisement, the cause produced its effect, and exhibited in the most unmistakeable shape the disagreeable force of an allusion that might, under other circumstances, have not been deemed uncomplimentary.

Nothing, says the old aphorism, is better than " well-timed wit and humour." There are, according to the sapient and philosophical Sydney Smith, occasions when mirth is marvellous in its effect, and productive of the most favourable consequences. But all that he could do —and he accomplished a great deal in his day, with his letters addressed to the broad-brimmed fraternity, on their doctrine of repudiation—never recompensed him in the smallest degree for his misguided American investments, though his admirable compositions have become a lasting memorial of his name. Had he lived to the present day, he would, however, have been compelled, reluctantly, to withdraw his prospective reflections upon securities, which were then supposed, not to be within the forecast of human probability.

Chinese debentures do not as yet exist, though it is possible they may, before long, come into the market as a negociable property; and Abyssinian bonds, despite the learned disquisitions of Captain Harris on the Hills of Ethiopia, have not yet made their appearance. But if this be not the case, has not the Crescent so struggled, that it has surmounted the scruples of the Cross; and have we not only the 4 per cent. Turkish guaranteed, but also the 6 per cents? Scarcely within the category of a great financial revolution had Peter Plymly ever presumed that propositions conceived in jest would become in reality fearfully earnest. Yet so it is; and even Tunisian 5 per cents. are not now a myth; though when he wrote, it was never imagined that such a security would be placed upon the Bourse.

Thus "drawing upon the imagination" is no ineffective work, and if only considered in relation to the past, it is not impossible events, as startling as those enumerated, with regard to the future, may still take place; but it is not to be expected that every one who predicates will be equally *clairvoyant*. The mystery in the present epoch of change is not who shall be right, but who shall be wrong; for, while prognostics of evil have been mentioned in all quarters concerning what has passed, and what will inevitably happen, the public, in the midst of the excitement, have apparently escaped with nearly a whole skin. It does not however follow, that if such has been the course of things up to the present moment, it will be hereafter perpetuated—since even the sound advice of Sydney Smith—to be satisfied with good before overflowing, lest it should turn acrid, and become disagreeable—may fail to command respect, and be slighted until it is too late.

How this venerable author, if he could "revisit the
glimpses of the moon," would be strangely puzzled to
select, either for investment or speculation, securities that
would, after his experience of the real days of infatuation
in the stocks and shares of the " stars and stripes," give
him real immunity from the fears that beclouded his
latter days, of the safety of anything in which money was
to be temporarily sunk! Confidence has certainly now
revived, and would seem to have taken the place of
previous doubtful apprehensions, particularly when we
look at the mammoth enterprises which, one after
another rear their heads, only to be succeeded by still
more towering schemes, the safe fruition of which is so
unhesitatingly predicted.

It is no " drawing upon the imagination" to believe
that there must be a limit to this; past success may
entail future failure. But the end has not yet come.
The very success of the strongest loans, enterprises, and
financial combinations, will in the end, prove the downfall
of the weaker undertakings, which have been brought
into existence through jubilant prospects of their
predecessors; and the consequences will of course be
extremely prejudicial. But out of this evil will proceed
a great deal of unmixed good, if every one will bear
their share of responsibility, and not attempt to cry
peccavi, when an exhibition of steady endurance is
required.

XXXIX.

WHITHER IS LIMITED LIABILITY LEADING US ?

Significant indeed is the fact, that limited liability has become "a power among men." It was not supposed that the Act, in its general acceptation, would have been received with such favour, when first it obtained the sanction of the Legislature. Vaunting, as were its authors, of its adaptability to the wants of the mercantile and financial community, it was several years before its privileges were made available; and when they were originally brought into operation, they did not shadow forth its advantages in the most encouraging light.

The early attempts to introduce its privileges—much as they were sopken of—eventuated, as it might be supposed they would, in the most lamentable failures; and then it was distinctly asseverated that so little were they suited to English taste, and English convenience, that they fell still-born, leaving the public dissatisfied with the experiment, and willing to abandon the new system for the old and better-working machinery of the general Joint-Stock Act. For a somewhat lengthened period "limited liability" was, so to speak, a dead letter, and notwithstanding provincial experience was rather more favourable to the development of the principle, it was difficult to get a metropolitan proprietary to organize undertakings, which should give it a proper or extensive trial.

Disheartening as were the prospects which were

associated with the progress of the movement, a few companies with small capitals were started, which essayed to
give vitality to the Act; and though these could not be
looked upon as more than additional crude experiments,
they made progress, and finally rendered the public
familiar with what was before considered a partially
impracticable dogma.

Although appeals were made to transatlantic knowledge, where the elements of success were so unmistakeably apparent, like every new notion based upon
theory rather than practice, our countrymen were most
slow to take the initiative. Into operation, however, the
principle came at last, and notwithstanding it was but by
steady and sure degrees, the multitude, when it was fairly
recognized, were only too ready and eager to adopt it.
The earlier undertakings that acknowledged its influence,
and made its provisions subservient to their purposes,
were those of a manufacturing description; and though
even after the first great break-down there were occasional difficulties through mismanagement, they were
ultimately counterbalanced by the more legitimate results
arising in other channels from this kind of co-partnery.

Nevertheless, doubts were still entertained if "limited
liability" would turn out the great boon that had been
predicted by its most ardent admirers, and none were
more averse to the new form of arrangement than the
Joint-Stock Banks and Private banking interests. Strange
to say, as is very frequently the case, and as if some fore-
shadowing of such a change were approaching, the Joint-
Stock and the Private Banks have probably more than any
other class, been affected by the revolution. The "limited
liability" rage made its first step in Manchester, and
there attacked the financial community in its stronghold,

by converting an old and influential bank to the tenets of the bill. Liverpool followed, and, with a prescience acknowledged in the locality, it was not long before Birmingham, refusing to be behindhand, did not wait for old banks to recognize the principle, but started one on this basis, which has since, although a creation of only a few years, proved one of the most thriving in the neighbourhood.

But people shook their heads, looked sombre, and were not then prepared to admit that there was the slightest prospect of the Act taking substantial root in London, or ever becoming thoroughly acknowledged. A short time, however, only elapsed before the plethora of money, occasioned by the curtailment of trade through the American war, opened a new field for the inventive genius of those, who considered themselves specially adapted to promote joint-stock enterprise, and they at once sought to make its principles subservient to their plans.

The dividends of the half-yearly meetings in 1861 and 1862 had been very favourable ; capital was seeking an outlet for employment; and though the supply of banking accommodation was large, it was nevertheless believed that it might he extended. The effects of unlimited responsibility were discussed, but notwithstanding they were considered the best applicable to banking, both as giving confidence to the public and customers, promoters themselves found that "limited liability" was more suited to their prospects and arrangements, and at a very opportune moment the vessel with the new name, showing new colours, was launched, not without, however, a little fear and trembling.

The period, it was soon ascertained, was propitious,

the current ran smoothly; and though occasional cries
of breakers ahead were heard, they never in reality appeared. Two banks were originally started, but the
names of the directors in either case being scarcely, in
City parlance, strong enough to float such institutions,
arrangements were made for effecting an amalgamation.
Before this one bank, under its altered appearance, and
with a strengthened board, could make its preliminaries
perfect for commencing business, the prospectuses of two
others appeared for public support—not, it is true, simul-
taneously, but following closely on each other's heels.
One, in the shape of share subscriptions, was a most decided success; the other speedily secured its capital, but,
measuring its worth by the market price, it was not so
great a favourite, either with the speculative, or the investing public as its competitor.

Previously to this, it should be mentioned, Discount
Companies had been started, with the same inscription on
their business banners, but in more prosaic terms, and
they were regarded for a period as banks in disguise,
though events subsequently showed the contrary. But
it was a partial struggle for them to succeed, and when
the great failures in the leather trade took place, predictions fatal to the lengthened existence of these institutions, were freely uttered. Their losses, it was certain,
were large, in common with the various banks and discounting establishments, which suffered through the
enormous mass of accommodation paper, put into circulation through the agency of Lawrance, Streatfeild,
& Co., and accruing when they were least able to bear
them, caused their balance-sheets, when printed, to exhibit a discouraging appearance.

The principal company stood their ground bravely,

the managers worked well and vigorously, and in the
space of two half years re-established their position,
much to the satisfaction of the proprietors, who manifested throughout, complete confidence in their directors. The other unfortunate company, guided by a timid
board, and assaulted by shareholders who, purchasing
stock at a depreciated value, found on investigating
the accounts, a profitable amount of assets to divide,
failed to recover its *status*, and it was not long before it
was determined to liquidate its affairs, which was gradually
and successfully accomplished. This was a blow to the
development of the principle of "limited liability" in the
financial circles of the Metropolis ; and, until the inaugura-
tion of the new banking movement, was the great argument always employed by the anti-limited liability
party.

But when it was so readily perceived that, with a
decided plethora in the money market, a revived taste
among the public for speculation, and encouraging prices
for shares, that limited liability would be accepted even
among the banking community, and that the experiment
would not be adopted on an unimportant scale, scarcely
any bounds were placed to the animation which now ensued, and "limited liability" soon became not only
patronized by banks, but by every other conceivable kind
of financial and industrial undertaking.

Not only, however, was the principle rendered applicable to banking in London and the provinces, but organizations were formed for extending its usefulness to the
more distant quarters of the globe. Hindustan and
China, Brazil and Portugal, Austria and Italy, the Cape
of Good Hope, Australia and New Zealand, were very
speedily accommodated, and in several of the more impor-

tant instances with every prospect of success. Even the
nearer relations of the United Kingdom were not neglected : France, Belgium, and the Netherlands being at
the same time completely supplied. The effect, as might
be supposed, was also to introduce those large and important finance credit companies which have since been
raised, with capitals more extended than those of the
banks. These again, striking into new paths and new
channels, have been accompanied by those exchange establishments, which are entering upon domains in the
territory of finance, before occupied alone by the leviathan
capitalists, whose names have been passwords throughout
Europe and the world, for wealth and resources, almost
defying competition.

It will be several years ere the true success of these
institutes will be established; but, regarding them as
agents working in circles, where they must come in
contact with the connections and operations of their
great predecessors, they will doubtless attempt to wrest
from their grasp, a portion of the enormous returns
and profits, they have hitherto exclusively appropriated to
their own benefit. Whether these private leviathan
houses will have to succumb in the open hostilities, which
may now be considered to have been declared between
themselves and the limited liability undertakings, cannot
be immediately determined; but it is reasonable to suppose that they will have to encounter strong competition
—stronger probably than was originally imagined.

But it is not in this direction solely that limited
liability is putting forth claims for universal support.
Everywhere now the adoption of the principle is encouraged, and from the highest to the lowest enterprise,
no other kind of foundation is permitted. Bold would be

the individual who dared in these days to propose to start an undertaking on the unlimited system, holding the shareholders, as in the case of many existing institutions, responsible " to his last shilling, and his last acre." That which seven or eight years ago was considered an experiment—and an experiment of a very dangerous character, even as applied to the most ordinary adventures, has at length become so popular, that it bids fair to over-ride antecedent interests, joint-stock and private, and throw them wholly into the shade. Indeed, it may be said to be an analogous expansion to that experienced in the period of railway history, when every route, every highway, or every canal, was to become auxiliary to the new interest, and be finally absorbed.

In the present instance the adaptation of the principle to the whole class of projects seeking popular support, leaves no chance for any other system to be developed, and when we see that vested interests, which were previously furious against the alleged innovation, ready to recognize its value, it may be fairly considered that limited liability possesses claims which cannot be altogether ignored. It would be all very well to say that the new principle might be regarded as an experiment, if its application were strictly confined to undertakings which were ushered into existence during the last two or three years; but when we discover, apart from this, that old and wealthy establishments—several of undoubted reputation and position —are making arrangements to dissolve their private partnership character, and array themselves in the apparel of the Hon. Mr. Lowe's Act, it must be allowed that either we are again in the midst of a most speculative epoch, or that the privileges offered, deserve to be fully tested.

Of course "limited liability" may in its extended form be carried beyond due bounds ; it may, like the railway system, be so expanded that the recoil from the shock may be felt detrimentally in some quarters when a collapse takes place ; but although this may occur sooner or later, it does not follow that " limited liability " as a principle will not turn out a success, and stamp encouraging traces of its handiwork upon many of the recently established financial and commercial institutions. The very excess of the preponderating influence, which has brought forward the late large crop of industrial enterprise, must at no distant date be relieved by reaction ; but although this will come, and its effect will be exhibited in a variety of localities, the result will not for ever prejudice the vitality of the principle.

Limited liability has at length made itself a name, and a position in the land; and though there may still be failures, and mischances in individual cases associated with its working, it will not be an easy task to divert it from its recognized channels. Limited liability, it has been jocosely remarked, has become our banker, our credit and finance purveyor, our armourer, our hotel-keeper, our brewer, our baker—not as yet our butcher, though there is no great reason why eventually this may not be the case—our bootmaker, our dairy supplier, and caterer for our most ordinary wants.

With this dominant tendency the power of the Act, now it has been so fully brought into play, must be severely felt, particularly by those who have hitherto endeavoured to stem the tide of its operation, and disinclined, as they even now may be, to receive its proffered assistance, they will not eventually escape its gradually absorbing powers. Limited liability is, therefore, established as a great principle; it may have its weak points, and defective arrangements will, in all probability, occasionally bring its development into disgrace; but, as a principle, it will outlive any such drawbacks as these, and finally extend its influence, if possible, even more widely than at present.

XXX.

SOME years ago—it must now be nearly twenty at least—
I started one fine midsummer evening on a voyage of
discovery. The visit I proposed to pay was to a *terra
incognita*, among high-ways and bye-ways, which then
were seldom explored except by the inhabitants, who
made these places their own special residence. The
object of my mission was of a public character, and the
public gained advantage from it ; but it is scarcely necessary to let my good readers into the secret of the manner
in which this was managed at so early a stage of the proceedings.

It was no common errand that sent me, after the
usual hours of business, some three or four miles' journey
into the very heart of a labyrinth of brick-fields, mud
huts, and newly-formed streets, to trace, if possible, the
link to a species of financial conspiracy which, while
carried on from a point near the great metropolis, was
supposed to involve the integrity of the great metropolis
itself. Sanguine as I was of being successful, I was not
quite satisfied that I should immediately fall upon the
scent of the parties engaged in the nefarious business,
and therefore I selected fine weather with the long evenings, for prosecuting an investigation, which I was induced
to believe would terminate much to the benefit of the in-

dividuals presumed to be compromised, and the discomfiture of those who had originated, and put into
operation, the plan of attack.

Notwithstanding I had received some information,
which furnished me with a clue to the whereabouts of
the dwelling of the principal ringleader, it was not of a
character which would prevent me from being deceived, or
thrown out of my reckoning, if I immediately followed
it up, since it was known that he was a most shifty party,
and one who, if he were suspected, would as freely
migrate to the Land's End, as direct his route simply
from Haggerston, to the lower end of Dalston. At the
time of which I speak, there was not the population now
existing in any of the suburban districts, and it was then
something more than an evening's walk to encompass the
neighbourhood into which I intended to plunge—first, to
discover if I could " spot " the delinquents ; and secondly,
eliminate the mode of working, and their peculiar system
of monetary accommodation.

The task I had set myself not only required perseverance but discretion, and by the exercise of these I was
eventually enabled to surmount difficulties which temporarily appeared unconquerable, and which threatened at one
moment to disarrange all my well-devised preconcerted
schemes.

When I started I was aware of the nature of the
locality towards which I was bending my steps ; but
when I arrived in the immediate vicinity it seemed that,
like the mariner at sea without chart or compass, I was
in a wilderness of distress. A wide, wild common on
one side, with yawning gravel-pits on the other, left in
the middle a small corduroy tract of road, which seemed
interminable. Marching along this I was understood to

be *en route* towards the establishment of a firm, the representatives of which, by circular throughout the provinces, informed the trading community that they could furnish them with mercantile acceptances of first-class character, in exchange for country or suburban bills, the sole remuneration required being a small commission, to be forwarded at the same time that the application for assistance was made.

The document also informed those to whom it was addressed, that the connections of the establishment were most extensive, centered as they were in the midst of bankers and others of high standing; but however picturesque and pleasant this might read, it was evident that I, now following out the address as lithographed in the Italian style, was far removed from the haunts of mercantile men, and was in great danger every now and then of breaking my neck or my legs, through contact with piles of Yorkshire stone, and collections of builders materials, waiting to be absorbed by the tenements in course of erection on the spot.

Still passing onward, the houses, where they were finished, exhibited a mean and disreputable appearance, and decidedly were not the abodes of wealth or credit; but what did that matter? the circular settled all such trifling considerations, by the mere assertion of any amount of accommodation in the shape suggested, being available, and few persons were prepared, like myself, to take the trouble to track the deception to its very stronghold.

Forward I went through quagmire paths, still seeking for the great house, the principals of which were ready to supply, on bills of exchange, such unlimited facilities to needy and paralyzed traders. Daunted every now and then I was, by the irregularity of the turnings, the doubtful *culs-de-sac* into which they led, and the apparent absence of defined direction ; but, nevertheless, with the great object in view of making the acquaintance of the partners, I did not hesitate to encounter numerous inconveniences before I arrived at the precise spot, where these enormous pecuniary engagements were conducted.

I did not imagine, after I had penetrated the lanes and streets which at length brought me to my destination, that the place of business would be palatial or imposing ; that would have been out of keeping with the habitations in the surrounding district ; I had, however, fancied, though I shrewdly suspected the legitimate tendency of the whole arrangements, that there would have been more of show, if not solidity, in the external appearance of the mansion.

A residence it certainly was—square-built and detached, with adjoining offices; but these were of a second-rate character, not affording any assurance of respectability, though it might be expected they were useful. Before the entrance was a sand screen of extraordinary dimensions, through which cement had been passed to assist in the plastering of neighbouring premises; and sundry trucks and wheelbarrows showed that repairs were proceeding in the neighbourhood on the most extensive scale. Certainly, the great firm, if it in reality existed—and I had not yet gained information disabusing my mind upon the point—could undoubtedly employ their resources in the locality, judging by the improvements going forward; and it seemed an unbounded stretch of generosity on their part to send into the provinces to distribute their wealth, particularly when they asked in return only a slight consideration to cover ordinary commission and postage.

I was weighing financially these circumstances in my

remembrance, and contrasting the dissimilarity of the situation for great monetary operations, with those I had quitted a few hours previously, when I thought I would commence my inquiries whether this firm, with its high-sounding name, in such a doubtful locality, was known or appreciated. The house was closed, the shutters were barred, and no sign was presented of a living soul being within. A letter-slip cut in the door was the receptacle for communications, and, as it was well worn, a good deal of business, it might be inferred, had been transacted. No knocker ornamented the dull lead-colour panels, but a bell-handle protruded from the wooden joist of the cornice, which made a faint tingle resound through the building when I gave it the ordinary jerk. Response there came none; and the great firm having thrown off the cares and labours of the day, might be reasonably imagined to have left the establishment to look after itself.

I was somewhat perplexed to find myself placed in this situation, because, although I was sure I was on the right spot, and no mistake could have been made about the name of the place, the complete isolation of the premises, and the manner in which they were evidently deserted, induced me to think for the moment that my visit had been paid a little too late. Determined not to be foiled in my endeavours to trace out the mystery, I strolled on; and desolate as the place was, and encumbered by surrounding buildings, I at length arrived at a beer-shop, the proprietor of which, struggling for a licence, made a greater display outside than he did within.

I soon obtained refreshment of a kind which, if not of the best, was sufficient for the taste of the neighbourhood, and it was served with an alacrity which showed what the poor fellow could have accomplished if there had been more numerous customers. I commiserated him on the small prospect of success in such a neighbourhood, and with so sparse a population. He at once entered readily into his griefs and his position— furnished me with a whole history of his disappointments in seeking the privileges of the trade, for it was his third application; assuring me that if he could obtain the ear of the coachman of the chief of the magistrates, his sorrows would be at an end; but how that was to be effected he could not divine, though somebody had promised to enlighten him shortly.

Having led him so far forward, I was enabled now to put a few questions in connection with the spot, and the purpose of my special journey. But I approached the topic in a most cautious manner, introducing in as gentle a manner as was possible, the name of the house transacting the financial business. At first he scarcely comprehended my meaning; he admitted he knew the parties, but he was not convinced that they had any kind of bill engagements. To use his own phrase, he thought they were "letter dodgers" (i. e., begging-letter impostors), and to this he attributed their frequent shiftings from place to place, though when it suited their convenience they invariably returned to the "Farm." This was the locality from which the circular was despatched, and near the spot where this very conversation was taking place. I elicited in a round-about way, much more circuitous than that in which I am detailing these simple facts, that there were three individuals engaged, a father, a son, and a daughter.

The father really owned the house, and the son and daughter occasionally stayed there; but after any business had been transacted they generally left for a fortnight or three weeks, and were not often long together.

"I thought there was something up," said the man, resuming his narrative after I had induced him to go into the matter, having unchained his memory by the appliance of his own ale and cigars; "I thought there was something up when 'old fur-collar' called yesterday, and said, if any inquiries were made, he had a pressing call into the country, and should not be back for some days."

"Then he was here so late as yesterday," I remarked.

"Yes," continued my informant; "and it seemed as if he had been doing something good, for he and his son had steaks and kidneys, and two pints of Mieklejohn's best, and talked of what further was to be done in the shape of *drawing*—drawing, as I supposed, from the soft people to whom they had written. The daughter was up in the evening; she usually pays her flying visits at night, to take whatever she may find in the letter-box."

"And so," I said, "you are quite sure that these are the people who inhabit, or at least have to do with the establishment close at hand?"

"Never fear," replied the landlord; "they are identically the same. 'Old fur-collar,' as I have called him before, is the individual who takes the lead in the business; and though the others may be only his tools, they are willing participators in the working."

"But when you allude to 'old fur-collar,' as you call him—he that is the principal in these arrangements—whether 'letter-dodging' or other operations of a doubtful character—how long is it, may I ask, you have known him, and has it always been in this same capacity?"

The man ruminated for a short time, and proceeded: "You see, I have been here about two years and a half, and they have been here all that time, if not longer. When I first came they were only small customers of mine, but latterly they have been rather more intimate. Originally, I believe, the old gentleman—for a gentleman he is in manners and appearance, if his line of life is not altogether satisfactory—was connected with some large City firm: but that failing, he has descended in the scale, and is glad to pick up a crust in the best manner he is able."

I had not yet let my friend into the whole preliminaries of the investigation I wished to carry out; but he, divining that I knew more than I was desirous of at once imparting, sought to arrive at the direct object of my mission.

I inquired cursorily of the time when it was most probable I could fall into the company of the senior of the party, or his son; the acquaintance of the daughter I did not desire to make, because I fancied it was not probable, if she only appeared in the character of a night messenger, that I should ever secure much information from her. I was, I confess, somewhat interested in the history of this " old fur-collar," who could, in the plenitude of his riches, make arrangements for assisting "country cousins" in the way he professed, especially with the small pretensions to resources, such as I had now discovered, and I therefore eagerly gleaned what more I could of his appearance.

" He is a most cautious bird," replied my loquacious friend, who was ready to answer my most minute inquiries, "and it is not at all to be expected that you would ever meet him, without it was purely by accident. Ever since I came here he has usually dressed in a singular style—a snuff-colour brown coat, with sable collar and sable cuffs; they are evidently the remnants of former days of prosperity, and he cherishes them, from the manner in which he smooths the wrinkles and the edges of the lappels, as a father would a darling child. He mounts spectacles—the school of the heavy round silver rim, which present more of a telescopic vision than those of the modern day; wears an old-fashioned but well-brushed hat, and gaiters of the most approved trim. This is his ordinary apparel. Occasionally he varies it; and if I now suspect the purport of your questions, it will throw some light upon what I have considered was a disguise, to throw people off a recognition, if it were desirable."

"How—in what respect? Pray, explain yourself," I continued.

"Why, thus," said the landlord: "I have known him come bustling down late at night in a suit of velveteen, but never without his spectacles; and at other times he has appeared as a country hawker, with the white smock frock covering his other garments, and leaving his gaiters visible, which gives him the most perfect air of innocence, and would induce any one to believe there could be no wrong in the man."

"But where were the son and daughter all this time?" I inquired.

"The son has been absent. I seldom see him. He is only occasionally with 'old fur-collar.' The daughter continues her flying visits, staying a night or a day, and then leaving."

"Did you never, all this time," I asked, "have any inquiries about an establishment that granted accommodation to poor, jeopardized traders, and which professed services of a most imaginative kind, on terms of an unexceptionable character?"

A few inquiries of the sort he confessed had been made, but not in a manner to arouse a strong impression that any *malfaisance* was being practised, though he thought it was possible that the family were obtaining a comfortable livelihood—for comfortable it really appeared to be—not in the most creditable manner. "Letter dodging," notwithstanding it was an ignoble pursuit, presented to his mind, rough and uncultivated as it was, a much less reprehensible mode of public plunder than anything associated with bill-dealing.

The landlord and myself by this time had established such mutual relations of confidence, that I considered there could be no harm in telling him the nature of my suspicions, and the grounds for my believing that the family, respecting which I had gleaned this information, constituted a nest of bill forgers of the most confirmed school. It was scarcely the right moment to endeavour to expose or prosecute them criminally ; and, therefore, having made him a friend, I returned to town very well satisfied with the progress I had made in testing the resources of this great establishment, and the power possessed of granting unlimited facilities.

For two or three days I refrained from revisiting the immediate locality. Nevertheless, in the meanwhile I energetically pursued the inquiries, which were essential to make myself acquainted with the description of business they could transact to secure the plunder, which it was evident they had obtained from individuals who, lured by their specious circular, had entrusted them with acceptances. The period was arriving when either they must be placed in the hands of the police, or I must retreat from the investigation, with the knowledge that the firm could not be legally dealt with, and that the special information could only be offered to the public in the shape of a warning, to deter others from following in the same path.

The statement upon which I had founded the inquiries had been sent to me by two poor deluded dupes of the house, who had not in reality suffered pecuniarily by their offer of assistance, but who had placed acceptances at their command, which, if negociated, would entail responsibilities of a heavy character, especially since they had not been enabled to obtain in return the exchange bills which the house proposed to supply, and which were necessary — foolish as they had been in relying upon those representations—to meet engagements that were about falling due. I had not failed to communicate to them my suspicions of the character of the hands into which they had fallen—thieves of the worst description by the way-side ; but as their affairs would be compromised if I adopted a precipitate course, I waited for their instructions before resorting to extreme measures.

My poor "country cousins"—for such they in reality were — became extremely sensitive when they discovered the trap into which they had been drawn ; and although it was a question of several hundred pounds, they expressed their desire to put up with the loss, rather than risk the penalty of an appeal to magisterial interference, which must bring out their names and abode in connection with such rascally transactions. Checked as I temporarily was by their wish to conceal an affair which exhibited in the clearest possible light, the machinations of "old fur-collar" and his accomplices, I was not prepared to allow the matter to drop without endeavouring to save their money, or obtain the return of the securities forwarded to the "Farm," and which, if not already placed through other hands upon the market, might, with a little strategy, be recovered before they in regular order became available.

The next link I traced in the conduct of these "extraordinary facilities" which were supposed to be granted in answer to the terms imposed, was the existence of a channel by which the prime movers in the conspiracy, when they obtained information of the position of unfortunate traders who sought their assistance, hastened to put themselves in communication with the chief creditors of their dupes, and thus place them in peril of legal proceedings, to thwart, if requisite, any direct attempt against themselves. By surrounding their unfortunate victims with difficulties, and encouraging those to whom they were indebted to press their claims, nervous traders would naturally strive to meet any outstanding engagements of a questionable kind, so as to prevent any stigma attaching to their names, or the opprobrium which would be sure to arise if bankruptcy or insolvency supervened.

It was sufficiently monstrous to ascertain that individuals might be victimized through an imprudent or a reckless action; but when I discovered that these auxiliary means were employed to cover the delinquency, I resolved more firmly than ever to root out the festering evil. Still, I had very difficult cards to play. On the one hand there were my relatives deeply involved through misguided judgment, and who, immediately they saw their error, appealed to me for relief. On the other stood arrayed the interests of the mercantile community, whose representative in a public capacity I was; and, while desiring to save the one, I determined, if possible, to serve the other.

My course of proceeding was soon chalked out. The weather, which had not been favourable, at last improved, and, once more, fully equipped with a stock of additional valuable information, I was on my way down the corduroy road, through the quagmire paths, to my friend who was struggling against fate for a licence. He received me in the most cordial manner possible, and instead of installing me in the ordinary parlour where our acquaintance first commenced, located me comfortably in a little back room, where, ensconced in cosy condition behind glowing red curtains, I found his wife and two chirpy children.

"I thought," said the landlord, after introducing me to the lady of the household, and a blue-eyed, fair girl, his eldest daughter, "you were never going to pay us another visit. The time passed so pleasantly when you were last here, that I have often said I should like to see you again, though good Bessie" (laughing at his wife) "said she feared I might be deceived in the stranger who wanted to know so much about 'old fur-collar' and his ways and doings. Women, you know, sir," he added, "are very suspicious; and she believed that it might be a plant of our old customer, to ascertain if we were too inquisitive."

I thanked him for his kindness, and also commended the vigilance of his wife. The latter darned away vigorously at some stockings, merely nodding approvingly at my concluding observations. In such a place, and with such neighbours, I asserted it was necessary they should exercise the utmost caution, since I believed I was now in a position, either to denounce the firm, or to put in motion the active powers of the law. I advised them by all means not to recognize "old fur-collar" or any of his gang,

except in the distant relation of visitors who paid for
refreshments like other ordinary customers, feeling
assured that the time was not far distant when an
explosion of the whole affair would take place, and perhaps place all participants under penalty of transportation
for their conduct.

The landlord promised to take my advice; and when
I told him who in reality I was, he said he could have no
further misgivings as to the correctness of what I had
stated.   Other indications had also been presented,
since I last visited the neighbourhood, confirming a
great deal of that which I now detailed to him; and it
was evident, from what had cursorily transpired, that
there were other branch depôts where similar operations
continued to be carried out.   " Old fur-collar " and
another friend, a new visitor, had been, he intimated, in
frequent attendance at the —— Farm, but never appeared
to transact business there.   They called for the contents
of the letter-box, and invariably repaired to his parlour,
where they talked over, and arranged their plans.   If
strangers were in the room, they ordered refreshment, and
waited till they left; they then required ink—pens and
paper they always appeared provided with; pumice-stone
and emery powder being likewise useful adjuncts.   They
never worked long at a time, and the preparation of two
or three letters seemed sufficient to satisfy them with their
course of operations for the day.   The daughter of " old
fur-collar" had apparently retired from the connection;
but my friend surmised that it was not improbable the
new comer was her husband, and had been imported into
the arrangement as more serviceable, particularly as he
seemed to be the great writer, and the busiest of the
two when pressing transactions had to be completed.

The reason for the landlord suspecting there were other places where the same nefarious business proceeded, was the fact that he had overheard " old fur-collar " say, on a recent occasion, when he was in and out of the room attending to his wants, that " if the Farm ever became so hot as the old shop near Stone Bridge Common, he fancied he should have to give up the trade altogether." To which remark, as they were busily employed upon their work, the friend had rather incautiously replied—" And no mistake, for those fellows in the Ten Towns were not to be lightly dealt with." Indeed, the landlord—all this conversation taking place in his closely-curtained private room—became so interested in the affair, that though his great grief of the want of a licence was not entirely suppressed, he volunteered to assist me in my plans of obtaining a return of the bills my poor friends had sent up, and of ultimately dispersing the gang itself.

I had not spent a week or ten days in ferreting out the greater part of the circumstances here related, without conceiving the measures I should adopt to secure my ends; but when I found my friend the landlord not merely ready to assist with his knowledge and advice, but likewise, if requisite, to act upon the spot, it would, I thought, be no difficult matter, both to learn the fate of the acceptances I was tracing, and eventually to place " old fur-collar" and his associates in such an unpleasant position, that they would either willingly abandon their disreputable practices, or bring themselves very speedily into the hands of the police.

The hour was getting late; the sky was dark and cloudy, but the stars, pale and shimmering, now and then broke out, and threw their silver gleams across night's murky pall.

The customers in the house had all left, and the great question was how soon I should depart; but, as we were much absorbed in our plans, I was anxious even to prolong my stay till two or three small arrangements were made. The gas was out in the parlour, the light against the door had been reduced, and that with the low, flickering flame which served to illumine the room in which we were seated, were the only indications of the hostelrie not beving entirely closed. We were in the midst of a deep discussion concerning what my friend the landlord should do the next time "old fur-collar" and any of his friends made a visit, with the view of breaking ground with them, when steps were heard approaching, accompanied by a low, short cough, and before the landlord could get to the door three distinct raps were given.

"Talk of a certain gentleman, and he always appears. What shall we do? It's them to a certainty," said the landlord, making towards the door.

Two men entered; they looked neither to the right nor to the left, but made straight for the room which I supposed they usually frequented. The landlord followed, and was for a short time engaged. At intervals I heard the same low, short cough, which, with its hard, dreary tone, struck gratingly on the ear.

The landlord again presented himself. "They are not in the best trim to-night—seem downhearted and disappointed, if I may judge from their order, and the way in which it was given: a pint of stout, with plenty of ginger, and a couple of pipes and a screw. There is a good deal to be learned of the character of your customers from their orders," continued my friend, as he drew the beer and arranged the pipes and tobacco on his tray, "and I frequently tell which way the wind blows from these trivial symptoms. I shall be back directly, and then, if you are disposed to stay, perhaps we shall be able to see our way clearer in this curious business."

I willingly acquiesced. It struck me that we were favoured by fortune in thus at once meeting with these worthies ; but I was not too ready to make their acquaintance, or arrange for an interview, unless the moment was opportune. The landlord returned, stating that they did not appear to be communicative, being, as he imagined, much occupied with the consideration of something that had proved a miscarriage, either of money or of a project in which they were interested. The only chance that existed of intruding upon their company was to risk another short delay, and seek to join them just before they left.

After due consultation with " mine host," I agreed it would be best not to attempt to open my especial case, but to allow them to have their swing with their own particular affair — the matter of moment that seemed to occupy their thoughts—and to leave him on a future opportunity to begin our campaign, when I was not personally present. The sole way that I could now be brought in contact with them, so as to make any observations which might be subsequently advantageous, was in the shape of an introduction as a friend of the landlord's, who had dropped in late, and proposed to take a cigar in his company. I confess I hated the scheme of deception employed, feeling that it would be more manly to grapple with the knaves then and there, and face them with a history of their delinquencies ; but the landlord was a good general, and I had no reason to regret the service of the *ruse* he suggested.

We boldly entered the room, and seated ourselves near

the black-dyed vagabonds who had deluded my poor relatives. Though not much disturbed by our unceremonious behaviour, they scrutinized me from head to foot. The landlord simply announced me as a friend who was passing, and had made a call, and having prevailed upon me to smoke, we preferred doing it in company in the public room, to suffocating his wife in their private apartment. The assurance of the landlord failed in the least to excite their curiosity. This I was not surprised at ; but "old fur-collar" and his friend every now and then darted out eagle glances at myself, as if they imagined there was more in my appearance than they could make out.

"Old fur-collar," as the landlord had described him, was gentlemanly but singular in his apparel, his "suit of sables," with which he was now adorned, being manifestly the remains of former greatness. At least sixty years of age, there was a sharp angularity about the lines of the face betokening natural shrewdness, while the abundance of iron-grey hair, joined to a certain regularity of feature, induced the impression that in early days he might have been reckoned a favourable specimen of humanity. But as he smoked, the low short cough returned, and it seemed not so much a physical ailment, as a hard, dry sound, which welled up, as it were, from some cavernous depth, and told, as plainly as words could speak, of utter hollowness and heartlessness within.

His friend and assistant—it will be seen hereafter the part he played—was an individual of a wholly different mould. He was short and flabby, but with just sufficient external appearance to raise him above the common level of mankind ; his visage, though partially disfigured through the effects of drink, exhibited strong symptoms of chicane and deceit. He had small and deep-set eyes, with a receding forehead, a squat nose, and strongly compressed lips, presenting a combination of disagreeable elements which it was impossible to regard with favour. Besides, it was a matter of difficulty for him to look straight, and with his pipe in his mouth, supported by a damp, heavy, red hand, he was constantly peering at the landlord and myself, and not only appeared to doubt the seasonableness of our presence, but also that of his venerable colleague and of his own into the bargain.

After our entrance, and when the first slight embarrassment had passed, they talked in a muttered whisper, every now and then interrupted by the low short cough of " old fur-collar."   The landlord and myself were not as scrupulously discreet. We chatted merrily and laughed heartily, but all our casual observations on men and things, only succeeded in eliciting monosyllables from the suspicious pair. When they had finished their refreshment, it was long after the hour of regular closing, but the landlord had not hurried them, because in the first place there was no loss of the great licence to fear, and in the next place it had afforded me the full opportunity of reconnoitring the appearance and physiognomy of the partners in this extensive and important financial firm, whose connections, according to the phraseology of their lithographic business announcements, " extended throughout the chief cities and towns in the United Kingdom."

Here had I been almost *tête-à-tête* in their society for an hour and more, but unwilling as I was, I was prevented from making close acquaintance with them, the moment being deemed inauspicious for the purpose. As they slunk away, turning round the corner after looking at the

Farm, and with shambling gait pursued their path towards the brickfields of Haggerstone for a quiet hiding-place in that neighbourhood, I merely regretted that an imperative reticence disarmed me from placing them without further to do, in the custody of the recognized authorities.

Wishing the landlord a hurried good night, although it was a mere compliment, for it was fast breaking into morning, I retraced my steps to the old City; not, however, before surveying the scene of my exploits from Kingsland Road Bridge, and feeling satisfied that my friend the landlord and myself would ultimately realize our most sanguine expectations.

Taking up a newspaper the following day, I was surprised to find that the arrangements of "old fur-collar" and his associates had at last attracted public notice. Reference was made in a disguised manner only to the kind of fraud attempted to be perpetrated; but it was quite evident from the paragraph, that if it did not apply to these very individuals, it must to some of their associates. The case alluded to was precisely analogous to the one I had under investigation; and had it not been for the mention of the district, and the amount involved, I should have almost declared that my " country cousins," dissatisfied with my exertions, were adopting independent steps to compass the downfall of the great financial firm at the " Farm."

The more I read, the more I was satisfied that the delinquency of the individuals would be shortly established. Scarcely had the evening set in before I was again on my road to the bewildering neighbourhood, where, at the peril of skin and bone, I once more explored its most intricate fastnesses. Although the day had been one of more than usual excitement, partially occasioned through my general pursuits, and partially through the desire to bring to a conclusion the inquiry into which I had thrown myself body and soul, I never in all my life was so resolutely cool as when for the last time I neared the fated locality.

I experienced a feeling of temporary anxiety, because it seemed that, with a premonitory warning in a newspaper, the birds might have flown ; and had this been the case, I should never have forgiven myself for presumed *laches*, when they had been for so long a time within my grasp. As I pictured to myself the antecedents of the dainty old villain " fur-collar," and the sanctimonious appearance of his assistant with the swivel eye and the heavy, damp, red hand, I became more annoyed than ever, in imagining that I might have allowed them, at the last moment, to elude my grasp ; and, with my natural habit, when vexed beyond control, I stamped with vehemence, and made the corduroy road, ballasted as it was with stone, ring again.

Judge of my surprise to see the two identical figures, " old fur-collar" and his associate, rapidly passing along, not in the direction of the house of my friend struggling for a licence, but in the opposite route, as if they were fleeing from detection. My first impulse was to rush after, and, at the risk of personal safety, seize them ; but before I had time to put my determination into execution I was stopped by my friend the landlord, who, with beaming face and animated gesticulation, beckoned me to him.

" There they go," he said, " and the sooner they are out of the way the better. They are at last traced, and the police, who have overhauled the Farm, will not be satisfied till they have them in custody."

" But surely you will not let them escape ?" I added ;

"the ends of public justice demand that we should aid in their arrest."

"Yes, yes, my good friend, public justice demands a great deal, but private interest a little more. You asked me to pursue a certain line of conduct, and I have followed it out to the very letter. Private interest having been served, public justice will nevertheless follow; for before the next two hours the whole gang will be secured. Not only has the Farm been thoroughly searched, but three other places between Dalston and Haggerstone; and the bill trade in which 'old fur-collar' and his friends have revelled, will from this time be entirely annihilated."

I was hardly prepared for this display of logical reasoning on the part of the landlord of the house where I had sojourned; but I made allowance for enthusiasm in a good cause, having worked him to a high pitch of excitement.

When he had sobered down a little, and I could approach the subject with delicacy, I inquired the fate of the bills which I apprehended had passed into other hands.

"By the way," he replied, "I tackled 'old fur-collar' on that point, when he called early this morning, and before the police had invaded his sanctuaries."

"And what did he say?" I inquired.

"Why, he gave one of his low, short coughs, and then told me, in a kind of half whisper, 'that he had not parted with the bills, and would return them, not because they were not negotiable, but because they represented the name of an old house, against whom he had already committed great wrong.' But even with this sort of compunction, he made a bargain that he was to be paid

£—— for giving them up. As you told me I was to do what I could, I jumped at the proposal; but before it could be settled, though he had passed me the bills, the police were at hand, and 'old fur-collar' and his friend were shortly in flight."

I grasped the hand of the landlord heartily, and thanked him over and over again for the judgment he had displayed. My poor "country cousins" were now relieved from the peril in which they had been placed, and I was, I hope, thoroughly grateful to the man who had so chivalrously assisted me in the hour of need. At the same time, however, I was burning with a desire to ascertain the prospects of the arrest of the gang— not that there was much fear that they would escape, the detectives being close on their track. My friend, the landlord, and myself waited to receive the duly authenticated report of the intelligence, which was brought by a paid messenger before the evening closed, and the sun shed his radiant beams no more upon "the name and mission of that great financial establishment."

The news of the capture of the subordinate delinquents was a fact that was speedily confirmed. The husband of the daughter—he with the doubtful countenance and the heavy, damp, red hand—was the first that succumbed to the power of the law; the woman was the next, and finally the son; the latter having been secured, when he supposed his appearance on the scene was that of an observer instead of a *particeps criminis*.

Within a short distance of the scene of their iniquities they were severally taken, seeking as they did a refuge in the very places where they had conducted their nefarious kind of enterprise; but prepared as they were to admit that they could not avoid the responsibility of the situation, the great difficulty was the apprehension of the prime originator of the huge conspiracy. He had escaped—"old fur collar"—the principal delinquent, the chief of the movement, and the arch-designer of the base fabric of accommodation that was now toppling to the ground; and satisfactory as it might be to destroy the lesser engines that had put into operation his wily schemes, it was certain that justice would be cheated of her due if he were permitted to go unscathed.

No sooner had the intelligence spread that the gang of bill dealers had been broken up, and that the assistance of the magistrates would be wanted to apportion them their acknowledged deserts, than communications from the provinces far and near were received, intimating how numbers of people had been fleeced, but how chary they were in making their special grievances known, for fear that the evil entailed, should be greater than the loss which the original transaction produced.

A short but summary inquiry at the nearest metropolitan police-court disposed of the three defendants, whose characters, when investigated, left not the slightest doubt of their complicity in the various charges preferred. The landlord, who was struggling for a licence, and myself were not unimportant witnesses in identifying the whole of the tribe, the writer with the swivel eye and the heavy, damp, red hand urging, nevertheless, that as far as he was concerned our recognition was to all intents and purposes a most egregious mistake. We ultimately had the satisfaction of ascertaining that subsequent evidence brought the cases endeavoured to be proved, most unmistakeably home to him and his two accomplices, and that they were committed for trial for the various frauds alleged against them.

My friend the landlord was not content with seeing them consigned to condign punishment, but he was anxious to follow up and discover, if possible, the concealment of "old fur-collar." We had, it should be stated, settled the transaction in which my country cousins had been concerned, and though I could have escaped the penalty of any payment had I been so disposed, considering the circumstances under which the bills had been obtained—a contract was a contract, and the sum promised was duly deposited with those who were employed to defend the son, the daughter, and the daughter's husband. The money, there was good reason to believe, was fairly expended; but hard as the case was fought in their favour there was no miscarriage, and the majesty of the law was, in that instance at least, vindicated in the most complete manner.

But where was "old fur-collar" all this time? Was it to be supposed that he could evade the officers of justice, and place at defiance the authority of those who were bent upon obtaining the custody of his person? Yes; he had determined to brave the great peril of apprehension, and to settle his account with nature in a way that satisfied his own scruples.

A man of stern resolve and hardened conduct, why should he fear "to shuffle off this mortal coil"? He already stood disgraced before the world, his habits and late course of living had long marked for him a desperate end. This exposure, if it came, and there was no hope of avoiding it, would be a more agonizing death than any species of self-immolation. And here the symphony of the low, short, hollow cough rose in all its discordant tones, to give him courage in the execution of a design that had often before presented itself to his mind, when overtaken by doubt or fear of discovery.

He had been concealed in an old out-house abutting on the canal, and there as he looked out upon the dark surrounding water, it required only a little nerve to accomplish that which he had often promised himself should be his fate, sooner than accept the responsibility of a trial. Since the time of his flight he was quite aware that he possessed one means only of escaping from the paths of his pursuers, viz., through the dread portals of death.

He was worked into a state of strong excitement through the fear of speedy arrest and imprisonment. The resolution once formed was soon carried out. An old but vigorous man, he mounted the scantling that could scarcely bear his weight. The moon was up, and her clear, bright rays threw a cold, still light athwart the stream; he plunged head foremost with a dull leaden sound. There was a momentary struggle, then he sank, and as his form was lost to view, heavy black clouds floated onward, overshadowing the scene of that dark but long meditated crime. A low, short, hollow cough seemed to rise from the depths of the waters, reverberating in mocking tones for an instant on the dull night air, and then there reigned the silence of death !

A reward was offered by the authorities for the apprehension of the delinquent, who was supposed to have evaded, through some mysterious influence, the strong meshes of the law. Bills were posted, describing him by name and person, and challenging, as they did, the attention of parties who were presumed to know his haunts and his practices, the inhabitants of the neighbourhood were all agog to surrender him to justice.

Little did they imagine that the dark, dank, stream which lazily took its way through the suburb in which they dwelt, covered the mortal remains of him they sought, or that within a stone-throw of one of his old tenements which had sheltered him in his hours of peril, was deposited the pallid corpse that only required a few turns of the lock-tide to bring it to the surface, and clear away the mystery.

Children at play on the borders of the canal spoke, with "bated breath," of the pleasure it would afford them if he could be discovered, and of the readiness they would exhibit in communicating his whereabouts, if it should fall to their lot to be the first to furnish the tidings to those who were interested. An old, broad-brimmed hat, battered and torn, disfigured by contact with the barges and billy-boy boats, at length floated near. It was weltered and puffed by submersion in its passage down the slow, turgid stream, and as it reached the edge of the canal some of these very mud-larking juveniles with the aid of their sticks brought it on shore. Made the sport of the moment, and tossed from hand to hand, it stood a fair chance of immediate destruction; but one boy, more inquisitive than the rest, took it up— and, lo! on a scrap of paper, fastened inside, were these ominous words, "*Seek, and ye shall find, near the spot where this floats, evidence of the last sad link in the history of the —— Farm.*"

The old weather-beaten hat with its singular inscription was shown to passers-by, and it was not long before the truth flashed upon the mind of more than one who had known "old fur-collar" in the days of his supposed prosperity. After a little delay the drags were procured, and the banks of the canal having meanwhile become crowded, in the presence of a motley assembly, among whom stood the indefatigable landlord, was brought, from the muddy depths of the opposite side of the stream, the body of the missing man, drenched and covered with the slime there accumulated.

The mystery of his surmised escape was at once solved; an inquest, with its formal but terse explanations, elicited all the requisite facts, and a verdict in accordance with the weight of testimony was returned. The gang was now fairly dispersed; "old fur-collar" had, by his summary process, made his exit for ever, and his companions in crime were deprived of the power of effecting additional mischief.

My friend the landlord, who had been so long struggling for a licence, happily had to struggle no more. Some good genius, perhaps propitiated by his active services in assisting to break up the doubtful financial establishment, introduced him, not to the coachman of the chief magistrate, but to that august personage himself; and, after one or two visits to a large white house, situated not far from Stamford Hill, the long-coveted privilege was obtained, and he has ever since been pursuing a thriving and lucrative trade.

I never pass mid-way between Haggerstone and Dalston without thinking of the weary hours spent in seeking out the history of this great "monetary firm," of the low, short cough of "old fur-collar," which still seems occasionally to resound in my ears, and of the damp, heavy red hand which was waved in wild defiance of me when its possessor was removed from the bar of the police-court, protesting his perfect innocence.

XXXI.

" A SOUTHERLY wind and a cloudy sky," according to the recognized rules of the chase, " proclaim a hunting morning." But, to whatever extent this may hold good in country sporting circles, which happily are becoming more general than ever, the simile scarcely carries weight when it is applied to the more proscribed domains of the metropolis, where every now and then we can witness without such accompaniments the exciting scene of what may not inappropriately be termed " a run with the Joint-Stock hounds."

In the one case, it may be very requisite to be booted and spurred in the most approved fashion, to mount the " pigskin," and turn out *cap-à-pie*, so as to suit the taste of those who are fastidious in such matters ; but the sport in the other case does not require the strict observance of any of these regulations, and a fair amount of modest assurance, with a favourable " scent," is all that is essential to give real zest to this recently much patronized pastime.

At the old familiar meet, in days gone by, in the midst of the crowd of well-groomed, sleek, and panting steeds, and strongly-proportioned and fine-featured patricians—" What is it ?" as they opened and spread, was the true Meltonian inquiry. " Dog fox, my lord ;" " Gone away ;" " Hark forward !" " Tally-ho !" resounded on all sides, and the hounds in full cry were up to their work, and no flinching, or woe betide any lazy, lagging fellow who came within the range of old Beppo's whip.

And then the chase itself—the break-neck, splitting pace, the ups and downs, 'cross country, the rasping fences, the quick-set hedges, the tough wattled gates, and the frightful croppers! What mettle and nerve it required to pull through the short hours that preceded the sure fate of poor Reynard, wily and artful as he might be in running to earth, or throwing the hounds off his trail! But greater the struggle to be in at the death, to reach there just in time to lose the "brush," and see some more favoured horseman bear away the trophy, though many had been left behind in endeavouring to secure it. Finally, the return home, the congratulations of your friends and yourself upon the numerous hair-breadth escapes, the joys of the field, and the beauty and courage of certain Dianas and Phillises, who had the temerity to break ground and go forward like men, compensate for ill-luck, or the knowledge that next time you had a "purl," it should be in company such as you are now so unwilling to leave.

Would to Heaven that a run with the Joint-Stock hounds could strike out such incidents, leave reminiscences so agreeable, and end in a way so manifestly healthful to all concerned! Not, however, the less exciting is it when the game is fairly in view, or when the object to be gained is sufficiently important to warrant the comparative hazard of the adventure. There is, it is true, nothing to be apprehended from the dangers usually associated with a hunting excursion of this class; though those dangers, by the acknowledged disciples of Nimrod, are considered to contribute part of the delights of the enjoyment ; but an exciting run within the proscribed limits of a mile of the Royal Exchange, with an occasional look-in at the lobby of the House of Commons—it has always been supposed rather difficult to entrap Peers—entails fatigue, expense, and frequent disappointment, second only to that experienced within the charmed circle of " merrie England," represented either in Leicestershire or Northamptonshire.

However my friends or myself ever became sufficiently infatuated to run in such a course is positively a marvel; but that they did do so, and induced me, with the notion of seeing a little of Joint-Stock life, to follow with them, need not be disguised. It will furnish matter for a page in history, and perhaps will not prove one of the most uninstructive that was ever penned.

Two of these possessed the basis of a project as *bonâ fide* as ever was constituted, but the great drawback that existed, as has been the case with many a sound and *bonâ fide* project before, was that directors could scarcely be obtained for love or money. A first-class board was necessary, a second-class would hardly be looked at; but the great embarrassment was, could either the one or the other be obtained? To place ourselves in connexion with some of the great promoters of the day would have been an easy task; to barter the scheme for a mere pecuniary advantage could have been done with profit to those who had taken the trouble to mature its details; but believing in the undertaking, and assured that it would supply an acknowledged want, we determined on risking, not precisely "life and limb," but a little time and money in having " a run with the Joint-Stock hounds."

How pleasantly the iris hues of a thriving and prosperous concern tinged our imagination. We did not go in for promotion money; that was simply vulgar and ungenteel. What we desired to do was to benefit the general community, and leave posterity to deal with the names of the founders of the institution, and, if need be, to erect monuments to their memories. We were so completely satisfied with our own position in the affair, that we were simply surprised the British public—and thank goodness one always can appeal to the British public—did not come with wings of pure Britannia metal, and bear our scheme to a safe haven of usefulness, so perfectly was it identified with philanthropic objects and a lasting and enduring name.

For months we had every day counted upon succeeding with the preliminaries to secure a board; but notwithstanding half promises, and as nearly as possible whole ones, were made, when we arrived at the moment of settling these things we found in reality we were as far off as ever. How long this project—which merely required the light of the day (at least so we thought) to render it one of the great luminaries in the Joint-Stock hemisphere—would have remained in a darkened dilemma it would be impossible to say, had not the services of one who was supposed " to know something about these things," been impressed for the special object of giving it vitality. There could be no doubt that the *Greenland Bank* (limited) with the co-operative establishment of the *Lapland Credit Foncier* (limited) would, when it was thoroughly known, attract subscriptions which must place it without the pale of rivalry with any other similar undertaking; but, though every endeavour had been exerted to secure it a favourable reception, it had been looked upon with comparative coldness, and as shadowing forth impracticable financial ideas.

Frigid as was the feeling in some quarters towards this enlightened and philanthropic endeavour, which was not only to give the inhabitants of those dreary regions proper banking facilities, but also to settle and convert upon a sound footing their territory—or that portion of it which might be considered capable of development, we felt that if the case were placed with discretion before the right individuals, they would, like ourselves, warm in favour of the character of the enterprise, and give it unbounded support. Statistics were at our fingers' end to illustrate the vast trade of the whale fisheries, the necessity of giving captains and their crews the advantage of monetary accommodation, and of the profits to be made from deposits during their several years' voyages. The freehold privileges of Lapland sites, the prolific nature of the crops during the short summer, and the economy with which agricultural operations were followed through the dead seasons, incontestably proved the perfect certainty of full returns from that source, the sole delicacy being the actual estimate of any dividend for fear it should be placed at a *minimum* instead of a *maximum* amount.

But now, having so far entered into the scheme, and being more or less determined to see how a board of directors could be secured, the next step was to take counsel with our sage adviser as to what was to be the mode of proceeding. Our good friend, Septimus Twilight—we fancied ourselves fortunate in obtaining the assistance of one, who was by name or other relations, partially identified with the locality of the project—considered the enterprise extremely sound, containing the germs of a great success, but he feared names would be difficult—at least such as he really liked, because the ground had been so harrowed, that of unqualified or qualified directors who were worth a rush, there were scarcely any left. He promised it his best attention, and that was guaranteeing something; for notwithstanding the three of us were thoroughly imbued with the importance and lucrative character of our great project, we could not, so far as we had tried, get anybody else to be of a similar opinion.

The "meet" had now commenced in real earnest—for though we had frequently before consorted together with the object of arranging a board of directors, we had invariably failed in getting beyond the solicitor, the secretary, and the auditors. These any of us could have at any time named, since we were all ready to appoint individual friends to lucrative posts of this description, and it did not require substantial interest to arrange nominations of this kind, further than that which was allied with the ordinary routine of filling up the prospectus with names likely to be useful, though the grand blank still remained, the list of directors.

Septimus Twilight was a man of consideration and judgment. The ornamental and useful he confessed he was pleased to recognize, but the great thing needed was a start with the board. It was not a mere myth, this desire to put into practical training the selection of individuals to carry out the project, for if it were ever to float—to use his own well-timed and properly-appreciated expression—it would be through the influence of a first-class list of directors. We ourselves thought that there was a great deal in the title and co-operative character of the enterprise, the *Greenland Bank* (limited) and the *Lapland Credit Foncièr* (limited); but he, with that remarkable intuition which could alone proceed from a thorough acquaintance with the subject, candidly informed us that had the scheme possessed more favourable attributes than those, which we had so glowingly set forth upon the various sheets of foolscap paper which constituted the sum of intelligence submitted to his consideration, it would have little chance with the purblind public, who were more desirous of obtaining, through direct or indirect means, a fair proportion of premium in preference to supporting legitimate undertakings.

At first it was proposed that we should give the patient British public their choice of supporting the undertaking, calculated as it was to set at rest all thought of dishonest rivalry or competition—seeing that the field of enterprise was far removed from where there could be supposed to be conflicting interests—without the magical presence of directors, and simply rely on its intrinsic merits of presumptive progress and profit, to secure the requisite subscription. This notion our sage adviser at once laughed to scorn, reminding us that it would be better to initiate our existence with even the great polar bear from the Zoological Gardens as permanent president, than seek the suffrages of the monetary world without a sufficient array of dignified and well-credited names.

It was necessary, therefore, under his special guidance, as we had so far consented to adopt the character, to take an ordinary run with the Joint-Stock hounds. The pack was not large in number, but consisting of ourselves and one or two others who knew the field, and whose services might be considered beneficial, we did not hesitate to take the earliest opportunity of breaking " cover," believing that our efforts would be crowned with the most signal success.

Shades of Tom Moody and Jonathan Oldaker spare me while I make the revelation. Never were endeavours to unkennel a fox rewarded with such ingratitude. But it is hardly perhaps at present the period to speak of the base insincerity of the British public who, with such a scheme displayed before their admiring gaze, perseveringly ignored its value, and unhesitatingly refused to provide the simple million sterling that would have satisfied the whole area of *Greenland Banking*, and set for ever on its legs that stable institution, the *Lapland Credit Foncier* (limited).

Septimus Twilight was a man of business. He had long revelled in the organization of public undertakings, and could only be " squelched" by a panic. Like the floating waifs and strays on a stream, he was ever buoyant when the tide ran strongest. His jewelled pendants and his general adornments gave evidence of his great achievements in this line of life, and a directorate was not worth having if it failed to produce a clear thousand pounds. His grand auxiliary, Horatio Coodove—the gentleman who volunteered his assistance in the amiable school, and who could do the soft and insinuating, and turn the heart of an adamantine director when it was least expected—was introduced to participate in the day's sport, and to show those qualifications just enumerated to the most perfect advantage. Though we ourselves did not altogether believe in these blandishments, we were distinctly informed that if we wished the great *Greenland Bank* (limited) and the *Lapland Credit Foncier* (limited) to go, we must be ruled by these suggestions, and their aid having been invited, it would, to say the least of it, have been uncivil at the last moment to refuse their services.

It is nothing but justice to allow that these gentlemen went about the affair in a most methodical manner, and that but for the obdurate inconsistency on the part of the British public, who are more frequently far behind than before their age, this important scheme, the general particulars of which have been referred to, would have been launched, and its paying capacities ere this fully tested. But perhaps, in indicating the course of events, I am in a degree forestalling a faithful record of a run with the Joint-Stock hounds.

We, the projectors of the great enterprise, were allowed to stand only in a secondary character, to the prime movers in the organization of the bank and the board. We had prepared the outline of the undertaking in its skeleton form, and furnished that mass of intelligence, which in every prospectus crops out and astonishes the weak nerves of expectant subscribers, whether shares float or not. Our friends, on the other hand, with supple freedom, were to mould this into shape, and what could not be proved would be taken for granted, only the estimated dividend must be first rate, and not in the least problematical. On this they based their notion of the result, in a sanguine manner it is true, but not more sanguine than we ourselves had pictured the fruition of the scheme if it were ever regularly launched.

And now the exciting period of the chase was at hand. The prospectus had been printed, temporary offices had been secured to give a status and locality to the enterprise, and solicitors', bankers', brokers', and auditors' names inserted with proper formality. A day was arranged, and the hour fixed, when we were to meet our sporting friends, the bold and adventurous Twilight, and the plausible and insinuating Coodove. They were to introduce an additional individual to show the ground, and if necessary, to act as whipper-in, as his special acquaintance with the whole of the houses associated with the Greenland and Lapland trades would, it was considered, be most invaluable in directing us in the right course.

It was convenient to the whole of us to have a final

preliminary assembly, at the private residence of our chief adviser, Twilight, to settle a few points of importance—for the project had now approached a stage that would render necessary a clear understanding relative to the proportion of promotion money, and other profits to be divided. Slightly verdant, as we the grand originators of the enterprise were, we nevertheless, in justice to ourselves, thought it desirable to set this straight, in order that hereafter, no difficulties might be raised among one another on the subject. The arrangement, therefore, to pay a morning call upon our friend in his apartments, not far removed from Belgravia, was agreeable to everyone, even including Horatio Coodove, and the taciturn and reserved Mr. Reachem, who now appeared actively on the scene for the first time. This gentleman had evidently been a strong ally of the courageous Twilight, for he had frequently insinuated how valuable the assistance of Mr. Reachem would be. It was clear from the moment of our introduction, that any information he possessed, or services he could give, would simply be for the benefit of Twilight, to assist in "screwing" as much as he could out of the *Greenland Bank* (limited) and the *Lapland Credit Foncier* (limited).

When we arrived at the apartments of Twilight—well situated and georgeously furnished,—Horatio Coodove and the reserved Mr. Reachem were busily employed in settling lists of directors. Coodove was extremely vivacious, and thoroughly satisfied with his own suggestions; but Reachem, who seemed dyspeptic and uncertain, did not agree altogether with his views. When, however, he did, he smiled, but it was a ghastly smile, that failed to invoke the least confidence. Twilight said he had prepared his list of directors—he appeared always to have everything cut and dried—and only waited for Coodove, with the assistance of Reachem to settle his; then we could compare names, and bringing our own individual experience to bear, see what would be our chances of obtaining a sufficient number to give due vitality to our project. Meanwhile Twilight was making capital of our astonishment at his style of living, of the success that he assured us had attended his past performances, and of the great prospects there were, of not only carrying out our undertaking, but a variety of others in which he was engaged. He spoke lightly of the simple £500 that was paid him as remuneration for his assistance in organizing the *Bantam Direct Railway Co.*, and intimated he was now much better up to his work, that having been his original essay in public undertakings. Directors, he considered, did not behave so liberally as they should, as he had discovered in the *Extra Mural Investment Co.* (limited), and therefore he would always advise friends in future to have their own lawyers, and insert promotion money without fear in the " Articles of Association." This would entitle them to stronger consideration, even if they chose subsequently to modify their claims.

The greatest slice he had ever made—but he had to fight hard for it—was, in the *White Sea Fishing Co.* (limited), when the chairman, an old retired Indian official, who was always ready to cut down other people's emoluments to increase his own, proposed instead of £1000 and 200 free shares, to reduce the whole to £250 in a money payment. That was a " scrimmage " and no mistake; but those on the direction who were in his interest, bravely supported his case, and he came off victorious; not only eventually beating poor Sicca Rupee, but assisting at his subsequent dethronement.

He pointed to his richly fashioned console tables; to his massive time-pieces in bronze; to his heavy damask window drapery; to his articles of *vertu*; and to his highly polished walnut furniture. Almost every item in the catalogue possessed a romantic history—a history connected with promotion arrangements, share transactions, and the other trifling guerdons proceeding from a close identity with joint-stock adventures. We listened patiently, but were thankful when he came to the end of his story.

It was amusing enough to hear it all without being critical, and startling as it was, I as well as my friends felt that if we much longer encountered the voice of the charmer, we should without doubt be ensnared. It was quite certain that he would expect to be well paid for his services if we were successful, and painful as it was to us before, to recognize our secondary position—the fact that we should be the least considered in any beneficial arrangement, became more strongly apparent than ever. We had not approached the delicate subject of a settlement, though it was understood it would be fully gone into; but Septimus Twilight guardedly alluded to the matter, and considered it would be best to endeavour to arrange directors, and ascertain something of the nature of our actual prospects. " Of course," he said, to use his precise language, "if the thing went, it would be a £8000 or £10,000 affair, and leave, after paying expenses, enough to satisfy everyone;" and we thought so to— but the latent apprehension had seized us of his intention to appropriate the lion's share. The memorandum of association was registered and defined, so far we were protected against ordinary designers, and then had merely to keep a vigilant look-out among ourselves.

Messrs. Coodove and Reachem were all this time engaged in making their list of directors, and though it had occupied longer than was imagined, it afforded the opportunity for the associate—perhaps accomplice would be the more appropriate word—to encouarge us with a laudatory account of his position, and to reduce, if possible, any estimate we might have formed of our own. We had not gone into the undertaking with the express purpose of making money—that we entirely repudiated —but if there was an advantage to be reaped, from a project which would elevate the character of Greenland and Lapland, as territories requiring and deserving financial support, we were scarcely prepared to allow either Twilight or his friends to run away with the whole of it. And now for the list of directors submitted for investigation—not that we had secured their promises, kind reader, or possessed any notion whether they would consent to act—but they were names well suited to give efficiency and life to our darling scheme, if a few only swallowed the bait presented to their consideration.

The list of directors brought under notice by Mr. Septimus Twilight was as follows, and included, as he euphoniously described it, "the trump cards of the pack," if their adhesion could be obtained. We scrutinized the names admiringly, and trusted we should succeed; but Mr. Reachem doubted it, because they comprised all "the top sawyers." If they were secured it could be alone through the indefatigable exertions of Twilight. Horatio Coodove imagined the list to be too good; the names were unexceptional, but who could approach them without channels were open, with which at present he had no acquaintance. After we had discussed

Mr. Twilight's list, Coodove would submit his—which if it did not contain the pick of the trades identified with our project, would, he thought, be useful, and might—a great thing in these days—be brought together.

LIST OF DIRECTORS PROPOSED BY MR. TWILIGHT.

Thomson Walrus, Esq., (Messrs. Walrus, Shingle, & Co.)
Andrew Pemmican, Esq., (Messrs. Pemmican, Snort, & Co.)
Richard Stunsail, Esq., (Messrs. Stunsail, Block, & Co.)
Benjamin Reefer, Esq., (Messrs. Reefer, Stevedore, & Co.)
Arthur Dyer, Esq., (Messrs. Harpoon, Dyer, and Lashing.)
Abraham Weather, Esq., (Messrs. Weather, Dunlop, and Passett.)
Duncan Overshot, Esq., (Messrs. Longspike, Overshot, and Ramadge)
Nathaniel Grampus, Esq., (Messrs. Grampus, Staunchion, and
   Lockbolt.)

All of us were satisfied with such a list of names, as, if secured, our labours would be most successful. Septimus Twilight intimated that if half could be "booked," he would be bound to have the whole capital subscribed in three days, and the shares at 5 premium. But the great drawback was how could we get them. I knew as well as my friends several of the influential firms put down, the difficulty was, the manner in which they could be approached to elicit their opinions, without directly offending them. This was the great obstacle that presented itself to Mr. Twilight. He could obtain introductions to the principals of the houses indicated, but the individuals, he apprehended, would not be seduced by a promise of "qualification," or any of the usual kinds of patronage which a seat at "a board" ensures.

Mr. Reachem having quietly canvassed every point, combatting some and defending others, at last manfully put it to us whether it would not be better to clear away all questions at once, by vigorously setting to work,

and either obtaining consents or refusals. At the same
time he suggested that it would be well to examine the
list prepared by our bland and insinuating friend, in case
in any of our rounds, we should be able on losing the
great fish to hook the small. True piscator as I am, I
immediately agreed to so reasonable a proposition; and
the others with all readiness assented. The names proposed by Horatio Coodove, in the place of those set down
by Septimus Twilight, if the latter could not be obtained, were :—

Henry Beaver, Esq., (Messrs. Beaver, Gordon, and Rush).
Edward Stargaze, Esq., (Messrs. Moondown, Stargaze, and Co.)
Thomas Darknight, Esq., (Messrs. Darknight, Hazy, and Black).
Frederick Yanlard, Esq., (Messrs. Yanlard, Tackle, and Brace).
Goodson Jollyboy, Esq., (Messrs. Jollyboy, Rullock, and Skip).
Jonathan Clewsail, Esq., (Messrs. Capstan, Clewsail, and Davit).
Brewster Flushdeck, Esq., (Messrs. Flushdeck, Brightspar, and
    Kinkle).

These seven names against the eight others, Mr. Coodove contended, were more likely than not to be procured;
first, because they represented several of the second-
class struggling houses, whose interest it was, to run a
muck against their wealthier compeers, especially since
the Yankees had so largely interfered with the fisheries.
Such houses as Walrus, Shingle, and Co.; Pemmican,
Snort, and Co.; or, Stunsail, Block, and Co., would not
join, it scarcely being to their advantage to do so. Their
fleet of vessels and outfit were paid for; they required no
accommodation, and made more from their captains and
crews, without the intervention of banking, than they
would with it. On the other hand, houses similar to those
in his list, such as Beaver, Gordon, and Rush; Darknight,
Hazy and Black; or, Capstan, Clewsail, and Davit, would

but be too glad to gain facilities, not merely for immediate purposes, but likewise to prepare against the exhausting process of long voyage accounts.

Arguments such as these could not be well resisted,
and before we severally took our departure with our lists
for the places indicated, each selecting the names he was
best acquainted with, or to whom he could get the most
favourable introductions, it was agreed that the amalgamation principle with the names, should be tried, rather than
not ensure the constitution of a working board. Septimus
Twilight, assisted by his old coadjutor Reachem, and one
of my friends, took one route; Horatio Coodove, myself,
and a third, followed another; but cover the ground
as energetically as we could, the first two days passed
with scarcely the slightest encouragement. We were
always tumbling over each other in our rounds—first it
was Twilight who had good news, which he hoped to
report on the morrow; he could not say a promise, but
nearly a promise, of one of the very best of his names.
Next it was Horatio Coodove, who, if he could not make
up a board of high-class names, felt satisfied, from the
manner in which the scheme was received and its prospects spoken of, that at least a fairly selected second-
class board would, in the course of a week, be obtained.

If anything, he was more sanguine than either Twilight or Reachem, but I could not tell precisely on what
grounds; for, notwithstanding we had trapesed Leadenhall Street, Limehouse, and Rotherhithe, to our hearts'
content, we had received little better than the cold
shoulder from the large Greenland interest; and the Lapland connection being comparatively exclusive, wholly
depended upon the satisfactory issue of our recognition in
the former quarter.

But, notwithstanding I despaired, Horatio Coodove would not be dismayed; he looked on the bright side of everything; he was sure we had made an impression in one quarter at least, though I must frankly avow I could not discover it; and if we only secured that director and his influence, he was perfectly convinced we should have very little difficulty in completing the board.

He referred to an interview that had taken place with the best of the names on his own list; but although I was in his company at the time, and the conversation that occurred was agreeable enough, the great Mr. Beaver had scarcely received our advances in the encouraging manner he described. I reminded him that I did not think the gentleman (he was a Rotherhithe ship-chandler) was altogether so favourably impressed with the scheme as he supposed; but he mildly reproved me, adding that he had watched the crafty individual, and could discern through his simulated abruptness, a hankering to be placed upon the direction. When I had worked so long in a similar pursuit to himself, I should, he said, become more acquainted with the particular idiosyncracies of the director-seeking fraternity. I imagined my rebuke was well merited, thanked him for the information, and determined silently to myself that he should always in future, while I was in company with him, take the lead in the field.

Twilight, Reachem, and my other poor friend—the latter very nervous—reported anything but sanguinely of the result of their exertions. The great Greenland interest, as represented by their list, were antagonistic to the last degree against any associated enterprise; directors were not obtainable, though every inducement had been held out to secure the junior members of the least important firms. If the Greenland interest could not be propitiated, what chance was there of bringing in the Lapland element ? Territorial acquisitions were all very well, and the basis of any arrangement that would include undisputed right over the enormous tracts remaining out of cultivation, should not be despised. But, separate and apart from the banking element, which could alone be provided through the Greenland trading community, it would be simply ridiculous to endeavour to mature the enterprise.

This was the fashion in which the question was argued by Twilight and Reachem. My representative on their route was so overdone by the supposed blank refusals they had received—for he was not at all times present at these interviews—that he could not advance a single word in reply, and his countenance only too plainly indicated how pleased he would be if relieved from a further run with the Joint-Stock hounds.

We were not prepared, however, to resign our quarry so readily. Coodove and Twilight—the one full of specious blandishment concerning the benefit to posterity that would accrue from the undertaking ; the other most meretricious and mercenary, with a strong eye to the all-prevailing consideration of £. s. d.—were not unwilling to continue their exertions, hoping that the scheme would eventually, with the purpose of serving their own views, come out all right. My friends and myself assuredly wished the same, but perhaps our notions on the subject were slightly dissimilar to those entertained by our trustworthy and most energetic coadjutors.

Brought up in the unromantic school, we rather shuddered at some of the bold devices suggested by Messrs. Twilight and Reachem, to ingratiate ourselves with individuals who, it was supposed, could exert influence upon names or connections required, and when we evinced the least alarm, remonstrating against any such proceeding, Coodove was always ready at hand to smooth down the difficulty, and propose some other plan of operations. Reachem, for a purpose that was subsequently discovered, unhesitatingly avowed he disliked timid men, who were unwilling to put in force every available stratagem to attain a desired end, and he very agreeably volunteered his advice that it would be better to abandon the thing altogether, than move forward in a doubtful manner.

Although this we believed was an endeavour to dispirit us, it induced increased exertion on our part; and Horatio Coodove, who more than ever professed to be enamoured of our project, declared he would put his shoulder to the wheel, and see if it could not, without further delay, be favourably launched. Another day or two's work, he considered, ought to put it in shape; and when the time for the due announcement of the *Greenland Bank* (limited) and the *Lapland Credit Foncier* (limited) arrived, what a neat festival would follow at the Albion, or the London Tavern !

Disappointed as we had been, we rallied at these fresh prospects ; we fancied once more that our scheme, Icarus-like, would soar at an unbounded elevation, and that the pinions of the British public, elastic usually as they appear to be, would support and give a vitality to its existence, sufficiently encouraging to recompense us for all our toil and annoyance.

" *Dum vivimus vivamus,*" says the old Latin proverb ; and so satisfied were we with this renewed assurance of success, that we anticipated the proposed little entertainment with the view of stimulating Horatio Coodove in the exertions required to surmount all difficulties. By some strange accident, neither Twilight nor Reachem could favour us with their company. Their absence afterwards was accounted for; they were probably better engaged; but "the feast of reason and the flow of soul" seemed wonderfully to agree with their patient companion.

The "scent" was once more gained. The next day we were hard at it; not, however, with much more actual results than had been previously ensured. Unfortunately, Twilight and Reachem were less punctual than usual in keeping their engagements. Another business Coodove intimated absorbed their attention; they had lost so much time in attempting to bring the *Greenland Bank* (limited) and the *Lapland Credit Foncier* (limited) to bear, that they were compelled to give some of their valuable assistance to another project that was to afford unparalleled advantages to the British public, and place new financial facilities at the command of those who might desire to make them available.

Lulled as we were into fancied security by these specious representations, we continued our labours, and our darling pet enterprise was more than once on the eve of completion—so, at least, Coodove asserted—requiring only the necessary finishing touches to settle the board, and place it in a condition to meet the broad light of day. Nevertheless, in our rounds—for we were still running in our approved character with the Joint-Stock hounds—we occasionally fell across Septimus Twilight, and that inseparate of inseparables, Mr. Reachem, who, though occupied with another undertaking, found it convenient to be on the same track, and, singularly enough, in the same neighbourhood.

For the moment it never struck us that there was any foul play or double dealing, and we communicated freely and confidingly the issue of the various inquiries we were making, and the probable chances of establishing our concern. Twilight was more enthusiastic than he had ever been before, and Mr. Reachem was particularly attentive and courteous. The scheme on which they were temporarily engaged was a secret—a profound secret, but as they were canvassing part of the same interests—the great Greenland and Lapland interests—they assured us that they believed they would be in a position in a few days, to throw the surplus of their strength into our current, giving us the kind of momentum which would be most essential, in placing us beyond the risk of all future failure.

Horatio Coodove was as well pleased as we were ourselves at these promises to put our vessel in trim for fair sailing, and the sincerity of Twilight was apparently second only to his generosity when he informed us, twirling his heavily-linked gold guard chain, and settling a huge diamond brooch in his cravat, that "the thing " upon which he was employed promised so well, that he should certainly not think of participating in our promotion money, and that we might arrange that affair in a manner to suit our own general convenience.

Coodove was extremely elated; he was now, with the appreciative feeling of men of his class, looking for a larger share of what was to be forthcoming when our highest aspirations were realized; but while he hesitated openly to avow the fact, he quietly insinuated there would be more to divide since Twilight had retired, and had, as a matter of course, taken Reachem with him. Still we worked, and worked with a will, and not the least suspicion was

entertained that we had been trepanned or treacherously
dealt with, until after having secured two directors—only
think of that, kind reader, two live directors—and seeking a third, who had already given a sort of semi-promise,
we discovered to our utter dismay that he had gone over
and joined another board, organized and nearly completed
by our staunch friend Twilight, and his ghastly ally the
redoubtable Mr. Reachem!

The sapient Mr. Grampus—for that was the identical
gentleman—informed us with most perfect coolness that
the name of the new undertaking having been imparted
to him confidentially, could not be divulged ; but this he
might communicate—viz., that the locality of operations
was nearly identical with our own, it being at the same
time intended to carry out arrangements on a very enlarged
basis.   The steady Mr. Grampus, in explanation to further
inquiries, condescended to state that the weight of the
Greenland and Lapland interest had been encompassed
by these very opponents, and that old Walrus, of Walrus,
Shingle, and Co., having gone with them, the best houses
in these respective trades would most certainly follow.

Here was a severe shock to our most sanguine expectations ; my friends and myself could hardly imagine
such villany possible.   Horatio Coodove, whose ordinary
forms of expression were typical of his name, broke into
most ungovernable fury, and strongly anathematized
professional promoters in general, and Septimus Twilight
in particular.   To restrain his ebulition of temper was a
task which we essayed, but essayed in vain, till we promised that, both for his and our own gratification, we
would seek out the base deceivers, and if we could not
obtain the requisite satisfaction, we would brand them in
the eyes of the British public as men without honour, and

a disgrace to society.   How strongly those terms sounded;
how we thought their free use would make the varlets
quail.   How differently the *dénouement* turned out, we
shall presently see; as also the consummate ease with
which the long-suffering British public is occasionally
bamboozled.

It required moderate perseverance only to follow up
the supposed delinquents in their retreat.   They had
exhibited an amount of moral turpitude which we considered deserved exposure, and though we were prepared
to find that they considered they were relieved from any
obligation of a connection with our enterprise, especially
after the intimation from Septimus Twilight, that we might
"apportion our promotion money as most convenient," we
were not inclined to allow them to escape, without fixing
them with the obloquy which we imagined they merited.

When we repaired to the private residence of our
quondam friend, and there discovered him engaged with
the imperturbable Mr. Reachem—for they were doubtlessly
occupied in drafting the very prospectus that was to
make their fortunes—it was some short period before we
could obtain an audience.   We ourselves were rather
annoyed at the want of respect paid to the announcement
of our names; but Horatio Coodove—the sucking turtle,
as we had considered him in all the relations associated
either with Septimus Twilight or his dreamy *confrère*—
grew positively pallid when it seemed we should be compelled to wait the pleasure of those gentlemen, surcharged
as they professed to be, with weightier business.

It was no small exercise of patience that induced us
to receive an intimation, proffered with the most cool
assurance, that we might wait or call again, with comparative grace, and had it not been for our feeling that the

emergency of the occasion warranted us in pursuing our inquiry, we should have retired in dudgeon, and taken other measures to have brought our competitors to book.

Gaining admission, after some little delay, to the *sanctum sanctorum* of the marvellous Mr. Twilight, he pretended to be most remarkably staggered at the circumstances which should have introduced us to his presence—assuming that we were most intently employed upon maturing our grand scheme, and that no other consideration could for the moment enter into our heads. Horatio Coodove and myself were the first to inform him of what we imagined to be a great breach of contract with regard to the *Greenland Bank* (limited), and the *Lapland Credit Foncier* (limited); and particularly on the rumoured intention of himself and Mr. Reachem to introduce to the public another scheme, based upon the very substratum of our project, with, probably, the identical names mentioned in our list, and the special information furnished through exclusive channels.

Never do I remember a man—hardened though he may have been—to have received a bill of impeachment with greater *sang froid*. It has fallen to my lot on many occasions to have seen individuals confronted in great and small peccadilloes, but certainly Septimus Twilight encountered "the attaint of treason" with a courage and nerve, that unless it had been witnessed, would never have been credited. While not in the least displaying temper, he denied that his conduct deserved the severe animadversion passed upon it, and he was only too ready to call Mr. Reachem, to assist in proving that his negotiations had been of the most disinterested description. Still, notwithstanding he admitted that his project would trench upon our ground, he was most careful to preserve its perfect *incognito*, believing that, as in the majority of cases, if the real facts transpired, that they would not merely compromise the enterprise, but also the very individuals connected with it.

Provoking, indeed, was it to perceive that although Horatio Coodove, myself, and my friends endeavoured to instil into the mind of Mr. Twilight that he had not behaved fairly or honourably to us, he was far from impressed with the absence of moral obligation in endeavouring to supplant us. The British public could, in its wisdom, adopt either of the projects it pleased; ours was pretty well known, having been freely ventilated —the other, to use a sporting phrase, was a " dark horse," but it might yet prove successful.

Hampered as Mr. Twilight and Mr. Reachem were in relation to the arrangements which they proposed to carry out, they rather appreciated the determined stand we made against being sacrificed, body and soul, to their interests. They promised munificently : their promises we did not care for ; and Horatio Coodove, sooner than consent to any terms of arrangement, would, to illustrate his own metaphor, have " seen them at the bottom of the sea."

It would be, to say the least of it, aggravating in the extreme to be foiled in our last endeavour to float the *Greenland Bank* (limited) and the *Lapland Credit Foncier* (limited), but we felt that we were now environed in a way, leaving scarcely any chance of escape. Our opponents possessed all our plans, they were thoroughly acquainted with the basis of operations, they were even completely aware of the origin of the undertaking. To find them, therefore, plotting against us in the noonday glare ; in fact, appropriating the very information

which was supposed to be simply intended for our mutual benefit, was something more than ordinary capacities
could tolerate.

Discussed as the question had been with Mr. Septimus
Twilight, and equivocal as seemed the position in which
he, with his friend, Mr. Reachem, was placed, they nevertheless possessed the brazen effrontery to imagine that
nature's law, "might not right," was the dominant prin-
ple, and by that they gravely said they would be guided.

If we, the quiet and unobtrusive individuals who had
selected the spot for these extraordinary banking and
credit operations, could place our scheme before the
British public in a proper manner, there would be every
chance of success ; but they, nevertheless, reserved to
themselves the right to make available their own resources,
and, if it should be deemed necessary, eclipse any and
every undertaking, that might be supposed to come into
competition with them.

Indeed, Septimus Twilight, in the *abandon* of the moment—for while perfectly at home sorting his papers and
giving instructions to his great ally and doubtful companion, Reachem, there was a *buffet* supplied with the
general course of refreshment—*naively* proposed that a
small refection, with a glass of Moselle, might set things
right, and lead to a more satisfactory understanding.

Myself and my friends, including the ever-vigilant
Horatio Coodove, at once scouted the proposition. We
discovered most completely the mesh into which we had
been drawn, and seeing the confidence our opponents
displayed, we were almost certain that they considered we
were at their mercy.

Our run, fatal as it had been, with the Joint-Stock
hounds, was nearly at an end. Although we had kept

up the pace, and braced our nerves to a pitch of excitement that had seldom, if ever before been equalled, we were not to be fortunate in the chase, and after manifold exertions and trials, were to be placed in the situation of being worsted by meaner hacks and less worthy sportsmen, who profiting by the expedients of the moment, were content to snatch a victory, through exceptional circumstances, which they had never properly earned.

It need scarcely be stated that we retired in deep disgust. The British public, long-suffering and patient as it is, might have the opportunity of subscribing to the *Greenland Bank* (limited) and the *Lapland Credit Foncier* (limited), but it appeared probable that another and more powerful company, was about to exhibit an attractive impersonation, with directorial names of the most distinguished calibre.

Was it surprising, then, that Septimus Twilight had in the generosity of his heart declined to participate in our promotion money, when he was well aware that the undertaking he was prepared to introduce would leave us, after an exhaustive career, " in at the death with the loss of the brush."

How shall we describe our feelings of mortified pride, when, a few days after the memorable interview—our worthy friends having at the last moment, made the most seductive promises of renewed exertions, to secure for us the certain realization of our fondest wishes—we encountered among the announcements of new undertakings—

THE ARCTIC AND ANTARCTIC BANK (LIMITED),

AND

THE KAMSCHATCA LAND AND TRADING COMPANY (LIMITED),

with an amalgamated board, from the pick of the names

which it was our duty to submit to those who proposed to enter into the great original scheme ?

Strong as our dissatisfaction had been at the proceedings of Mr. S. Twilight, and his close associate, Mr. Reachem, much more strongly was it enunciated when we discovered the real arrangement intended. The capital of the *Greenland Bank* (limited), and the *Lapland Credit Foncier* (limited), was simply a million. The capital of the *Arctic and Antarctic Bank* (limited), and the *Kamschatca Land and Trading Company* (limited), was two millions, with power to increase; and the prospectus contained, in a highly elevated and intensified form, the principal statistics, which we, at much cost and labour, had collected !

Although the promoters and the directors will no doubt use their best exertions to get the funds subscribed, we, as a favour, ask the British public to pause. It is not often that a scheme is presented to its notice for nothing; but we weary of the task of propitiating directors, and at the same time being most grievously disappointed with the result of our run with the Joint-Stock hounds, most willingly surrender the *Greenland Bank* (limited) and the *Lapland Credit Foncier* (limited) for its behoof, believing, as we most sincerely do, that it possesses all the elements of success, and requires a much smaller capital to develop it, than its tricky rival the *Arctic and Antarctic Bank* (limited), and the *Kamschatca Land and Trading Company* (limited), and, finally, that there will be less anxiety of ulterior consequences, should the sudden thaw in commercial enterprise, which is so perseveringly predicted, ever strongly set in.

The British public—as a British public—has the

opportunity afforded it of wisely discriminating, and it is confidently presumed, that of two evils it will chose the least. We candidly confess our object is to thwart the indefatigable endeavours of Mr. Septimus Twilight to make a market of the aforesaid British public, which, through either the one or the other institutions, would, if banking and credit facilities be required in such extreme regions, be equally well served. Let it not be supposed that ours is any other than the most disinterested proposition for protecting the British public— which, as a body, is so powerful and all-seeing as not to be able occasionally to protect itself.

XXXII.

THE public are deeply interested in a subject which has caused loud complaint for some time past, but which received no check till the Committee of the Stock Exchange took action, and passed, a short period since, a special regulation respecting the necessity of an increased amount of capital and deposit, being provided on the shares of new companies, before a settlement was permitted, or quotations were allowed in the official lists. Indeed, the facilities which were afforded for the issue of a limited number of shares, and the means taken to "manipulate" them, have so long been questions of dissatisfaction among the share-dealing public, that it is rather surprising some strong demonstration has not taken place before. The Committee of the Stock Exchange having at length interfered, it has brought the matter to a simple issue, and a high range in premiums, or activity in "rigging," is not for the present to be again expected.

The enforcement of this new law has already checked the success of several new undertakings, which presented prospects, when they were first announced, of the most encouraging character. Scarcely had they been announced before the shares were quoted at a strong elevation, but no sooner was this measure agreed to—shadowing forth a stringent policy—than down went the values, and they have not since sensibly recovered.

Although these undertakings have been remodelled, and the promoters are justified in continuing their labours to carry out their organization, the effect has been for the present discouraging, and it seems likely that the partial success of future schemes will be compromised. But this state of things must be viewed, more with regard to its premium-bearing prospects, than in relation to its active working when satisfactorily and honestly developed.

The Stock Exchange Committee have done perfectly right in passing the new rule ; and as it will hereafter become part of the recognized regulations of the establishment, it will prevent much of the mischief, hitherto made a ground of animadversion. The alteration has not been effected a moment too soon ; the only question is, should it have been allowed to apply retrospectively, instead of prospectively ? The general opinion seems to be, that the committee were scarcely wise in thus arranging for the operation of the change. Had they decided upon adopting the arrangement, and carrying it out without delay, they would have passed the rule, and fixed a date from which it should have taken operation, of course excepting those projects already announced.

They have, nevertheless, resolved otherwise ; and the principle now being adopted, it remains to be seen what its future effect will be upon the miscellaneous share market. Till some method of rearrangement shall be discovered by talented promoters, it is exceedingly probable it will restrict the formation of new undertakings ; first, from the larger number of shares which will have to be created to represent the half paid-up capital ; and, secondly, from the increased amount of deposit necessary to provide the capital subscribed. The allotment, through these means, will be spread over a wider surface, and will scarcely allow any trafficking in shares, and in the next £3 and £5 calls will entail a larger amount of risk than the public will, in the majority of cases, choose to incur.

This resolution will, therefore, during the time being at least, restrict much of the late animation, and success will not now so greatly depend upon the way in which a company is brought out, as it will upon its real and distinctive merits. So far, this must be admitted to be completely satisfactory, and it will be one of the first things which will assist in establishing a more healthy order of affairs, though it may for a time interfere with the current value of new shares, and the profits of the general school of operators.

The most desperate case of rigging which has long been known, is that associated with the shares of a new steam company introduced, and which has reached such a serious pitch, that the Committees of the Stock Exchange of London, Liverpool, and Manchester have been called upon, for the credit of the respective establishments, to investigate the case. Now, this business, it must be understood, does not arise from any arrangement with respect to the number of shares or to the amount paid, but simply occurs through competitive influence between rival promoters in Liverpool. At least this is the report circulated in London. In Liverpool, there may be rumours in which the same charge is alleged against London. The Manchester operators may probably like to divide the responsibility, and take their fair share of what is considered the blame of the movement.

Certain it nevertheless is, that the company was ushered into existence with very fair chances of success; but the shares not being subscribed so rapidly as was anticipated, the Liverpool people were inclined to support the undertaking by extensive purchases. This they did, and the quotation advanced. Another antagonistic party—also identified with a steam shipping company—endeavoured by sales to depress values, and, having undertaken a course of transactions between Liverpool and London, to a great extent accomplished their supposed object. Meanwhile subscriptions were received for the shares, and it then transpired, through one channel or other, that very few allotments would be sent out, and that in cases where such favours were conceded, the holders must consent to retain them five or six months, so as to support the market, and prevent the sellers from attaining their ultimate end—the depression of the price to a discount.

Owing to this state of things, a struggle between Bulls and Bears went on for at least two months, till the quotation, through the efforts of the former, was carried to a high premium, and the price from its strength now seems to be safe against further assaults from opponents. The questionable manner in which this value has been secured has naturally excited comment, and a number of individuals—of course among them many who have lost by adverse transactions—seek to appeal to the Committees of the Exchanges in London, Liverpool, and Manchester against the ratification of outstanding bargains. It must be admitted *in limine* that the conduct of the parties is reprehensible, and that the plan deserves the strongest condemnation. But it is the system that is to blame, and not the individuals who avail themselves of it. Do away with the system, which can easily be effected by the concurrent action of the several Exchanges, and there will be no more outcry on the subject.

Persons who sell that which they do not possess, must

always stand at a disadvantage against those who are either identified with, or know the course, that will be adopted by a particular company, and consequently they should avoid dealing with such contingencies staring them in the face. It is, no doubt, very annoying to make losses of this character; but if individuals will endeavour to secure shares, and before they have the opportunity of knowing whether they can obtain them, do not hesitate to sell, they must bear the brunt of such a doubtful proceeding. On the other hand, directors, when they invite subscriptions for 5000, 10,000, or 15,000 shares, should, if they receive extensive applications, apportion them as nearly rateably as possible, to prevent the frequency of complaints with regard to favouritism in such arrangements.

If directors would do this it would have a very encouraging effect upon the public mind, and the outside public would manifest a greater desire to support general undertakings than it does at present, in consequence of the shabby tricks it has been served when seeking, in a limited degree, to participate in the presumed returns from good enterprises. In every mania however, the same evil has had to be encountered as that now experienced; and whilst the Stock Exchange literally lives, in a great measure, upon this kind of excitement, it will scarcely seek to take active measures for its repression, unless the movement springs through pressure from without. To such an extent has the excitement been carried on the present occasion, that it has been a matter of serious consideration, and while the Bulls and the promoters are deserving of great blame, the Bears have not altogether exercised a wise discretion.

It was not to be imagined, with interests at stake as

important as those involved in a settlement, or an
arrangement of the account, that the occasion would be
lost, to see how far the Committee of the Stock Exchange
might in reality be inclined to take cognizance of the
question. Desperate as had been the exertions of former
promoters and their friends, to carry the price of shares
to an undue elevation, here was a case so patent to the
world that the application to secure a day for the adjustment of transactions was not likely to be considered, without a strong resistance on the part of those who believed
they were aggrieved by the conduct of parties, endeavouring to advantage themselves by the fictitious rise.

The Committee of the Stock Exchange have been
called upon to enquire into the merits of the case, and
they have very readily consented. The investigation
will be a long one, and it may elicit facts which will not
prove creditable to either side. In the zeal to secure
their respective causes, the parties identified with these
exceptional proceedings may have overstepped the bounds
of discretion, and while the Bulls have to all intents and
purposes purchased much more extensively than the
exigency of their situation warranted, the Bears, rushing to the other extreme, have doubtlessly forced the
market without the least notion of the danger they were
so signally incurring. Like their great prototype, in the
" Beggar's Opera," may they not exclaim, " Brother,
brother, we are both in the wrong ;" and taking counsel
from past experience if they find themselves, either
through a compromise or other expedient, relieved from
present difficulty, promise never to transgress so seriously
again.

It is nevertheless for the Committee of the Stock
Exchange, having decided this all-important case, to

adopt further measures for the regulation of dealing in the shares of public companies. The basis of their judgment in this instance has of course been founded on the particular evidence adduced; but it will be much more satisfactory if they endeavour to frame some such supplemental regulations as will prevent a recurrence of so disagreeable a *contretemps*.*

Many suggestions have been made, but none seem more feasible than that which proposes that the Stock Exchange shall prohibit operations in the stocks or shares of new enterprises, until the allotment has been regularly made, and the first deposit satisfied. If the speculators and dealers will operate in anticipation—and it is hardly to be hoped that any bye-law will in these days of competition restrain them—let it be entirely on their own responsibility, with no claim on the individual with whom they may negotiate the special business, save that of good faith among themselves.

When it is brought to such a pass as this, many of the more respectable brokers and jobbers will decline business of the sort, till after the period of allotment and payment of the deposit, and consequently if the evil which is now so great a matter of complaint be not wholly remedied, it will hereafter assume much less formidable proportions. It must at the same time be admitted, that while this speculative activity exists it will be impossible to legislate satisfactorily to suit all classes; and the dexterity of many will still be employed to evade the rules of the House, well intentioned and framed though they may be for the general protection of the public.

---

* While this chapter is passing through the press, the Committee of the Stock Exchange announce that they " refuse the settlement."

XXXIII.

IT is the year 186— (excuse the blank in the date, kind reader, for it is not always safe to be precise in a per-diction), and the mania for banking enterprise, financial and credit undertakings, may be supposed to have run its career, and I have returned home, weary and faint with the excess of arduous duties, to taste the comforts of the domestic hearth, with its attendant felicities.

I have struggled hard, and in vain, to keep my vision clear against the inroads of fatigue and exhaustion; but succumbing at length to the effects of a more than average day's toil, I gradually but surely sink into the arms of Morpheus. My couch is not richly caparisoned with silks from India's clime; my apartment is not fur-nished in regal state, nor is there any symptom of pomposity in the *entourement* of any of its appointments. It is nevertheless "Home, sweet home," and as I recline, not on buhl fretted work, but on real well-seasoned mahogany, the train of reflection runs lightly, if not pleasantly, upon the present, past, and the future.

Old Captain, the name of a prime favourite in the family, is keeping "watch and ward" within sound of another in-door trusty companion, Wales (named in honour of the good Prince that some day shall ascend the throne), to catch the remotest alarm from Rifle—one of the best of the canine race, who, safely housed outside, will at the sight of a policeman's bull's-eye, or the flutter of a servant's apron, send a sound through the welkin that would disturb the slumbering peace of the seven sleepers, were they ever so disposed to ignore a claim upon their attention.

So guarded, so cared for, what have I to do but to indulge my fancy, and, despite any of the cankering cares of life, to look out boldly at the fire, nod serenely at my lamp, and wish a calm adieu to the noisy, busy turmoil of commercial agitation for the next twelve hours?

But though I have dropped such cares and anxieties as are acutely experienced in mixing with the current where it seethes the strongest, even nature's sweet restorer, "balmy sleep," will not allow me to throw off wholly the responsibilities of the situation. My sensuous faculties, continuing to keep pace with, and overweigh the state of repose, into which I have so comfortably subsided, conjure up pictures of events and circumstances, which having happened before, may, in all human probability, happen again.

I fancy, and remember, kind reader, it is merely fancy, for imagination here is strongly brought into play, that a cloud, no bigger than a man's hand, is looming in the future, which portends a storm. The sky is blue, and clear, and the bright appearance of the high vault of heaven would induce every one to believe that the present will be as the past, all smooth and agreeable. In my steady dozing state this seems the prospect, but how long it will continue is the reflection which persistently arises. I, in the comatose condition, endeavour to shirk the answer; the interrogatory is nevertheless repeated and repeated with force, till I am compelled, as it were, to look with undisguised fear into the future.

The small dark cloud has assumed more noticeable proportions ; the sky, so brilliant and free from haze, has become overcast, and birds scud across the horizon as if imbued with a presentiment of approaching danger. I relapse once more, after a slight disturbance through these atmospheric influences, and feel relieved when the shadow, impalpable almost as it is, has passed.

Anon my sleep is fitful, and I turn reluctantly, to be again seized with still more alarming apprehensions. The raven of Denmark, one of the birds seeking refuge from elemental strife, is pursued by the double-headed eagles of Austria and Prussia, which, with extended wings, sharpened beaks, and outstretched talons, are evidently determined to wage war against their less well-armed adversary.

The Gallic Cock is prepared to ring his note of warning through all ranks, but the British Lion, with un-ruffled mane and depressed tail, stands in the rear per-plexed what situation to assume. The Russian Bear, askance in the distance, eyes the whole proceeding, dis-satisfied somewhat at the opportunity lost of reckoning up old scores with false and truckling friends.

Is the fable of Reynard the fox to be presently intro-duced into the scene, with the view of creating an European imbroglio, which shall increase the fertile plains of Italy, " one and undivided," preserve the strongholds of Denmark, and arrest the progress of German unity ?

In the midst of these fanciful imaginings—and recol-lect, courteous reader, they are merely the wild surmises of an over-taxed brain—the scene once more changes, and I am hurried into the presence of physicians who are

suddenly gathered together in the chamber of a valetudi-
narian, yclept Speculation. He is extremely plethoric—
hale and hearty, as it would seem, but the rude robust-
ness of his nature has made him the prey of virulent
disease.

Not but what symptoms of recovery are perceptible, if
the patient be properly attended to—and there are those
who, completely identified with his position, would risk
any amount of wealth to restore him, the only misgiving
being that he has made too free with a good constitution,
and compromised the chances of a successful treatment
by self-reliance on the efficiency of that, which is deno-
minated the "recuperative process."

Like all vigorous individuals, who scarcely know how
far they may tamper with their strength, he appears to
have played with his energies and toyed with the innate
force of his powers, till, struck down with partial paralysis,
the apprehension is aroused whether or not he may survive
the shock. Arraying himself in purple and fine linen, feast-
ing on the fat of the land, and seemingly never satisfied,
he has persistently ignored all premonitory warnings,
and hesitated to recognize the necessity of abstinence
until it was too late ; and when the period in reality arrives
for retirement from his exciting career, refuses to leave
until advised professionally that depletion is absolutely
necessary.

In my mind's eye I find this stalwart champion of
finance in its best days, reduced at last to the miserable
plight of being placed on a bed of sickness, surrounded
by his parasites, and his "medicine men," loud in their
wail at the unforeseen occurrence, and palavering as to
the remedies which shall be adopted to restore health
and vitality to the constitution, which has been so ruth-

lessly struck down. Struggling as the victim does—for, like the Indian overweighted with jewels and bangles, this very *embarras des riches* produces a serious reaction—he endeavours to throw off the burden which sorely distresses him; but at last, in his futile attempts to escape the responsibility of his situation, succumbs to its influence, and is almost buried in the dust.

But it appears to me—and, of course, it is only in the shape of dream haziness that I discern any of the supposed marvels here revealed—that this great Titanic form is reduced to mere nothingness from his own involuntary spasmodic movements to save himself. The well-proportioned figure of old Speculation, when I first viewed him, swathed as he was in furs from Astracan, fine linen from Calicut, and robes of Tyrian dye, has sadly diminished under the care of the selected notables called in to consult respecting his general state of health.

That figure, originally so commanding, and which, supported by a kind benignity, gave life and position to his name, might have been called the very Atlas of the commercial community, but now, notwithstanding the most sapient advice, and the most careful resort to palliatives, has become shrunk and withered, without the least flesh and muscle to afford it adequate support.

That countenance, formerly so buoyant and animated, with full swelling cheeks and flashing eyes, has steadily dwindled, and become pinched and wan, and there remains simply the shadow of what he was, contrasted with what he might have been, had his career proved more circumspect, and his flatterers less urgent in forcing him down the road to ruin.

My fancy ranges again, and I imagine that while in the multitude of counsel it is supposed there is wisdom, doctors, like other ordinary mortals, can be found to disagree. Numerous in attendance, each one fortified with his own particular panacea, they do not despair of effecting a speedy cure.

Exhausted circulation in the one case, it is suggested, shall be renovated by a legitimate increase; in another, the plethoric condition of the patient shall, it is gravely proposed, be reduced by a further course of depletion, the San Grado theory being considered wonderfully applicable, leaving the sufferer to the chances of a slow, if not certain recovery.

Others suppose that intermediate measures may be resorted to, but everything is uncertainty, and at the fated moment when all are looking for the turning point in the attack, a tremulous shudder through that dilapidated frame, accompanied by a convulsive sigh, unmistakeably tells that the worst has passed.

A great cry arises—a tumult of voices utter forth in piercing tones the sombre fact that Speculation, old Speculation, is dead. Still dreaming, the announcement is conveyed to me in a solemn manner, and I fancy, with the knell of the event ringing in my ears, a scene of the most intense hurly burly follows.

What crowding is that of staid men in streets that I am supposed to witness; what whisperings are those I am presumed to hear of the difficulties of mammoth establishments, which have raised their heads in periods of fancied security, and now, with the first blush of adversity, are suddenly toppling down! What whitened sepulchres are those of mighty buildings, erected in days of plenty and apparent prosperity, but which, when the tide has turned, can scarcely find tenants for their high vaulted apartments!

What symptoms of decay and wretchedness are presented even in the blazoned panels of the door and side posts, the armorial bearings in brass and zinc, neglected and defaced ! What evidence everywhere furnished of exhausted means, and no immediate hope of recovery !

I am startled by this surprising hallucination, and collecting together my scattered senses, am strangely pleased to discover, when I awake, that the precise illustrations of this peculiarly absurd phantasy are at present far from being realized. May they not for a very lengthened period be experienced.

APPENDIX.

It is curious to notice that in almost every period of speculation, the current takes a very similar course. It may be either railways, banks, or general enterprise, but there are usually the same original features in the move-ment, with almost parallel incidents in the collapse. Here collected together, are some statements and statistics, the first identified with the railway mania, before the break up of the speculation; the second with the progress and development of the late loan, banking, and miscella-neous company movement, which cannot fail hereafter to be useful for reference.

§ 1.—THE GREAT RAILWAY MANIA.

(*From the " Circular to Bankers."*)

We now proceed to bestow a few observations for the purpose of distinguishing this extraordinary speculation from some of those which have preceded it, equally marking in their day an excited and diseased state of the public mind, when stimulated by the de-signs and interests of brokers, the association of numbers, and the eagerness of gain. The speculation of 1824-5 took all directions —colonial produce, all raw materials of manufacture, public com-panies for all imaginable purposes, from steam-washing and cow-keeping, to making Ireland a silk-producing country, and covering the sea with ocean steamers—bad and good schemes of all sorts. But its boldest and most conspicuous flight was over the Atlantic, to invest money in the mines of South and Central America. It is impossible to state how large was the whole capital which was sent in this direction; Mr. Huskisson made it the theme of a discourse, in which he represented the clear loss at from three to four millions sterling. But the peculiar character and manifestation of that speculation, are the important and instructive circumstances that we have now to consider, for the purpose of showing their bearing, by force of contrast, on the mania now prevailing.

The source of all these speculations is a reflux of money to the centre, after a period of commercial and manufacturing distress, and low prices. That of 1824-5 was wide-spread, and it fastened on many objects; but its most striking feature was mining enterprises, which also involved the greatest amount of ultimate loss. During the highest state of the fever, the premiums on the shares of some of the South American mining companies, rose to more than a thousand times the nominal value of the shares. In this there is a striking contrast to that which has taken place in railway shares, in none of which has the premium amounted to the nominal value of the shares, when the affair was in the state of projection. The reason is this :—supposing the spirit to have the same strength and intensity, and to be supported by the same amount of power in 1824-5 as in 1844-5, at the former period no one object presen ed itself on which alone the speculation could live and prosper. Gold and silver mines are limited in number; their situations are remote from the centre of power; the people of England were not familiar with such enterprises, and nothing but high mercantile names, could have induced the nation to adventure its money in such novel and hazardous undertakings. The spirit was rife and eager to be led, but the leaders could not create objects fast enough to satisfy the cravings of the spirit; and so it fastened on many absurd schemes, which men of lower grade, and inferior authority, brought forward for it to feed on. If mines had been like railways, equally familiar to the public observation and approbation,—if mines could have been presented in unlimited number, and some leading men had been willing to lend their names, influence, and authority, to the formation of a score of companies at once, as they do now in the case of railways, the speculation of 1824-5 would have been confined as exclusively to mining enterprises, as the speculation of 1844-5 is confined to railway enterprises. Ingenious men observe the craving of the monster, and they find no difficulty in creating a thousand railways for the purpose of satisfying it. In 1824-5 there was no such prolific field of creation: and, consequently, the shares in the few mining companies brought out, rose in some cases, to more than a thousand-fold of the amount of capital proposed to be laid out.

The next succeeding period of speculative prosperity, 1835-6, more nearly resembled, in its characteristics, that of 1825 than does the present one. North American credit, garnished with banks, railways, and other public improvements, was in this case the tempting bait. Substantially, the objects then presented for investment were of sounder foundation than four out of five of the railway projects that have been brought out for public patronage in the year 1845; and we firmly believe that the shareholders in canal and railway property, and in loans to municipalities in the United States, and on the other hand, in the new railways of England, will admit the validity of this conclusion when they compare accounts in the year 1855. The range of enterprise for British capitalists in 1835-6 was extensive, for it had the whole of the United States for its theatre. It was then, as now, confined mainly to one field abroad, but in England it took the direction of forming joint-stock banks, opening large streets, and constructing new ones, building public edifices, laying out parks with villas, as at Clapham and near Manchester, and generally it created a spirit of speculation in mills, mines, manufactures, and the raw materials of manufacture. On attempting to draw a parallel between the two periods of excitement, 1824-5 and 1835-6, we find the great feature of the first was, that the principal stream of speculation was directed to South and Central America, and that of the latter was, that the great stream was directed to North America. In other respects there was no striking characteristic of difference in the two, except what relates to joint-stock banks, which, in 1825, the state of the law precluded from being formed.

We now come to the speculation of the present time, to make the examination more intelligible. The object of the current speculation is principally, almost exclusively, confined to railways here and abroad. Its range, however, is as great as in the two former cases, probably far more extensive, but it is in great part limited to home, and the money it calls out is spent in great part on ourselves. We rejoice that it is so; it must be productive of public benefit by drawing out hoarded, and, as it lay, useless treasure, and giving employment to labourers. But, we are considering the matter as a speculation, and endeavouring to trace out some of its probable consequences. As such, in what respect does a railway differ from a mill that is built in times of stimulation, and is sold for one-fifth of its cost in times of distress, because the owner cannot pay the expense of working it? The mill is better property than a railway, because the latter can be applied to one only purpose. In both cases the architects, dealers in materials, and labourers of the structures, were benefited whilst they were in course of being constructed, but, after that, so long as the structures will not pay for working them, the capital expended is almost wholly pure waste. Of what use to the public or the proprietors is the capital expended in the Junction Railway? We believe that is the name of one for which an Act was obtained ten years ago, to bring the traffic of the existing railways to a point somewhere about Gray's Inn Lane, and which was partly constructed. The ground has been forfeited to the original owners of it long since, according to the terms of the Act. Of what use will be some of the five railways projected to be formed between London and York? Not one additional railway can be formed without injuring the revenue of that which is in operation. Some of them must be closed for the want of power to pay the working of them; for, to render them all productive of profit, the wealth and population of the country must be at once quintupled. If, in a small country like this, you lay out fifty millions of money in railways, the outlay may be judicious, pay the proprietors well, and benefit the public; but if you lay out one hundred and fifty or two hundred millions, one half of that sum may be pure waste, because the railways that represent it, cannot be worked in consequence of the current expense of working them being greater than the gross current earnings, and they can be put to no other use.

Wasteful expenditure, whether it be made in war, warlike implements, useless canals, or useless railways, has the same malign bearing on the welfare of a country, whatever may have been its object. In the case of wasteful expenditure in war, the State provides that the capitalist who advances money as it is wanted, shall receive his stipulated usance for it by taxes levied on the whole community; in the case of a wasteful expenditure in

useless railways—say of fifty or a hundred millions, which cannot
be worked because of the expense of working being more than the
income—there is no State or Power to guarantee the annual usance
to those who supply the capital; consequently, although the public
burden must be less than that for expenditure caused by war, or
nothing at all, the individual misery caused by abortive railway
schemes, with their outlays, must be so great as to baffle all power
of description. Neither are there wanting evidences even in this,
the infancy of the system, to prove that three or four out of every
five of the new projects—especially those for the east, south, and
south-west of England, remote from the sources of mineral wealth
—must fail. To say nothing of the wrecks passing under the
titles of the Peak and the Moreton-in-the-Marsh Railways, there
exists the Whitby and Pickering Railway (a single line, with
sidings, of twenty-four miles) as a warning. There is no railway
that runs over such a proportionate length of waste and worthless
land; there is no railway more needed, for Whitby is a populous
and wealthy town, situated in a deep and remote *cul de sac*, the
nearest market town being twenty miles distant, and the inter-
vening space in every direction being moorland. Two beautiful
valleys approximating near to midway between Whitby and Pickering present the most favourable basis for the construction of a
railway. The one now worked has been constructed—badly constructed we admit—and in operation many years. The owners
never, we believe, received one farthing in the shape of dividend
or interest for their capital, and the expense of working the line
was with difficulty defrayed—the operations were frequently on
the point of being stopped for this reason. Here there was no
competing line, no competing carrying power worth alluding to,
except that provided by the sea; and, we repeat, no circumstances
can be imagined more favourable for a railway enterprise except
dense population and mineral treasures. Not one in five of the
new projects is to be compared with it, all circumstances considered. Mr. Hudson's keen practical eye has perceived this, and
he has bought the Whitby and Pickering Railway, which, as an
adjunct to the York and Scarborough and the York and North
Midland, now all one, will prove in his hands an important feeder
for competition is out of the question in such a locality.

We have adverted to these illustrations furnished by brief

experience in working a novel system, for the purpose of suggesting the improbability of more than one in four of the new projects paying any interest to the adventurers. It would be useless to multiply examples, or they might be adduced from the plight and miserable dividends exhibited by some of the southern railways, working without competition. Then what will be the effect of all this speculation on the monetary power, is the only remaining section of the matter on which we shall at present offer any observation. We said a fortnight since that the thing as a speculation must break down within six months, or subside, leaving shoals of adventurers helpless on shore when the tide ebbs. Prophets, with a particle of foresight and discretion, will take an ample margin when prophesying; and a third part of six months may be sufficient to realize this prophecy. Whenever that time comes, there will be a rush to obtain the possession of money to keep the speculation afloat. A few only of the speculators will succeed in this; for there never was a speculation in which the Directors of the Bank of England generally, and those who influence and control monetary operations in the city of London, stood more aloof than they do in this railway speculation. The Bank will not be controlled by railway magnates, as it was controlled by the great merchants and merchant-bankers at the two former crises of 1825 and 1836.

This leads to the inference, that the manufacturing and mercantile operations of the country will be less interfered with at the next convulsion than at any preceding one; and this appears to us a just inference. Still there will be a very large sum of money abstracted from its mercantile and ordinary uses, which will make the market for supplying it to those uses scarce and "tight." We can perceive no difference between locking up money in a useless railway in Pennsylvania, and locking up the same sum in eight useless out of ten projected for Southampton. America being always the debtor country on the balance, it would be rather less disadvantageous to our manufacturing interests to waste English money there than for such purposes at home; at home it would cause less to be spent in English manufactures than in the United States, and more to be spent in such imports as tea, coffee, tobacco, sugar, wine, rice, and food—especially in the period of projection and laying out of schemes. A secondary clerk to an engineer has, we know, been paid seven guineas a-day for his services; and this fact marks the objects on which an increased expenditure for railways, in this stage of their progress, is likely to be squandered. The great question for consideration is, what will be the effect of all this speculation combined with augmented imports on the Bank of England?

On this last question we know far too little to justify us in saying more than we have said at present. We understand that the Directors count on the probability of losing two or three millions of their treasure. Such a drain, we believe, would not stop at the assumed point, but even that small sum would be quite sufficient to sink three out of four of all the new railway projects, to produce greater stringency in the administration of money, and very guarded conduct on the part of all bankers.

1824 AND 1825 CONTRASTED WITH 1844 AND 1845.

(*From " The Economist.*")

It is at all times a painful thing to refer to periods of misfortune, and it is especially distasteful, in the midst of an extraordinary flush of prosperity, which people generally believe will be as permanent as it is unprecedented. There have, however, been two periods within the memory of most who are now engaged in the active business of life, which were in some slight degree similar to the present times, as far as regards the extraordinary new and sudden creation of wealth. We know that opinions generally exist that at the periods referred to, there were some peculiar and unhappy characteristics which caused the wealth which was then suddenly made to disappear as suddenly; and it is believed, that at this time happily no such reason exists which can in any way endanger the permanency of the present state of things. It is said that the objects of the present speculations are all tangible, and well tried, and have proved to be a most profitable investment for capital; further, it is said that the money required will be all expended in the country, and will be no inconvenience, as it will only change hands. We do not in this place offer any opinion on these points, but it may be very interesting and instructive to our readers, if we lay before them the simple facts connected with the two former periods and the present, which each may turn to any use he sees fit. These periods of the greatest flush of prosperity known in modern times were 1824 and part of 1825; 1834, 1835, and part of 1836; and 1844 and 1845 so far.

Then for the facts. We have before us parliamentary documents, from which we glean the following statement of the transactions of 1824 and 1825. We have separated the foreign from the home engagements, as it is believed that they are so essentially different, and that our readers may see the amount of the objectionable and unobjectionable schemes at the different times.

PUBLIC UNDERTAKINGS IN 1824 and 1825.

Foreign.

	£
Total of foreign Loans, nominal value £34,278,571, contracted for at	23,722,000
Foreign Mining and other Companies of all kinds, on which a deposit of 10 per cent. was paid . . .	24,467,000
Total of foreign liabilities undertaken . .	48,189,000

Great Britain, Jan. 1824 to Jan. 1825.

Mining companies	10,400,000
Railroads	21,942,000
Canals, Docks, Tunnels, and Bridges . .	14,134,000
Fire and Life Insurance Offices at the nominal capital £32,040,700, of which was only required to be paid .	3,204,700
Waterworks	2,680,000
Gas companies	7,370,000
Loan, pawnbroking, investment, annuity, and banking companies	22,160,000
Colonial companies	2,000,000
Steam navigation, building and bath companies . .	3,680,000
Provision, milk and flour	3,160,000
Sundry companies, after Jan. 1825 . .	66,047,930
Total subscribed capital on home schemes .	156,778,630

Total of 1824 and 1825.

Foreign loans, mining companies, and other schemes .	48,189,000
Home schemes of all kinds, to be expended in the country .	156,778,630
Total subscribed	204,967,630
On which was paid up in 1824 and 1825 . .	35,014,698

Besides these, there seems to have been one hundred and thirty-three schemes advertised, on which it does not appear what amount, if any, has ever been paid.

Note.—The chief banking house to these companies has long been extinct.

	£
Bullion in the Bank, Feb. 1824 . . .	13,810,060
,, ,, Feb. 1826 . . .	2,459,510

From the same parliamentary papers we glean the following transactions of 1834, '35, and '36 :—

PUBLIC UNDERTAKINGS IN 1834, 1835, and 1836.

		Capital.			Shares.
Railway .	.	£69,666,000	.	.	590,920
Mining companies	.	7,035,200	.	.	447,730
Packet and navigation	.	3,533,000	.	.	127,390
Banking companies	.	23,750,000	.	.	670,000
Conveyance ,,	.	500,000	.	.	50,500
Insurance ,,	.	7,600,000	.	.	68,000
Investment ,,	.	1,730,000	.	.	23,900
Newspaper ,,	.	350,000	.	.	46,000
Canal ,,	.	3,655,000	.	.	14,400
Gas ,,	.	890,000 .	.	.	72,400
Cemetery ,,	.	435,000	.	.	24,000
Miscellaneous ,,	.	16,104,500	.	.	403,450
Total .	.	135,248,700	.	.	2,538,690

On which the deposit per share averaged from £2 10s. to £3, and taken at the latter, the deposits were £7,616,070.

The above schemes are thus divided :—

						£
Foreign	.	.	.	.	.	6,175,000
British	.	.	.	.	.	129,073,700
						135,248,700

These documents do not state the amount of the American loans of this period, but we may add to the above £6,175,000 foreign projected undertakings, about £15,000,000 more on various accounts, making—

		£
Home undertakings, to be expended in the country		129,073,700
Foreign		21,175,000
		150,248,700

Note.—Bullion in the Bank, Feb. 1834		.	10,142,000
„ „ Feb. 1837		.	4,221,000

The Parliamentary document before us gives a list of twenty individuals who were engaged in the above Companies as Directors, and states the number of Companies in which each was so engaged. We will apply letters in place of the names.

A	Director of 6 Companies.	L	Director of 8 Companies.
B	„ 5 „	M	„ 8 „
C	„ 3 „	N	„ 2 „
D	„ 7 „	O	„ 3 „
E	„ 8 „	P	„ 4 „
F	„ 9 „	Q	„ 3 „
G	„ 5 „	R	„ 7 „
H	„ 6 „	S	„ 11 „
I	„ 10 „.	T	„ 8 „
K	„ 5 „	U	„ 4 „

A. B. and Co., Bankers to 27 Companies.
C. D., Engineer to 13 Companies.

The Bankers referred to have some time since given up their business. Of all the above list of names, we observe only ONE at present prominently before the public, or holding a similar position as in 1836.

The next period to which we will refer is from Jan. 1844 to the present time.

RAILWAY UNDERTAKINGS in 1844 and 1845.

	Capital.
Railways of which the Acts are passed, and which are in the course of construction	. £55,862,200
Railways projected in 1844, and of which the plans were deposited last year, besides the above . .	. 67,000,000
Carried forward . .	. 122,862,200

Brought forward . . 122,862,200

Projected in 1845, to the 8th of October :—

	Total number.	Amounts known.	Capital.
A . .	6 . .	6 . .	. £5,040,000
B . .	45 . .	32 . .	. 27,450,000
C . .	37 . .	35 . .	. 29,490,000
D . .	33 . .	26 . .	. 38,840,000
E . .	25 . .	24 . .	. 19,470,000
F . .	3 . .	1 . .	. 3,000,000
G . .	42 . .	41 . .	. 58,710,000
H . .	11 . .	8 . .	. 7,300,000
I . .	11 . .	11 . .	. 10,300,000
K . .	7 . .	6 . .	. 7,115,000
L . .	60 . .	54 . .	. 54,830,000
M . .	22 . .	20 . .	. 21,055,000
N . .	39 . .	36 . .	. 28,450,000
O . .	8 . .	8 . .	. 7,000,000
P . .	8 . .	5 . .	. 3,250,000
R . .	10 . .	10 . .	. 8,400,000
S . .	42 . .	36 . .	. 32,020,000
T . .	14 . .	13 . .	. 12,550,000
U . .	2 . .	1 . .	. 500,000
W . .	39 . .	36 . .	. 31,775,000
Y . .	4 . .	3 . .	. 4,300,000
Estimated various .	.	. .	. 2,155,000
	468	412	413,000,000

Additional Lines from the 8th to the 12th Oct.   20,400,000

Capital of 56 Lines, not included in the above

   sum, at the same rate . . . 56,000,000

——————— 489,400,000

Total of British Railways in progress and projected . . £612,262,200

FOREIGN RAILWAYS to the 8th Oct.

41 Lines, of which the capital of 39 ascertained amount to . £79,250,000

Home Railways, to be expended in the country £612,262,200
Foreign   79,250,000

Total . . . £691,512,200

On which the deposits may be thus stated :—

> 10 per cent. on the Lines passed, independent of calls £5,586,220
> 5 per cent. on the Bills of last Session remaining over,
> of which most are now increased to 10 per cent.   .   3,350,000
> 10 per cent. on the projections of 1845 to Oct. 15th.   }
> Taking Foreign Railways only at the same rate   . }   69,512,200

Total deposits paid or to be provided .	£78,448,420
Bullion in the Bank, January, 1845 . .	£14,801,621
„ „ June, „ .	16,500,000
„ „ last week „ .	14,865,000

The following is a *resumé* of the three periods :—

	Home Schemes. £	Foreign. £	Total. £	Paid up and Deposits. £
1824 and 1825 . . .	156,778,630 . .	48,189,000 . .	204,967,630 . .	35,014,698
1834 to 1837 . . .	129,073,700 . .	21,175,000 . .	150,248,700 . .	22,616,070
1844 and 1845 so far	612,262,200 . .	79,250,000 . .	691,512,200 . .	78,448,420

BULLION IN THE BANK.

February, 1824	£13,810,060
„ 1826	2,459,510
„ 1834	10,142,000
„ 1837	4,221,000
January 1845	14,801,621
June, „	16,500,000
October, „	14,865,000

We will only add, that the *premiums* upon undertakings, which have as yet not received an act of Parliament, cannot be estimated at less than £40,000,000, which at this moment figures as increased wealth hanging on opinion during the present year. We leave these facts in the hands of our readers, to make such application of them as they may appear to deserve.

§ 2.—LOANS CONTRACTED IN 1862.

January.

Five per cent. Moorish loan of £501,200, at 85, secured (with a sinking fund for extinction at par within 20 years) by hypothecation of 50 per cent. of the Customs' duties of the empire. The British government entered into a convention to appoint commissioners at the various ports. The operation very successful.

February.

Five per cent. Italian loan of £1,338,000, at 74, to complete Maremmana Railway. Introduced by Messrs. Hambro and Son, and the whole subscribed; but the stock did not long maintain its price.

March.

Six per cent. Turkish loan of £8,000,000, at 68, or £5,440,000 sterling, arranged by the Ottoman Bank and Messrs. Devaux and Co. The revenues hypothecated were £1,885,220. The applications represented £34,949,860. The principal of the loan was to be redeemed by a sinking fund in 23½ years, and the proceeds to be applied to the redemption of the floating debt.

April.

Seven per cent. Egyptian loan of £2,195,200, or £1,811,040 sterling, at 82½, secured with interest and sinking fund by the hypothecation of the revenues of the Delta. Messrs. Fruhling and Göschen arranged the transaction, the applications reaching £9,635,200.

Five per cent. Russian loan of £15,000,000, introduced through Messrs. Rothschild Brothers, at the price of 92, £5,000,000 having previously been placed, £10,000,000 were offered and subscribed in the markets of London, Paris, Frankfort, Berlin, Amsterdam, etc.

July.

Three per cent. Portuguese loan of £5,000,000, offered through Messrs. Knowles and Foster at 44, for railway purposes, which was immediately subscribed, the total applications reaching £21,500,000.

Seven per cent. Egyptian loan, additional issue to the extent of £1,097,000, distributed among the holders of the former stock.

Four and a-half per cent. Peruvian loan of £5,500,000, at 93, by Messrs. Heywood, Kennard, and Co., on the security of the British and Belgium guano contracts. All the existing Peruvian debt in the London market, amounting to about £2,700,000, was absorbed by this issue.

Six per cent. Venezuela loan of £1,000,000, was arranged by Messrs. Baring and Co. at 63, the security being a mortgage of 55 per cent. of the Customs' duties at La Guyra and Porto Cabello, to be paid weekly to the British Consul and the agent of Messrs. Baring and Co.

FLUCTUATIONS IN CONSOLS AND THE BANK BULLION IN 1862.

The extreme range of Consols during the year 1862 has been only 3¾ per cent., while that of the preceding twelve months was 5⅜ per cent. The lowest price, 91, was at the commencement, and the highest price, 94¾, was touched in July. The difference between the opening and closing quotations of the year shows an improvement of 1½ per cent. In railway shares an average recovery has been established of about 5 per cent., a decline of about 10 per cent. having occurred in 1861. American Federal stocks show a decline of about 3 per cent., while Virginia State Bonds have slightly improved, and railway shares generally show a recovery. The Bank of England bullion has slightly decreased. At the commencement it was £15,961,439; it touched its highest point, £18,448,443, on the 30th of July; its lowest, £14,823,063, on the 17th of December; and it is now £14,870,795. At the

Bank of France the total at the commencement was £12,970,000; it declined to £11,816,000 in November, and is now £12,760,000. On the Paris Bourse the movements in French Rentes have resulted in establishing a rise of 3 per cent. The changes in the Bank rate of discount, which were 11 in number in 1861, have this year been only 5. On the 1st of January the rate was 3 per cent., at which it now again stands, after a period of three months during which it was as low as 2 per cent. In the cotton-market there has been excitement throughout, and the price has again nearly doubled. In the wheat-market there have been no very important fluctuations, but a gradual and continuous decline, owing to the extraordinary extent of the arrivals from America and elsewhere.

LOANS CONTRACTED IN 1863.

February.

Five per cent. Danish loan of £500,000, at the price of 91, introduced by Messrs. Hambro and Son, for assisting in the construction of railways.

March.

Five per cent. Italian loan of £3,000,000, introduced by Messrs. Rothschild at 71, or 69½ reckoning allowances. This amount was part of £28,000,000 debt to be created by the Italian government, of which the Rothschild family took £8,000,000, the remainder being intended for Paris, Turin, etc.

Seven per cent. Confederate loan of £3,000,000 at the price of 90, introduced by Messrs. W. H. Schröder and Co., of London, and Messrs. Erlanger and Co., of Paris, for the markets of London, Paris, and Frankfort, secured by cotton, and deliverable at sixty days' notice at 6d. per lb.

June.

Six per cent. Venezuela loan of £1,000,000, at 60, brought forward by Messrs. Matheson and Co. Half the proceeds to be invested in Consols as security for a National Bank, to be established at Caraccas. The operation was completed, but ultimately withdrawn, in consequence of the unsatisfactory state of the country.

October.

Four and a-half per cent. Brazilian loan of £3,300,000, announced by Messrs. Rothschild and Co. at 88, principally for the purpose of paying off Brazilian loans held in London.

Three per cent. Portuguese loan of £2,500,000, at 48, introduced by Messrs. Stern Brothers, which was most perfectly successful.

December.

Three per cent. French loan of £12,000,000 inaugurated under the authority of M. Fould, to provide for deficiency in the Budget.

§ 5.—PUBLIC COMPANIES IN 1862.

Subjoined is a list of the principal new companies brought forward in 1862. A considerable proportion of them failed to raise their capital, owing to the doubtful profits they exhibited. On the other hand, many were completely successful:—

Company.	Capital.
Albion Marine, Mortgage, and Insurance .	£1,000,000
Alliance Bank of London and Liverpool ...	2,000,000
Anglo - Indian Steam Navigation	50,000
Algerian Cotton Land and Irrigation ...	1,000,000
Adelphi Hotel... ...	150,000
Anglo-Danubian Steam and Colliery... ...	220,000
Aërated Bread ...	500,000
Anglo-Indian Cotton ...	500,000
Atlantic Telegraph ...	600,000
Anglo-Portuguese Bank	1,000,000
British Columbia Overland Transit ...	500,000
Buenos Ayres Great Southern Railway ...	750,000
British and Eastern Steam Navigation ...	750,000
British Fire Prevention and Insurance ...	500,000
British Columbia and Vancouver's Island Banking and Gold Company	250,000
Bristol Port, Railway, and Pier Company ...	125,000
Bere Charter Mining Company	20,000
Bantry Bay Slate and Slab Company ...	15,000
Bombay Gas	250,000
Bank of Hindustan, China, and Japan ...	1,000,000

Company.	Capital.
Bank of Canada, Nova Scotia, and New Brunswick	£1,000,000
Bank of Queensland ...	1,000,000
Bank of Buenos Ayres	500,000
Brighton Hotel ...	75,000
Belfast, Holyhead, and Bangor Railway ...	115,000
Brandon Walls Lead Mining	18,000
British Paper Pulp ...	50,000
Canadian Native Oil ...	100,000
Continental Company for Boat-building by Machinery	50,000
Channel Islands Hotel	80,000
Ceylon Company ...	500,000
Cape of Good Hope Telegraph	62,000
Cork Carpet	100,000
Chartered Bank of British Columbia and Vancouver's Island ..	250,000
Compagnie Générale Transatlantique ...	80,000
Cape(Eastern Province) Railway	1,200,000
Charing Cross Hotel ...	160,000
Cambrian Consolidated Gold Mines	150,000
Clifton Hotel	40,000
Cape of Good Hope Copper Mining ...	150,000
DagenhamThames Dock	300,000
Dolfrw y nog Mining...	20,000
Eastern Bengal Tea ...	100,000

Company.	Capital.
East India Cotton Agency	£500,000
Ely Merthyr Colliery...	25,000
East Blonfloyd Silver Lead	10,000
English and Irish Bank	2,000,000
East Cambrian Gold ...	50,000
Fortune Copper Mining Company (West Australia)	80,000
FlintshireLeadand Zinc	150,000
Farnborough and Aldershot Freehold Ground-rent Society...	75,000
Gefle Gas	50,000
Gilvach Coal ...	30,000
Great Copper Lode of Huaycavo ...	200,000
General Steam Fuel ...	30,000
General Rolling Stock	150,000
Glanrheidol Silver Lead	12,000
General Ventilation and Atmospheric Fire Grate	30,000
Grays Chalk Quarries...	50,000
Glyn Neath Steam Coal and Iron	50,000
Greenland	100,000
Great Devon and Bedford Mining...	25,000
Great Laxey Mining ...	60,000
Italian Irrigation	1,000,000
Imperial Bank	3,000,000
Indian Branch Railway	500,000
London and Middlesex Bank	1,000,000
London and South of Ireland Direct Telegraph	100,000
London and Colonial Bank	500,000
London India-rubber...	75,000
London Cab and Conveyance	200,000
London and Brazilian Bank	1,000,000
London and Northern Bank	1,000,000
London, Birmingham, and South Staffordshire Bank ...	1,000,000

Company.	Capital.
Land Investment	500,000
Laguna Silver Mining	20,000
LlantwitVardre Colliery	20,000
Leeswood Cannel and Gas Coal	100,000
Langham Hotel	150,000
Londonderry and Lough Swilly Railway	60,000
Lagunazo Sulphur and Copper	30,000
Mincing-lane Investment...	100,000
Mount Rose Copper (South Australia) ...	120,000
Metropolitan Dairy ...	60,000
Metropolitan Railroad Carriage	100,000
Metropolitan Cab and Carriage	100,000
Moelfra Slate and Slab	50,000
Midland Gas ...	25,000
Moldavian Railways ...	3,440,000
Maretzo Company	50,000
North London Park and Land	250,000
Northern Counties Bank	2,000,000
Northern Railway of Buenos Ayres	210,000
North Sea Fish Guano	60,000
Nova Scotia Land and Gold-crushing	100,000
New Zealand Land and Trust	500,000
Oil-wells of Canada ...	75,000
Oriental Commercial ...	200,000
Otea Copper ...	50,000
Ottoman Gas	100,000
Oriental Canal and Irrigation	250,000
Oxygen Gas ...	100,000
Prize Medal Flour ...	50,000
Permanent Lime Light	120,000
Park Gwyn Tin Mining	25,000
Peninsular Irrigation...	300,000
Para Gas	100,000
Plantation Company of West Hindustan ...	170,000
Queensland Cotton Cultivation	100,000
Queen's Hotel, Ryde...	50,000
QuebradaLand & Mining	170,000

Company.	Capital.
Queensland Wool ...	£200.000
Rue Lafayette	1,000,000
Ross of Mull Granite...	50,000
Rolling Stock Company of Ireland	200,000
Rio de Janeiro Improvements	850,000
Royal Forest of Dean Mining	55,000
River Navigation of India and China ...	500,000
Roaring Water Mining	18,000
Strand Hotel	100,000
Sea-Coast Hotel ...	150,000
St. David's Gold Mining	100,000
Steven's Patent Bread Machinery	60,000
Southsea Pier Hotel ...	60,000
SouthGreenland Mining	60,000
South Kensington Hotel	100,000
South Essex Waterworks	80,000
South Foxdale Mining	25,000
South African Irrigation	1,000,000
Singapore Gas ...	100,000
Silver Mountain United Mines	25,000
St. Lawrence & Ottawa Land and Railroad...	600,000
Spring Creek Copper (South Australia) ...	100,000
Standard Bank of South Africa	1,000,000
Sovereign Gold Mining	50,000
Scinde, Punjaub, and Delhi Bank	1,000,000
St.Cuthbert Lead Smelting	75,000
Societé Financière d'Egypte	600,000

Capital.	Company.
Thames Express Steam Boat...	£75,000
Thames and Humber Iron Shipbuilding ...	500.000
Toplitz Colliery ...	60,000
Upper Norwood Hotel	50,000
Union Bank of Ireland	1,000,000
United Kingdom Shipowning	300,000
Universal Club and Permanent Exposition Company	100,000
Upper Assam Tea ...	250,000
Union Bank of England and France	1,000,000
United Kingdom Railway Rolling Stock ...	100,000
Vancouver Coal Mining	100,000
Victoria (London) Mining	25,000
Ventnor Harbour ...	20,000
Varna Railway ...	800,000
Ventilation and Sanitary Improvements...	50,000
Victoria Hotel of Pau...	140,000
Vistula Colliery ...	60,000
Warmley Colliery and Spelter	70,000
West London Land ...	125,000
Westminster Chambers, Tontine	200,000
Western Australia Cotton	220,000
Western Neilgherry Coffee, Tea, and Chinchona Plantation ...	50,000
West Africa	250,000
Yudanamutana Mining (South Australia) ...	45,000

PUBLIC COMPANIES IN 1863.

(From the " Times.")

Subjoined is a complete list of the new Joint-Stock Companies brought out during the year 1863. The total capital thus proposed to be embarked appears to be exactly 100 millions sterling :—

" 19, Gresham Street, London, Dec. 30.

" Sir,—We beg to hand you herewith a statement showing the number of joint-stock companies brought out during the year 1863, with particulars as to capital authorized, capital offered (or first issue), number and amount of shares and deposit, with analysis showing the capital required for each particular class of companies.

" As an illustration of the extent to which the principle of limited liability is being adopted, it may be noticed that out of a total of 263 companies, only two are with unlimited liability. The proportions are as follows :—

	Number.	Capital Authorized.	Capital offered.	Deposit.
		£	£	£
Companies (limited) ...	246	92,807,000	70,889,000	8,006,200
Companies in which the liability is limited by special acts of Parliament...	15	7,116,000	7,116,000	843,350
Companies unlimited ...	2	130,000	130,000	26,000
Total	263	100,053,000	78,135,000	8,875,550

" Should you consider the statement of sufficient importance we should be much obliged by its insertion in your columns.

" We remain, sir, your obedient servants,

" SPACKMAN AND SONS."

New Joint-Stock Companies brought out during the Year 1863, with Analysis, showing the Capital required for each Class of Companies.

Name of Company.	Capital Authorized.	Capital Offered.	Amount of Share.		Deposit.		Total Deposit.
	£	£	£	s.	£	s.	£
Abertham Mining (lim.) ...	150,000	150,000	5	0	2	0	60,000
Adelaide (North Arm) Port and Railway Extension and Land (lim.) ...	400,000	200,000	20	0	1	0	10,000
Agricultural Hotel (lim.)...	100,000	100,000	10	0	2	0	20,000
Alamillos (lim.)	70,000	70,000	2	0	0	10	17,500
Albion Marine Insurance (lim.)	1,000,000	1,000,000	20	0	2	0	100,000
Alexandra Hotel (lim.) ...	120,000	120,000	10	0	3	0	36,000
Alexandra Slate and Slab Quarry (lim.)	25,000	25,000	10	0	3	0	7,500
Alhambra Palace (lim.) ...	100,000	50,000	5	0	2	0	20,000
Anglo-Austrian Bank ...	2,000,000	2,000,000	20	0	4	0	400,000
Anglo-Indian Cotton (lim.)	500,000	100,000	5	0	1	0	20,000
Anglo - Parisian Brewery (lim.)	200,000	100,000	20	0	5	0	25,000
Anglo-Parisian Hotel (lim.)	200,000	200,000	—		—		—.
Anglo - Prussian Mining (lim.)	100,000	100,000	5	0	1	0	20,000
Asia Minor (lim.)... ...	500,000	100,000	10	0	2	0	20,000
Australian Mortgage Land and Finance (lim.) ...	1,000,000	500,000	25	0	2	0	20,000
Bank of Gibraltar and Malta (lim.)	250,000	250,000	100	0	2	0	5,000
Bank of Great Britain(lim.)	2,000,000	500,000	100	0	3	0	15,000
Bank of Otago (lim.) ...	500,000	500,000	100	0	5	0	25,000
Bank of Wales (lim.) ...	1,000,000	500,000	100	0	2	0	10,000
Beckenham, Lewes, and Brighton Railway ...	225,000	225,000	—		—		—
Bedford Hotel, Brighton (lim.)	100,000	100,000	10	0	2	0	20,000
Birmingham and District Gas (lim.)	250,000	250,000	10	0	0	10	12,500
Blaencennant Silver Lead Mining (lim.)	25,000	25,000	1	0	0	5	6,250
Bois de Boulogne Hotel and Land (lim.) ...	120,000	60,000	20	0	2	0	6,000
Brazilian and Portuguese Bank (lim.)	1,000,000	1,000,000	20	0	2	0	100,000
Bridlington Quay Hotel (lim.)	80,000	80,000	10	0	2	10	20,000

(New Joint-Stock Companies continued.)

Name of Company.	Capital Authorized.	Capital Offered.	Amount of Share.		Deposit.		Total Deposit.
	£	£	£	s.	£	s.	£
Brighton Club and Norfolk Hotel (lim.)	40,000	40,000	10	0	1	0	4,000
Bristol City Hotel (lim.) ...	30,000	30,000	10	0	1	0	3,000
Bristol College Green Hotel (lim.)	40,000	40,000	10	0	2	0	8,000
Bristol Sugar Refinery (lim.)	100,000	50,000	10	0	—		—
British and American Exchange Banking Corporation (lim.)	1,000,000	500,000	50	0	2	0	20,000
British and Colonial Brush (lim.)	50,000	50,000	1	0	0	10	25,000
British and Foreign Domestic Machinery (lim.)	50,000	50,000	5	0	2	0	20,000
British and Foreign India-rubber (lim.)	100,000	100,000	5	0	2	10	50,000
British and Foreign Marine Insurance (lim.) ...	1,000,000	500,000	20	0	2	0	50,000
British Flax (lim.) ...	100,000	100,000	10	0	1	0	10,000
British Honduras Cotton (lim.)	200,000	200,000	10	0	2	0	40,000
British Indian Tea (lim.)...	250,000	250,000	20	0	2	0	25,000
British Sewing Machine (lim.)	50,000	50,000	1	0	0	10	25,000
Building Material Improvement (lim.)	30,000	30,000	5	0	2	10	15,000
Buxton Hotel (lim.) ...	50,000	50,000	10	0	1	0	5,000
Cader Idris Slate and Slab (lim.)	20,000	20,000	1	0	0	10	10,000
Cambrian Stone and Slab (lim.)	20,000	20.000	10	0	5	0	10,000
Cannes Hotel (lim.) ...	120,000	120,000	20	0	2	10	15,000
Cape of Good Hope Copper Mining (lim.)	150,000	150,000	10	0	2	0	30,000
Castle Hotel, Richmond (lim.)	60,000	60,000	10	0	3	0	18,000
Cavendish Hotel, Eastbourne (lim.)	70,000	70,000	10	0	2	0	14,000
Central Darjeeling Tea (lim.)	75,000	75,000	10	0	2	0	15,000
City and County Assurance (lim)	500,000	500,000	20	0	2	0	50,000
City Discount (lim.) ...	1,000,000	500,000	50	0	2	10	25,000
City of Glasgow Union Railway	650,000	650,000	10	0	1	0	65,000

(New Joint-Stock Companies continued.)

Name of Company.	Capital Authorized.	Capital Offered.	Amount of Share.		Deposit.		Total Deposit.
	£	£	£	s.	£	s.	£
City of London and General Fire and Life Insurance (lim.)	500,000	500,000	25	0	2	10	50,000
City of London Hotel (lim.)	50,000	50,000	10	0	2	10	12,500
City of Norwich Hotel(lim.)	50,000	50,000	5	0	1	0	10,000
Clarence Hotel, Dover(lim.)	75,000	75,000	10	0	2	0	15,000
Clifton Hotel (lim.) ...	40,000	40,000	10	0	2	0	8,000
Clowance Wood Copper Mining (lim.)	25,000	25,000	1	0	0	5	6,250
Commercial Navigation of India (lim.)	300,000	150,000	50	0	5	0	15,000
Do., B stock	43,000	43,000	—		—		—
Company of African Merchants (lim.)	400,000	400,000	10	0	1	0	40,000
Consolidated Bank (lim.)...	2,000,000	2,000,000	10	0	4	0	800,000
Consolidated Discount(lim.)	1,000,000	500,000	50	0	3	0	30,000
Constantinople and Alexandria Hotels (lim.) ...	300,000	100,000	20	0	1	0	5,000
Continental Bank Corporation (lim.)	1,000,000	500,000	100	0	3	0	15,000
Continental Gas and Water (lim.)	100,000	50,000	10	0	1	0	5,000
Contract Corporation (lim.)	4,000,000	2,000,000	100	0	3	0	60,000
Copenhagen Railway (lim.)	160,000	60,000	10	0	2	10	15,000
Cotton Plantation of Natal (lim.)	150,000	150,000	10	0	2	0	30,000
Credit Metropolitan (lim.)	3,000,000	1,000,000	50	0	3	0	60,000
Crenver and Wheal Abraham United Mining(lim.)	150,000	150,000	5	0	2	10	75,000
Crosier Valley and Port Madoc Freehold Slate (lim.)	60,000	40,000	10	0	1	0	4,000
Crystal Palace and South London Junction Railway	675,000	675,000	10	0	2	10	168,750
Cwt-y-Bugail Slate Quarry (lim.)	50,000	30,000	50	0	10	0	6,000
Dartford Creek Paper Mill (lim.)	150,000	150,000	10	0	3	0	45,000
Deep Dale Mining (lim.) ...	20,000	20,000	2	0	1	0	10,000
Discount Corporation (lim.)	2,000,000	1,000,000	100	0	2	10	25,000
Dublin Cattle Market (lim.)	40,000	40,000	10	0	2	0	8,000
Dublin Metropolitan Railway	556,000	556,000	10	0	1	0	55,600

(New Joint-Stock Companies continued.)

Name of Company.	Capital Authorized.	Capital Offered.	Amount of Share.		Deposit.		Total Deposit.
	£	£	£	s.	£	s.	£
Dunaburg and Witeps Railway (lim.)	2,600,000	2,600,000	100	0	10	0	260,000
East Bottallack Consolidated Mining (lim.) ...	18,000	18,000	3	0	1	0	6,000
Eastbourne Hotel (lim.) ...	40,000	40,000	10	0	2	0	8,000
East Great Work Tin Mining (lim.)	30,000	30,000	5	0	1	0	6,000
East Kent Flour Mill and Bakery (lim.)	25,000	25,000	10	0	5	0	12,500
East London Bank (lim.)...	600,000	600,000	50	0	5	0	60,000
East Norfolk Railway ...	200,000	200,000	10	0	1	10	30,000
East Pant Du United Lead Mining (lim.)	30,000	30,000	5	0	1	0	6,000
Edgware, Highgate, and London Railway ...	220,000	220,000	10	0	1	0	22,000
Egyptian Commercial and Trading (lim.)	2,000,000	2,000,000	20	0	2	0	200,000
El-Chico Silver Mining and Reduction (lim.) ...	75,000	75,000	5	0	2	0	30,000
Empire Marine Insurance (lim.)	1,000,000	200,000	10	0	2	0	40,000
English, Belgian, and Netherlands Bank (lim.) ...	1,000,000	500,000	50	0	3	0	30,000
English and Russian Bank (lim.)	2,500,000	2,500,000	100	0	5	0	125,000
English and Swedish Bank (lim.)	2,000,000	1,000,000	50	0	3	0	60,000
English and Scottish Marine Insurance (lim.) ...	1,000,000	1,000,000	100	0	2	0	20,000
Equitable Furnishing (lim.)	50,000	50,000	2	10	1	10	30,000
Export and Inland Coal (lim.)	100,000	100,000	10	0	2	10	25,000
Factage Parisien (lim.) ...	200,000	200,000	20	0	2	0	20,000
Financial, Industrial, Commercial	500,000	500,000	—		—		—
General Auction and Rent Guarantee (lim.) ...	50,000	20,000	2	0	1	0	10,000
General Credit and Finance of London (lim.) ...	2,500,000	2,500,000	20	0	2	0	250,000
General Floating Dock (lim.)	200,000	120,000	10	0	2	0	24,000
General Petroleum (lim.)...	200,000	200,000	10	0	2	0	40,000
General Steam Cultivation (lim.)	250,000	100,000	10	0	1	10	15,000

(New Joint-Stock Companies continued.)

Name of Company.	Capital Authorized.	Capital Offered.	Amount of Share.		Deposit.		Total Deposit.
	£	£	£	s.	£	s.	£
Glan Alyn Mining (lim.)...	5,000	5,000	1	0	0	5	1,250
Gloucestershire Smelting (lim.)	70,000	70,000	5	0	0	10	7,000
Gold Com. of the Approu-ague, French Guiana ...	80,000	80,000	4	0	2	0	40,000
Great Indian Peninsular Extension Railway (lim.)	1,000,000	1,000,000	20	0	2	0	100,000
Grenville, Delabole, and Trehane Slate and Slab (lim.)	30,000	30,000	10	0	2	10	7,500
Hafod Hotel (lim.)	30,000	30,000	10	0	2	0	6,000
Havan Silver Lead Mines (lim.)	25,000	25,000	5	0	1	10	7,500
Hayling Railways... ...	50,000	50,000	10	0	3	0	15,000
Hercules Fire and Life In-surance (lim.)	100,000	100,000	2	0	0	10	25,000
Ilfracombe Hotel (lim.) ...	20,000	20,000	10	0	2	0	4,000
Imperial Royal Privileged Union Bank of Austria (lim.)	2,000,000	2,000,000	—		—		—
Indian Tea Company of Cachar (lim.)	100,000	80,000	10	0	2	10	20,000
Indian Tea Company of Darjeeling (lim.) ...	60,000	60,000	10	0	2	10	15,000
Inns of Court Hotel (lim.).	100,000	100,000	10	0	1	0	10,000
Intercolonial Bank of Aus-tralia and New Zealand (lim.)	750,000	750,000	100	0	3	0	22,500
International Financial (lim.)	3,000,000	3,000,000	20	0	2	10	375,000
Irish Iodine and Marine Salts Manufacturing (lim.)	50,000	25,000	1	0	0	5	6,250
Italian Irrigation Canal (Canal Cavour) (lim.) ...	1,000,000	1,000,000	—		—		50,000
Jersey Imperial Hotel (lim.)	40,000	40,000	10	0	1	10	6,000
Joint-stock Discount (lim.)	1,000,000	1,000,000	25	0	2	0	80,000
Kenyon Colliery (lim.) ...	40,000	40,000	10	0	5	0	20,000
Kinsale Hotel and Baths (lim.)	10,000	10,000	5	0	1	0	2,000
Kyffhauser Mining and Smelting (lim.)	200,000	200,000	20	0	2	10	25,000
Lancashire Steel (lim.) ...	150,000	150,000	20	0	2	0	15,000
Land Mortgage Bank of India (lim.)	2,000,000	2,000,000	20	0	2	0	200,000

(New Joint-Stock Companies continued.)

Name of Company.	Capital Authorized.	Capital Offered.	Amount of Share.		Deposit.		Total Deposit.
	£	£	£	s.	£	s.	£
Leasehold Investment (lim.)	100,000	100,000	10	0	1	0	10,000
Life Association of England (lim.)	500,000	125,000	5	0	0	10	12,500
Littlehampton, Havre, and Honfleur Steamship (lim.)	75,000	75,000	10	0	1	0	7,500
Llanberis Slate (lim.) ...	50,000	50,000	5	0	1	0	10,000
Llanfair Green and Blue Slate (lim.)	50,000	50,000	5	0	2	10	25,000
Loan Trust and Agency of South Africa (lim.) ...	500,000	250,000	20	0	2	0	25,000
London and African Trading (lim.)	500,000	100,000	25	0	2	0	8,000
London and Caledonian Marine Insurance (lim.).	500,000	500,000	25	0	3	0	60,000
London and Hamburg Exchange Bank (lim.) ...	1,000,000	500,000	100	0	3	0	15,000
London and Lisbon Cork Wood (lim.)	100,000	100,000	5	0	2	10	50,000
London and Paris Hotel (lim.)	400,000	200,000	20	0	2	0	20,000
London and South American Bank (lim.) ...	1,000,000	500,000	100	0	2	0	10,000
London and Suburban Land and Building (lim.) ...	50,000	50,000	10	0	2	0	10,000
London and Westminster Assurance Corporation (lim.)	100,000	100,000	10	0	2	0	20,000
London and Westminster Wine (lim.)	50,000	50,000	5	0	2	0	20,000
London Bank of Scotland (lim.)	1,000,000	1,000,000	100	0	3	0	30,000
London Financial Association (lim.)	1,000,000	1,000,000	50	0	5	0	100,000
London General Depository (lim.)	20,000	20,000	5	0	1	5	5,000
London India-rubber (lim.)	75,000	75,000	10	0	2	10	18,750
London Laundry (lim.) ...	10,000	10,000	2	0	0	15	3,750
London Paper-making (lim.)	50,000	50,000	10	0	3	0	15,000
London Permanent Exhibition (lim.) ...	50,000	50,000	5	0	1	0	10,000
London Scrap Iron Works (lim.)	25,000	25,000	1	0	0	10	12,500
London Tavern (lim.) ...	120,000	60,000	10	0	2	10	15,000

(New Joint-Stock Companies continued.)

Name of Company.	Capital Authorized.	Capital Offered.	Amount of Share.		Deposit.		Total Deposit.
	£	£	£	s.	£	s.	£
Lundy Granite (lim.) ...	100,000	100.000	5	0	1	10	30,000
Madrid Bank (lim.) ...	1,200,000	600,000	20	0	2	0	60,000
Manchester Villa and Cottage (lim.)	50,000	50,000	10	0	0	10	2,500
Margate Terminus Hotel (lim.)	50,000	50,000	10	0	1	0	5,000
Marine Investment (lim.)...	500,000	250,000	25	0	2	0	20,000
Martin's Patent Anchor (lim.)	50,000	50,000	5	0	2	0	20,000
Mauritius Land Credit and Agency Company (lim.)	250,000	250,000	20	0	1	0	12,500
Mauritius Gas (Lim.) ...	100,000	60,000	5	0	1	0	12,000
Mediterranean Hotel (lim.)	100,000	100,000	20	0	2	10	12,500
Medoc Railway	400,000	400,000	20	0	4	0	80,000
Mercantile and Exchange Bank (lim.)	1,000,000	1,000,000	50	0	2	0	40,000
Mercantile Credit Association (lim.)	2,000,000	1,000,000	50	0	3	0	60,000
Mercantile Union Assurance (lim.)	1,000,000	500,000	50	0	2	0	20,000
Merchant Banking of London (lim.)	1,000,000	1,000,000	100	0	2	10	25,000
Metropolitan Lavatory (lim.)	60,000	60,000	5	0	1	10	18,000
Metropolitan, Tottenham, and Hampstead Railway	500,000	500,000	10	0	1	0	50,000
Metropolitan Zinc Rolling (lim.)	50,000	50,000	10	0	2	10	12,500
Midland Counties Union Banking (lim.)	500,000	500,000	100	0	3	0	15,000
Mining of Italy (lim.) ...	50,000	50,000	5	0	1	10	15.000
Muntz's Metal (lim.) ...	600,000	600,000	20	0	5	0	150,000
Natal Central Railway (lim.)	600,000	600,000	20	0	0	3	4,500
National Armoury (lim.)...	100,000	50,000	5	0	2	10	25,000
National Bank of Liverpool (lim.)	1,000,000	1,000,000	100	0	2	0	20,000
National Steam Navigation (lim.)	2,000,000	2,000,000	100	0	2	0	40,000
National Union Life Assurance	100,000	100,000	5	0	1	0	20,000
Neath and Pelenna Colliery (lim.)	65,000	65,000	5	0	2	0	26,000

(*New Joint-Stock Companies continued.*)

Name of Company.	Capital Authorized.	Capital Offered.	Amount of Share.		Deposit.		Total Deposit.
	£	£	£	s.	£	s.	£
Neustadt Charcoal Iron Works (lim.)	230,000	230,000	20	0	2	0	23,000
New Concord Silver, Lead, and Copper Mining (lim.)	30,000	30,000	3	0	1	10	15,000
New City Club (lim.) ...	25,000	25,000	5	0	1	0	5,000
New Mansfeld Copper and Silver Mining (lim.) ...	100,000	100,000	10	0	2	10	25,000
Newport Dry Dock, Wood, and Iron Ship-building and Ship-repairing (lim.)	100,000	100,000	20	0	3	0	15,000
New Theatre (lim.) ...	125,000	125,000	25	0	3	0	15,000
New Zealand Banking Corporation (lim.) ...	600,000	300,000	100	0	3	0	9,000
Nice Hotel (lim.)	150,000	150,000	10	0	2	0	30,000
North and South Staffordshire Junction Railway...	130,000	130,000	10	0	1	0	13,000
North Delabole Slate and Slab (lim.)	50,000	50,000	5	0	2	0	20,000
North Warwickshire Worsted and Woollen Spinning and Weaving (lim.)	25,000	25,000	5	0	2	0	10,000
North - Western Railway Rolling Stock and Plant (lim.)	100,000	100,000	10	0	2	10	25,000
Norwich Flour Mills (lim.)	50,000	50,000	10	0	3	0	15,000
Nottingham and District Gas Consumers (lim.) ...	100,000	100,000	10	0	0	10	5,000
National Provincial Aërated Bread (lim.)	250,000	100,000	10	0	2	0	20,000
Norwegian Copper (lim.) ...	100,000	100,000	2	0	1	0	50,000
National Volunteer Hotel (Wimbledon) (lim.) ...	120,000	120,000	10	0	2	10	30,000
Oilseed Crushing (lim.) ...	500,000	100,000	20	0	2	10	12,500
Oriental Hotels (lim.) ...	250,000	125,000	10	0	2	0	25,000
Oriental Tea (lim.) ...	250,000	250,000	20	0	2	0	25,000
Ottoman Cotton (lim.) ...	100,000	100,000	10	0	2	0	20,000
Palleg Anthracite Coal and Iron (lim.)	20,000	20,000	4	0	2	0	10,000
Para Gas (lim.)	100,000	100,000	—		—		—
Patent Concrete Stone (lim.)	100,000	50,000	10	0	2	10	12,500
Patent File (lim.)	100,000	100,000	10	0	1	0	10,000
Patent Lubricating Oil and Grease (lim.)	60,000	60,000	10	0	2	0	12,000

(New Joint-Stock Companies continued.)

Name of Company.	Capital Authorized.	Capital Offered.	Amount of Share.		Deposit.		Total Deposit.	
	£	£	£	s.	£	s.	£	s.
Patent Ventilating Granary (lim.)	100,000	100,000	20	0	5	0	25,000	
Pertusola Lead Mining and Smelting (lim.)	250,000	250,000	10	0	3	0	75,000	
Philharmonic Rooms (Southampton) (lim.) ...	20,000	20.000	20	0	1	0	1,000	
Photogenic Gas (lim.) ...	200,000	100,000	20	0	3	0	15,000	
Plym River Slate and Slab (lim.)	60,000	30,000	6	0	2	0	10.000	
Pneumatic Despatch (lim.).	125,000	125,000	10	0	2	10	31,250	
Portugal Iron and Coal (lim.)	100,000	100,000	10	0	2	0	20,000	
Princess Alexandra Silver Lead, and Zinc Mining (lim.)	6,000	6,000	5	0	1	10	1,800	
Prince of Wales Hotel (lim.)	100,000	100,000	10	0	2	0	20,000	
Public Works Credit of London and Paris (lim.).	200,000	100.000	20	0	1	10	7,500	
Queensferry Alkali (lim.)...	50,000	50,000	100	0	25	0	12,500	
Ramsey Lead Mining and Smelting (lim.)	100,000	100,000	5	0	0	10	10,000	
Ramsgate and Broadstairs Hotel (lim.)	100,000	100,000	10	0	2	0	20,000	
Residential Clubs (lim.) ..	130,000	65,000	5	0	1	0	13,000	
Richmond-Hill Hotel (lim.)	100,000	50,000	10	0	2	0	10,000	
Royal Bellevue Hotel at Aberystwith (lim.) ...	30,000	30,000	5	0	1	10	9,000	
Royal Marine Hotel of Kingstown (lim.) ...	100,000	100,000	5	0	1	10	30,000	
Royal Sardinian Railway...	1,000,000	1,000,000	20	0	3	0	150,000	
St. James's Hotel (lim.) ...	50,000	50,000	10	0	2	0	10,000	
St. Thomas Floating Dock (lim.)	100,000	100,000	10	0	2	0	20,000	
Sardinian Mining (lim.) ...	100,000	100,000	10	0	2	0	20,000	
Skara (Norwegian) Silver Mining (lim.)	50,000	50,000	2	0	1	0	25,000	
Southampton Imperial Hotel (lim.)	100,000	100,000	10	0	2	0	20,000	
South Blackpool Hotel (lim.)	50.000	50,000	5	0	1	10	15,000	
South Essex Waterworks	80,000	80,000	10	0	1	0	8,000	
South Kensington Hotel (lim.)	100,000	100,000	10	0	1	0	10,000	

(New Joint-Stock Companies continued.)

Name of Company.	Capital Authorized.	Capital Offered.	Amount of Share.		Deposit.		Total Deposit.
	£	£	£	s.	£	s.	£
South Pary's Copper Mining (lim.)	20,000	20,000	2	0	1	0	10,000
Southsea Pier Hotel (lim.)	60,000	25,000	5	0	1	0	5,000
Stafford and Uttoxeter Railway	130,000	130,000	10	0	2	0	26,000
Staffordshire Joint - Stock Bank (lim.)	1,000,000	1,000,000	100	0	5	0	50,000
Staffordshire Rolling Stock (lim.)	50,000	50,000	10	0	2	0	10,000
Star and Garter Hotel (lim.)	120,000	120,000	10	0	3	0	36,000
Storm's Breechloader Small Arms (lim.)	100,000	100,000	50	0	2	0	40,000
Suburban Hotel (lim.) ...	50,000	50,000	—		—		—
Sutton Royal Hotel (lim.)...	10,000	7,000	5	0	1	0	1,400
Tal-y-Drws Slate (lim.) ...	20,000	20,000	10	0	2	0	4,000
Tan, Gas, and Charcoal (lim.)	20,000	20,000	5	0	1	0	4,000
Terriccio Copper Mining (lim.)	50,000	50,000	2	0	1	0	25,000
Thames, Mersey, and Humber Shipping (lim.) ...	250,000	250,000	25	0	2	0	20,000
Titanic Steel and Iron (lim.)	360,000	280,000	{ 10 0 { 100 0		1 0 —		8,000 200,000
Tobacco, Cigar, Snuff (lim.)	100,000	50,000	5	0	2	0	24,000
Torquay Hotel (lim.) ...	70,000	70,000	10	0	2	0	10,000
Tregurtha Downs Mining (lim.)	40,000	40,000	2	10	1	0	16,000
Turnhurst Hall Colliery and Ironstone (lim.) ...	75,000	75,000	5	0	1	10	22,500
Tywarnhaile Mine... ...	30,000	30,000	5	0	1	0	6,000
Union Marine Insurance (lim.)	2,000,000	2,000,000	20	0	2	0	200,000
United London Newspaper (lim.)	20,000	20,000	1	0	0	10	10,000
Universal Mercantile Association (lim.)	50,000	50,000	1	0	0	5	12,500
Vallanzasca Gold Mining(li.)	50,000	50,000	1	0	0	5	12,500
West Central Horse and Carriage Repository(lim.)	50,000	50,000	5	0	2	0	20,000
West Cornwall Consols Tin and Copper Mining (lim.)	30,000	30,000	5	0	1	0	6,000
West India and Pacific Steamship (lim.) ...	1,000,000	1,000,000	50	0	2	0	40,000

(New Joint-Stock Companies continued.)

Name of Company.	Capital Authorized.	Capital Offered.	Amount of Share.		Deposit.		Total Deposit.
	£	£	£	s.	£	s.	£
Westminster and South-wark Bank (lim.) ...	1,000,000	500,000	100	0	2	0	10,000
West of England Woollen Manufacturing (lim.) ...	100,000	100,000	10	0	2	0	20,000
Weston-super-Mare Hotel (lim.)	75,000	75,000	10	0	2	10	18,750
West Surrey Tanning (lim.)	50,000	50,000	2	0	0	10	12,500
West Wheal Friendship Copper Mining (lim.) ...	30,000	30,000	1	0	1	0	30,000
Whittington Freehold Colliery (lim.) ... }	135,000	135,000	{ 10	0	4	0	40,000
			10	0	10	0	35,000
Western Fire Insurance (lim.)	1,000,000	250,000	10	0	1	0	25,000
Yorkshire Railway Waggon (lim.)	30,000	30,000	10	0	1	10	4,500
Total	100,053,000	78,135,000					8,875,550

ANALYSIS.

Companies.	No. of Cos.	Capital Authorized.	Capital Offered.	Deposit.
		£	£	£
Banking	27	31,900,000	25,000,000	2,171,500
Financial and Discount...	15	19,000,000	13,150,000	1,082,500
Manufacturing & Trading	65	14,455,000	10,400,000	1,786,750
Railways	17	9,496,000	9,196,000	1,064,850
Insurance...	14	10,300,000	7,375,000	692,500
Shipping	6	4,168,000	3,768,000	142,500
Hotel	47	4,320,000	3,522,000	625,150
Mining	49	3,019,000	3,019,000	989,050
Gas	6	670,000	580,000	38,500
Miscellaneous	17	2,655,000	2,125,000	282,250
Total	263	100,053,000	78,135,000	8,875,500

FLUCTUATIONS IN CONSOLS AND BANK BULLION IN 1863.

The extreme range of Consols during the year 1863 has been $3\frac{7}{8}$ per cent., while that of the preceding twelve months was $3\frac{3}{4}$ per cent. The lowest price, $90\frac{1}{8}$, was on the 3rd of December, and the highest, 94, was on the 5th of May. The difference between the opening and closing quotations of the year shows a decline of $1\frac{1}{4}$ per cent. In railway shares a further average improvement has been established of about 5 per cent. American Federal stocks show a decline of 6 per cent. The Bank of England bullion stood in 1862 at £14,635,555, and was at the end of last year £14,362,605, showing a reduction of £272,950. It touched its highest point, £15,494,219, on the 2nd of September, and its lowest, £13,008,617, on the 9th of December. At the Bank of France the total at the beginning of 1863 was about £13,000,000, and at the close it had fallen to a point lower than had been touched during the twelve months—£7,400,000. The specie in the American banks on the 1st of January, 1863, was £7,200,000, and at December last it was £5,300,000. On the Paris Bourse the movements in French Rentes resulted in establishing a fall of $3\frac{1}{2}$ per cent. The changes in the Bank rate of discount, which were only five in number in 1862, were last year twelve. On the 1st of January, 1863, the rate was 4 per cent.; on the 30th of April it was down to 3 per cent. and on the 3rd of December it was at 8 per cent., with an extra charge of 1 per cent. in the case of temporary advances. On the 31st December it was 7 per cent. In the cotton-market there was excitement throughout. The price of fair Surat at the commencement of last year was $17\frac{1}{4}d.$ per lb.; on the 5th of March it was down to $15\frac{1}{2}d.$; on the 27th of October it touched $24\frac{3}{4}d.$; and on the 31st of December it was at $23\frac{3}{4}d.$ The stock in Liverpool was, in 1862, 392,500 bales; at the close of 1863 it was 281,300. In the wheat-market there was almost uninterrupted heaviness. The opening price was 45s. 10d., and an advance took place to 48s. 4d. up to the 24th of January. A steady decline then ensued, until the lowest quotation, 39s. 10d., was touched on the 14th of November.